T0305267

Green Fiscal Reform for a Sustainable Future

CRITICAL ISSUES IN ENVIRONMENTAL TAXATION

Series Editors: Larry Kreiser, *Cleveland State University, USA*, Hope Ashiabor, *Macquarie University, Australia and* Janet E. Milne, *Vermont Law School, USA*

The *Critical Issues in Environmental Taxation* series provides insights and analysis on environmental taxation issues on an international basis and explores detailed theories for achieving environmental goals through fiscal policy. Each book in the series contains pioneering and thought-provoking contributions by the world's leading environmental tax scholars who respond to the diverse challenges posed by environmental sustainability.

Previous volumes in the series:
Original book published by CCH Incorporated

Volumes I–IV published by Richmond Law Publishers

Volumes V–VIII published by Oxford University Press

Volume IX onwards published by Edward Elgar Publishing

Recent titles in the series include:

Green Fiscal Reform for a Sustainable Future

Reform, Innovation and Renewable Energy

Edited by

Natalie P. Stoianoff

Professor of Law and Director of the Intellectual Property Program, University of Technology Sydney, Australia

Larry Kreiser

Professor Emeritus of Accounting, Cleveland State University, USA

Bill Butcher

Director of Coursework Programs, Taxation and Business Law, University of New South Wales, Australia

Janet E. Milne

Professor of Law, Vermont Law School, USA

Hope Ashiabor

Associate Professor of Law, Macquarie University, Australia

CRITICAL ISSUES IN ENVIRONMENTAL TAXATION
VOLUME XVII

 Edward Elgar
PUBLISHING

Cheltenham, UK • Northampton, MA, USA

Published by
Edward Elgar Publishing Limited
The Lypiatts
15 Lansdown Road
Cheltenham
Glos GL50 2JA
UK

Edward Elgar Publishing, Inc.
William Pratt House
9 Dewey Court
Northampton
Massachusetts 01060
USA

A catalogue record for this book
is available from the British Library

Library of Congress Control Number: 2016938584

This book is available electronically in the **Elgar**online
Law subject collection
DOI 10.4337/9781786431196

ISBN 978 1 78643 118 9 (cased)
ISBN 978 1 78643 119 6 (eBook)

Typeset by Servis Filmsetting Ltd, Stockport, Cheshire

Printed and bound in Great Britain by
TJ International Ltd, Padstow, Cornwall

Contents

PART I FISCAL CARBON POLICY DEVELOPMENT

PART II TRADE, TAXATION AND SUSTAINABILITY

Figures

Tables

Editorial review board

The 13 chapters in this book have been brought to publication with the help of an editorial review board dedicated to peer review. The 20 members of the board are committed to the field of environmental taxation and are active participants in environmental taxation events around the world:

Chair:
Natalie P. Stoianoff
University of Technology Sydney, Australia

Members:
Hope Ashiabor
Macquarie University, Australia

Patricia Blazey
Macquarie University, Australia

Bill Butcher
University of New South Wales, Australia

Jacqueline Cottrell
Green Budget Europe, Germany

Damien Giurco
University of Technology Sydney, Australia

Wayne Gumley
Monash University, Australia

Ann Hansford
University of Exeter, UK

Larry Kreiser
Cleveland State University, USA

David Leary
University of Technology Sydney, Australia

Soocheol Lee
Meijo University, Japan

Roberta Mann
University of Oregon, USA

Janet E. Milne
Vermont Law School, USA

Anna Mortimore
Griffith University, Australia

Sven Rudolph
Kyoto University, Japan

Rahmat Tavalali
Walsh University, USA

Dodo J. Thampapillai
National University of Singapore, Singapore

Stefan Weishaar
University of Groningen, the Netherlands

Jian Wu
Renmin University, China

Yan Xu
The Chinese University of Hong Kong, Hong Kong

Contributors

Cristina Brandimarte, Italian National Institute of Statistics, Italy

Jan Brůha, Kolin Institute of Technology, Czech Republic

Hana Brůhová-Foltýnová, Kolin Institute of Technology, Czech Republic

Lorenzo del Federico, University of Chieti-Pescara, Italy

Agime Gerbeti, Gestore Servizi Energetici, Italy

Silvia Giorgi, University of Trento, Italy

Evgeny Guglyuvatyy, Southern Cross University, Australia

Sally-Ann Joseph, National University of Singapore, Singapore

Claudia Kettner, Austrian Institute of Economic Research (WIFO), Austria

Daniela Kletzan-Slamanig, Austrian Institute of Economic Research (WIFO), Austria

David Leary, University of Technology Sydney, Australia

Yuko Motoki, Mizuho Information & Research Institute, Inc., Japan

Aya Naito, Mizuho Information & Research Institute, Inc., Japan

Prafula Pearce, Curtin University, Australia

Vítězslav Píša, Kolin Institute of Technology, Czech Republic

Natalie P. Stoianoff, University of Technology Sydney, Australia

Seck L. Tan, National University of Singapore, Singapore

Xiao Wang, Renmin University of China, China

Sarah Wright, University of Wollongong, Australia

Jian Wu, Renmin University of China, China

Zhe Yang, Renmin University of China, China

Preface

In 2015 we saw the introduction of the United Nations' Sustainable Development Goals, building on their predecessors, the Millennium Development Goals. These 17 goals were adopted while the 16th Global Conference on Environmental Taxation was being held in Sydney and six of these goals directly relate to our environment and natural resources: clean water and sanitation; affordable and clean energy; sustainable cities and communities; climate action; life below water; and life on land. All these goals require national fiscal measures to help fund their achievement.

In Volume XVII of the *Critical Issues in Environmental Taxation*, environmental tax experts review the development of fiscal carbon policy, consider the impact of green taxation on trade and competition, analyse the lessons learned from national experiences with fuel and energy pricing, and evaluate a variety of green economic instruments. Green fiscal policies not only help provide needed financing but also serve the sustainable development goals.

We hope you enjoy reading these studies and find them to be worthy of serious consideration by policy makers right round the world.

Natalie P. Stoianoff, Lead Editor
Larry Kreiser, Co-Editor
Bill Butcher, Co-Editor
Janet E. Milne, Co-Editor
Hope Ashiabor, Co-Editor

PART I

Fiscal carbon policy development

1. A good FACT for climate change mitigation

Cristina Brandimarte*

1.1 INTRODUCTION

The global degree of carbon dioxide (CO_2) concentration in the atmosphere – a direct cause of global warming – has reached worrying record levels, and is continuing to rise along a steep upward trend. Global Carbon Budget (GCB) estimates[1] point out that carbon concentration in the atmosphere increased by 85 parts per million (ppm) from 1959 to 2015, nearly 40 per cent of which was over the last 15 years, and that combustion of fossil fuels is the dominant and growing anthropogenic source of emissions.

GCB figures also point out that stabilizing or, even more, reducing CO_2 concentration would require drastic global emissions abatement, considerably above 50 per cent. Such a great reduction, besides being difficult to attain within a reasonable time horizon, would entail huge costs for developing countries. Indeed, as International Energy Agency (IEA) figures show,[2] non-OECD countries actually emit the greatest share of CO_2, and the recent emissions' increase was driven by positive and desirable catching-up phenomena, with poorer countries experiencing mortality rate reductions and increases in well-being. Indeed, increases in global population and gross domestic product (GDP) per capita have been the main forces driving upward trends in CO_2 emissions, while global emissions intensity has been progressively decreasing.

For these reasons, most recent guidelines[3] suggest large-scale integrated approaches combining measures to both strengthen efforts to reduce emissions and boost carbon sequestration. Following these guidelines, a proper approach should be, for example, to price carbon and to use revenues to promote protection and development of carbon sink ecosystems. Hence, it becomes particularly important to adopt anti-emissions measures that do not harm the economy and free up resources to strengthen the climate change fight.

3

Among market-based instruments, literature indicates that carbon taxes are one of the most cost-effective for emissions reduction. In particular, upstream (or production-based) CO_2 taxation – a tax levied at the point where the source of emissions enters the economic system – is suggested as it has low administrative costs and ensures great coverage. If imposed unilaterally, however, this kind of tax could entail significant economic costs, mainly through competitiveness losses, and could become environmentally ineffective due to carbon leakage phenomena. Suggested co-measures, such as border tax adjustments or proper reuse of revenues, might not be sufficient to avoid these problems and to make a production-based carbon tax an easy win–win solution.

Literature then suggests as a viable alternative a different carbon tax design: namely the CAT (carbon-added tax), a downstream, or consumption-based, carbon tax modelled on value-added tax. It has the advantage of protecting competitiveness of domestic producers as it is levied on imports and reimbursed on exports.

In this chapter, the implementation of a fuel-added carbon tax (FACT) – a duty levied on fossil fuel embodied in goods and services and patterned after VAT– is considered and compared with a tax on fossil fuel purchases (FCT), the simplest and most common upstream carbon tax. In particular, macroeconomic effects of both taxes are estimated for Italy, using MEMo-It, the macroeconometric model of the Italian National Institute of Statistics (ISTAT).

The remainder of the chapter is organized as follows. Section 1.2 briefly reviews characteristics and implications of production-based carbon taxes. Section 1.3 examines downstream taxation and describes the FACT. Section 1.4 deals with differences between FCT and FACT both from theoretical and empirical points of view. In particular, the effects of their implementation in Italy are analysed and compared. Some conclusions follow in section 1.5. A technical appendix on FACT simulation concludes the chapter.

1.2 UPSTREAM TAXATION OF CO_2 EMISSIONS: PRODUCTION-BASED CARBON TAXES

Theoretical literature suggests imposing taxes directly on, or close to, environmental damage and proportional to the specific environmental cost.[4] According to theory, a carbon tax on fossil fuel emissions should fall at different points of the production–consumption chain, where the fuel is burned, and should equal the *marginal* damage. Considering administrative costs, relative to measurement, management and control, it can, however, become optimal to impose the tax farther from the emissions and set it equal to the *average* damage.[5] For these reasons, the most common carbon tax takes the form of a duty on fossil fuel purchases. It falls upstream, when fossil fuels enter the system, involves low administrative costs and is effective in the short and long run, inducing economic agents' behavioural changes and technological innovations that lead to structural emissions reduction. It should be noted that, even if imposed upstream, the price signal must reach consumers in order to fully achieve such desired effects. It is widely recognized[6] that the major risk arising from the implementation of a unilateral production-based carbon tax, and the most important obstacle to its implementation, is the competitive disadvantage that can lead to shifting production abroad. This phenomenon, called carbon leakage, undermines the global emission reduction target, by reducing national emissions in the abating country but increasing emissions in non-abating ones, and poses a major challenge for designing effective unilateral policies aimed at mitigating global climate change. Finally, production-based carbon taxes have important, and inequitable, international burden-shifting implications.

1.2.1 Carbon Leakage

Carbon leakage may occur through several channels. First of all, the reduced demand for fossil fuels in the unilaterally abating country causes an international fuel price decrease, which means a demand increase and then an increase of emissions in countries with no or lower carbon pricing. The second channel works in the medium to long term and occurs because energy-intensive and trade-exposed industries in the unilaterally abating country lose competitiveness and their production is relocated to areas where abatement costs are lower. A further channel happens through substitution of domestic products with cheaper imported ones. Finally, the last channel, less considered in literature, affects the economy in the short to medium term and becomes important if the exchange rate is not fully flexible and costs are indexed. It is due to the 'cascading effect' on costs that occurs through both wages indexation and increases in prices of domestically produced inputs. This results in further competitiveness losses and therefore in additional incentives to move production abroad. If entrepreneurs anticipate this development, a stronger carbon leakage effect should happen in the short term.

Theoretical and empirical literature widely agree that economic costs from a unilateral carbon tax the main obstacle to environmental taxes implementation. To overcome these limits, several anti-leakage measures have been proposed: border tax adjustment, industry exemption, subsidies and rebates, and reuse of revenues to reduce other more distortive taxes ('double dividend' literature).[7] Anti-leakage proposed measures are, however, second-best instruments that could lead to reduced environmental benefits, provide little or no incentive to cut emissions, and result in protection of sectors with greater emission intensity with respect to the rest of the world.[8]

Among instruments aiming to reduce carbon leakage without reducing environmental benefits of a unilateral carbon tax, border tax adjustments (BTAs) are widely regarded as the most effective instruments. They are aimed at levelling the playing field between the national regulated industries and unregulated industries abroad, usually taxing imports to the same extent as domestically produced goods and exempting exports. This solution has, however, some important limits. First of all, a correct implementation of BTAs could be excessively complicated and could have extremely high administrative costs.[9] Second, BTAs do not avoid increased prices of domestically produced inputs and the ensuing negative effects on competitiveness. Finally, compliance of BTAs with World Trade Organization (WTO) rules is highly controversial, as such border adjustments might be considered a barrier to international trade, by discriminating against some imports in favour of domestic products or other imports, or by restricting trade between developed and developing countries.

1.2.2 International Burden-shifting Implications

In a context where about one-quarter of the carbon released is associated with production of internationally traded goods and services,[10] the upstream carbon tax has important implications for international burden distribution. The tax burden, indeed, will weigh differently on countries, according to their production characteristics and their position along the so-called carbon supply chain.[11] Carbon supply chains follow goods' flows according to their embodied carbon, that is, CO_2 emissions that are needed to produce them, from extraction or production of raw materials and intermediate goods, up to final consumption, including transport activities. This approach enables consideration of 'the geographic separation of consumers and the pollution emitted in the production of the consumable items'[12] and shows that within a single country there could be significant differences between 'produced emissions' and 'consumed emissions'.

Countries can indeed be distinguished into three main groups: at one end, countries that are net exporters of fossil fuels; in the middle, countries

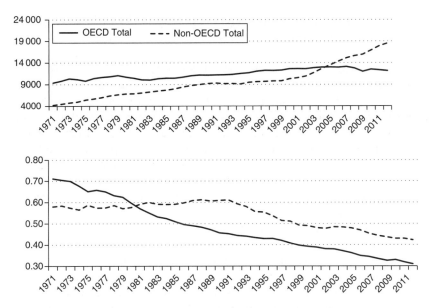

Source: CO$_2$ *Emissions from Fuel Combustion* (2014 edition), Paris: IEA.

Figure 1.1 CO$_2$ emissions from fossil fuels (a) million tonnes of CO$_2$ and (b) in percentage of GDP (using purchasing power parities Kg CO$_2$/US$, 2005 prices)

that are net exporters of embodied carbon (manufacturing countries); and countries that are net importers of embodied carbon (consumer countries) at the other end of the chain. Countries located at both ends of the international supply chain evade environmental responsibility by shifting emissions associated with their consumption to countries in the middle of the chain.[13] Since the beginning of the century, most CO$_2$ from fuel combustion has been emitted by developing countries (located in the middle of the chain), while the share of emissions by developed countries has significantly declined, as shown in Figure 1.1.[14]

Implementation of a production-based carbon tax would fall heavily on poorer countries, disproportionately compared to national consumption choices, with severe implications in terms of global equity.[15] Furthermore, the implementation of production-based carbon taxes in countries at the end of the chain has little environmental effectiveness.

1.3   DOWNSTREAM TAXATION: CONSUMPTION-BASED CARBON TAXES

An alternative measure to production-based carbon taxes suggested by the literature is downstream taxation, that is, a tax imposed on final consumption.[16] A consumption-based carbon tax is imposed on carbon embodied in final goods and services and shifts the responsibility from territorial to consumption emissions. Pricing carbon downstream has the advantage of protecting competitiveness of domestic producers and can be more easily implemented. Furthermore, other countries are stimulated to price carbon to retain border tax revenues.[17] Literature suggests the carbon-added tax (CAT), that is, a tax based on carbon embodied in products and modelled on VAT.

The major criticisms of consumption-based carbon taxes are the possible conflict with international trade law and an extremely complicated implementation, as with BTAs.[18] However, a growing body of legal experts agree on compliance of well-designed consumption-based approaches with WTO rules and it can be argued that, as in the case of upstream taxation, second-best solutions can be found to facilitate its implementation and minimize administrative costs. For example, a consumption-based tax on fossil fuels could be much simpler to manage with respect to taxes on carbon content and can be a viable alternative to common taxes on fuel purchases.

1.3.1   Fuel-added Carbon Tax

A fuel-added carbon tax (FACT) is a duty levied on the fuel that is added at each stage. Like VAT, the product is taxed at the end of each stage on its cumulative fuel content to that point, and credit is allowed for tax paid on fuel embodied in purchased inputs and refunded if net liability is negative. At the final stage, the tax is on the cumulative fuel used and is equivalent to the sum of the fuel-added carbon taxes at each stage.

In the case of exports, the tax accumulated will be rebated, so that the tax does not impact international competitiveness. At the same time, a fuel tax will be levied on the imported products. Ideally, this tax should be based on imports' real fuel content but, where it is not known, imports will be taxed to the same extent as homogeneous products that are domestically produced by the predominant production method.

FACT is similar to a duty on fuel purchases with border tax adjustments. Both of them aim to level the playing field between domestic and foreign firms, trying to convert origin-based fuel prices to consumption-based prices and limiting competitive disadvantages for the imposing country. But important differences lie between the two. First of all, FACT is imposed not only on fuel goods but also on non-fuel goods, according to their fuel content. In other words, it is levied on all goods that are domestically consumed, wherever they are produced.[19] Second, the FACT burden falls directly and entirely on domestic final consumers and does not affect prices of intermediate products, limiting negative effects on competitiveness. Further, FACT reduces incentives for tax evasion and provides incentives for exporting countries to adopt their own carbon prices, especially if it involves the refunding of CO_2 taxes already paid abroad on imported goods.

Last but not least, there are stronger arguments in favour of FACT's compliance with WTO rules, as it can be considered as a VAT with flexible rates, where rates vary in order to reflect fossil fuel content following production improvements and technological progress.

1.4 UPSTREAM VS DOWNSTREAM FUEL TAXATION

Major differences between the FACT and the FCT are related to tax bases and price effects. We may analyse these differences starting from the following equation, expressing a country's fossil fuels budget:

$$FC = FE + FM - FX \tag{1.1}$$

where:
FC = total final fuel consumption;
FE = total fuel domestic extraction;
FM = total fuel imports;
FX = total fuel exports.
Each addendum in expression (1.1) is referred to the total fuel and may be disaggregated into fuel and non-fuel products as follows:

$$FCf + FCnf = FE + FMf + FMnf - FXf - FXnf \tag{1.2}$$

where:
FCf = fuel final (direct) consumption;
$FCnf$ = final consumption of fuel embodied in non-fuel products;
FMf = imported fuel;
$FMnf$ = fuel embodied in non-fuel imported goods and services;
FXf = exported fuel;
$FXnf$ = fuel embodied in non-fuel exported goods and services.

Table 1.1 Effects on prices of FCT and FACT

	Production Prices	Consumer Prices	Import Prices		Export Prices
			FMf	FMnf	
FCT	X	X	X	–	X
FACT	–	XX	X	X	–

Note: Dashes signal no effect. XX indicates a much stronger effect than X.

Tax bases can be then expressed as follows:

$$FCT\text{'s tax base} = FE + FMf - FXf$$

$$FACT\text{'s tax base} = FE + FMf + \mathbf{FMnf} - FXf - \mathbf{FXnf}$$

The tax base's difference (bold addenda) depends on the trade balance of fuel embodied in non-fuels products. As developing countries, located in the middle of the carbon supply chain, have a negative balance, in those countries FCT's tax base is larger than FACT's tax base. The opposite happens in developed countries.

With regard to short-term impacts on prices, these are shown in Table 1.1.

FCT affects the firm's purchase price of fuel and then has the effect of increasing production prices and export prices. Consumption prices are affected directly by the tax levied on final consumption of fossil fuels and indirectly through the translation of production price increases.

FACT has no effect on production prices or on export prices. Consumer prices are directly affected through two channels: the tax levied on final consumption of fossil fuels and the tax levied on fuel embodied in non-fuel products consumed by final consumers.

1.4.1 Empirical Evaluation for Italy

In this section empirical evaluations for Italy are presented. Macroeconomic effects of both FCT and FACT have been simulated over a four-year time horizon using the ISTAT (Italian National Institute of Statistics) macroeconometric model (MEMo-It).[20,21]

Fiscal measures amount to 1 percentage point of GDP in the ex ante evaluation[22] for FCT and tax rates are set equal in the two simulations. The ex post macroeconomic effects[23] are evaluated with respect to a baseline scenario based on the May 2014 ISTAT official forecast.

Simulation exercises are based on the following hypotheses:

- The country is small and belongs to a single monetary area. That means that nominal interest rates and nominal exchange rates remain unchanged with respect to baseline.
- Wages are indexed to consumer prices.
- Income taxation is progressive but income brackets are indexed, so that a fiscal drag does not occur.
- Entrepreneurs do not expect significantly restrictive effects on domestic demand or on competitive position and react to the lower real interest rates and the introduction of fuel tax, increasing investments.
- Fuel intensity of goods and services is assumed to be the same, on average, for imported, exported and domestically produced goods.

Results are shown in Table 1.2.

In the first exercise the introduction of the FCT (duty on fossil fuel purchases) is simulated.[24] Results indicate that two periods can be distinguished: the first two years are characterized by a slightly positive effect while in the following two years a depressive effect on the economy occurs. In the first period, restrictive effects come from the reduction of households' real disposable income and are offset by expansive effects coming from terms of trade gains[25] and from the real interest rate reduction. Moreover, negative effects on exports are limited by low (estimated) elasticities of both the export deflator to changes in fuel prices and foreign demand of Italian products to export deflator. In the second period, the effects of higher inflation on production costs, in particular on indexed labour costs, result in a significant loss of competitiveness, which is mainly reflected in an increase in imports, since consumption of domestic goods is reduced in favour of cheaper imported ones.

In the second exercise the introduction of a FACT is simulated. Some relevant differences with respect to FCT simulation are evident. In the first period, inflation is higher and reduction of households' real disposable income is stronger, but they are associated with a stronger reduction in imports, as the tax is levied not only on fuels, as in the case of FCT, but also on non-fuel imported goods. Exports remain unchanged, as in the FCT simulation. As a result, expansive effects on GDP are stronger. In the second period, exports are not hit and imports continue to shrink. No carbon leakage effect occurs and investment and GDP growth are still positive. Higher real economic growth and higher inflation exert positive effects on public budget balance and on households' disposable income.

Table 1.2   Simulation results for FCT and FACT effects in Italy (differences from baseline)

	Tax on Fuel Purchases (FCT)				Fuel-added Carbon Tax (FACT)			
	2015	2016	2017	2018	2015	2016	2017	2018
GDP	0.1	0.0	−0.2	−0.2	0.2	0.1	0.1	0.0
Domestic demand	−0.1	−0.2	−0.1	−0.1	−0.2	−0.3	−0.1	0.0
Household consumption	−0.1	−0.4	−0.1	0.0	−0.2	−0.5	−0.1	0.0
Investments	0.1	0.2	−0.3	−0.4	0.2	0.5	0.2	−0.1
Exports	0.0	0.0	−0.2	−0.2	0.0	0.0	0.0	−0.1
Imports	−1.1	−1.1	0.2	0.4	−1.2	−1.5	−0.5	−0.3
GDP deflator	0.7	0.6	0.5	0.3	1.0	0.8	0.6	0.5
Consumer deflator	1.0	0.6	0.3	0.2	1.4	0.8	0.5	0.3
Export deflator	0.0	0.0	0.3	0.3	0.0	0.0	0.0	0.4
Employment	0.3	0.1	0.0	−0.1	0.4	0.2	0.0	0.0
Fuel tax/GDP	0.6	0.4	0.3	0.2	0.5	0.3	0.2	0.1
Net lending/ GDP	0.7	0.7	0.6	0.5	0.7	0.8	0.7	0.7
Gross debt/ GDP	−1.8	−3.2	−4.1	−4.7	−2.2	−4.0	−5.4	−6.8
Real disposable income (% change)	−0.8	−0.1	0.1	0.0	−1.1	−0.1	0.1	0.1
Real disposable income (% difference with respect to baseline)	−0.8	−0.9	−0.8	−0.8	−1.1	−1.2	−1.1	−1.0

1.5   CONCLUSIONS

Empirical results indicate that in Italy, a small country belonging to a monetary area that is a net importer of fossil fuels, the implementation of a FACT should be more effective and less costly with respect to a tax on fuel purchases.

Without competiveness losses, benefits coming from terms of trade gains and the stimulus to invest in new, fuel-saving technologies can be fully exploited, with positive effects on both the economy and the environment. Public finance conditions improve too, and resources then become available to strengthen efforts to reduce CO_2 atmospheric concentration, for example enhancing carbon sink ecosystems. A further simulation, not shown here, indicates that recycling revenues to promote sustainable development, for example, boosting forest management and linked economic activities, should help to reach multiple environmental and socioeconomic targets without worsening public finance.

NOTES

*   The views expressed in this study are those of the author and do not represent those of the Italian National Institute of Statistics (ISTAT), with whom she is affiliated.
1.   Global Carbon Budget Archive (2014), accessed 5 April 2016 at http://www.globalcarbonproject.org/carbonbudget/archive.htm#CB2014.
2.   IEA (2014), *CO_2 Emissions from Fuel Combustion Highlights 2014*, accessed 5 April 2016 at http://www.iea.org/publications/.
3.   Intergovernmental Panel on Climate Change (2014), *Fifth Assessment Report: Climate Change 2014*, accessed 5 April 2016 at http://www.ipcc.ch/report/ar5/wg2/.
4.   Pigou, A.C. (1920), *Economics of Welfare*, London: Macmillan; Heine, D., J. Norregaard and I.W.H. Parry (2012), 'Environmental tax reform: principles from theory and practice to date', *IMF Working Paper WP/12/180*.
5.   Baumol, W.J, and W.E. Oates (1971), 'The use of standards and prices for the protection of the environment', *Scandinavian Journal of Economics*, **73**(1), 42–54; Pearce, D.W. (1991), 'The role of carbon taxes in adjusting to global warming', *Economic Journal*, **101**(407), 938–48.
6.   Intergovernmental Panel on Climate Change (2008), *Fourth Assessment Report: Climate Change 2007*, accessed 5 April 2016 at https://www.ipcc.ch/pdf/assessment-report/ar4/wg2/ar4_wg2_full_report.pdf; OECD (2014), *Competitiveness Impacts of Carbon Pricing: A Review of Empirical Findings COM/ENV/CTPA/CFA(2014)20*.
7.   A large body of literature has analysed the possibility of getting a double dividend by recycling carbon tax revenues, but the issue is still largely debated and no certain and agreed conclusions have been reached.
8.   Literature shows that environmental effectiveness of anti-leakage measures heavily depends on differences between abating and non-abating countries.
9.   Pauwelyn J. (2012), 'Carbon leakage measures and border tax adjustments under WTO law', working paper, accessed 5 April 2016 at http://papers.ssrn.com/sol3/papers.cfm?abstract_id=2026879.
10.   Peters, G.P., S.J. Davis and R. Andrew (2012), 'A synthesis of carbon in international trade', *Biogeosciences*, **9**, 3247–76.
11.   Davis, S.J and K. Caldeira (2010), 'Consumption-based accounting of CO_2 emissions', in *Proceedings of the National Academy of Sciences of the United States of America*, **107**(12), 5687–92; Harrison, K. (2015), 'International carbon trade and domestic climate politics', working paper, accessed 5 April 2016 at http://depts.washington.edu/envirpol/wp-content/uploads/2015/02/Colloquia_Harrison.pdf.
12.   Peters, G.P and E.G. Hertwich (2008), 'CO_2 embodied in international trade with implications for global climate policy', *Environmental Science and Technology*, **42**(5), 1401–7.
13.   Many fossil fuel exporters have clean economies and are net importers of carbon

embodied in non-fuel products. See Harrison, K. (2015) 'International carbon trade and domestic climate politics', working paper; at http://depts.washington.edu/envirpol/wp-content/uploads/2015/02/Colloquia_Harrison.pdf.

14. Davis, S.J., G.P. Peters and K. Caldeira (2011) 'The supply chain of CO_2 emissions', in *Proceedings of the National Academy of Sciences of the United States of America*, **108**(45), 18554–9.

15. Economic activity in manufacturing countries could be very strongly damaged by imposing an unilateral, production-based, carbon tax: the competitiveness loss would suddenly lead to a drop in demand of domestically produced goods, to carbon leakage phenomena and to a strong reduction of economic activity and fiscal revenues. A global uniform carbon tax, on the other hand, would suddenly delete the competitive advantage that has driven poorer countries' economic growth, with negative consequences that could hardly be eliminated without an international redistribution of carbon tax revenues.

16. Christian, A.C. (1992), 'Designing a carbon tax: the introduction of the carbon-burned tax', *UCLA Journal of Environmental Law and Policy*, **10**(2), 221; Duff, D.G. and M. MacDonald (2013), 'Towards a destination-based carbon tax', *Proceedings of the 14th Global Conference on Environmental Taxation*, Kyoto, Japan, 17–19 October; Harrison, 'International carbon trade and domestic climate politics'.

17. Harris, P. and J. Symons (2013), 'Norm conflict in climate governance: greenhouse gas accounting and the problem of consumption', *Global Environmental Politics*, **13**(1), 9–29.

18. For a detailed critique, see McLure, C.E. Jr (2010), 'The carbon-added tax: a CAT that won't hunt', *Policy Options Politiques*, 1 October, accessed 6 April 2016 at http://policyoptions.irpp.org/magazines/obama-at-midterm/the-carbon-added-tax-a-cat-that-wont-hunt/.

19. Tax rates being equal, FACT leads to higher inflation.

20. For a synthetic description of the model and its transmission channels see Brandimarte, C. (2014), 'Macroeconomic effects of environmental tax subsidy reform: an evaluation for Italy', in L. Kreiser et al. (eds), *Environmental Taxation and Green Fiscal Reform –Theory and Impact, Critical Issues in Environmental Taxation Volume XIV*. For a detailed description see Bacchini, F. et al. (2013), 'Building the core of the ISTAT system of models for forecasting the Italian economy: MEMo-It', *ISTAT Rivista di Statistica Ufficiale*, **2013**(1), 17–26.

21. The methodology used to simulate the fuel-added carbon tax is explained in the Appendix to this chapter.

22. Ex ante evaluation means that economic agents do not change their behaviour in response to the introduction of the tax.

23. Ex post macroeconomic effects account for direct and indirect effects.

24. For a similar exercise see Brandimarte, 'Macroeconomic effects of environmental tax subsidy reform: an evaluation for Italy'. The main difference with respect to that simulation lies in a more optimistic reaction of private investments.

25. Imports decrease more than GDP and internal demand, since consumption of fuel, largely imported, decreases, and consumption of national products increases.

APPENDIX

In this Appendix the methodology used to simulate fuel-added carbon tax (FACT) with the ISTAT macroeconometric model is explained. The approach followed is to consider differences from the tax on fuel purchases (FCT), already modelled in MEMo-It, and to accordingly amend the relevant equations. FACT differs from FCT in two respects: effects on consumer prices and effects on revenues.

Effects on prices   Differential effects on prices are modelled considering the FACT's additional effect on consumer deflator growth with respect to FCT and to baseline. This additional effect reflects the tax on fuel embodied in non-fuel goods.[1] It is calculated assuming that fuel intensity is the same, on average, for imported, exported and domestically produced goods.

Effects on revenues   To estimate revenues from FACT, we face the problem of calculating the tax base. FACT's tax base differs from FCT's tax base by the balance between fuel embodied in non-fuel exported and imported goods. These variables are expressed in the model in nominal and real terms, but not in quantity (barrels) of fuel content, as required to estimate revenues. We need a conversion factor to transform variables expressed in real terms to variables expressed in barrels of embodied fuel, the same unit as the FCT's tax base.

This conversion factor (gamma) is estimated by combining the following two different ways to calculate FACT's revenues: in differential terms with respect to FCT revenues; multiplying the tax rate times total fuel final consumption expressed in barrels. Formally:

$$FACT = FCT - t * I * (X - Mnf) \qquad (A1.1)$$

$$FACT = t * CFf * gamma + t * I * CFnf \qquad (A1.2)$$

where:
FACT indicates revenues from the fuel-added tax;
FCT indicates revenues from the tax on fuel purchases, where *FCT = t * FUEL* and *FUEL* indicates total fuel goods (barrels) that are domestically purchased, both by firms and final consumers;
t is the tax rate (applied to fuel barrels);
I indicates fuel intensity of goods: it is assumed to be the same, on average, for imported, exported and domestically produced goods and services;
X indicates total exports (volume);
Mnf indicates imports of non-fuel goods;

CFf is the final fuel consumption (volume) and (*I**CFnf) is the fuel embodied in final consumption of non-fuel goods expressed in barrels.[2]

Once gamma is calculated, FACT's revenues are easily estimated with equation (A1.1).

How to calculate conversion factor gamma   As stated above, gamma is calculated by combining equations (A1.1) and (A1.2):

$$gamma = (FUEL - I * (X - Mnf) - I * CFnf)/CFf)$$

where the numerator represents the number of barrels embodied in final fuel goods[3] and denominator the same quantity expressed in volume (*CFf*). As numerator and denominator represent the same quantity expressed in the two different units, gamma is the number of barrels per volume unit (conversion factor).

How to calculate fuel intensity (I)   *I* represents the fuel embodied in goods and services and it is assumed to be the same (on average) for domestically produced, consumed, exported and imported goods. *I* expresses the number of barrels used by firms to produce a unit of goods and services (volumes):

$$I = (q * FUEL)/(Y - k * C)$$

where:
q is the share of fuel barrels used by firms and it is obtained residually, after estimating the share of fuel that is directly consumed;
Y is total product (in volume);
C is total consumption (in volume);
k is the ratio between direct fuel consumption of households and total household consumption (as in national accounts).[4]

Notes

1. Mainly imported non-fuel goods.
2. *CFf* times gamma is final fuel consumption expressed in barrels.
3. Indeed: *FUEL* = purchased fuel (barrels); *I* * *X* = total exported fuel (directly or embodied in exported goods and services), expressed in barrels (if *I* is expressed in barrels too); *I* * (*Mnf*) = fuel barrels embodied in imported non-fuel goods; *I* * *CFnf* = fuel barrels embodied in final consumption of non-fuel goods.
4. These simplifying assumptions are not very restrictive as, even with changing of shares between direct and indirect consumption of fuel by household, revenues would not change significantly. A further assumption is that the proportion between firms' and households' consumption of fuel (direct or embodied) does not vary. In other words, if tax rates increase, fuel consumption decreases in the same proportion everywhere (direct consumption of households, manufacturing activities, exported products).

2. Tax credit hypothesis to coordinate the EU ETS and EU energy tax systems

Lorenzo del Federico and Silvia Giorgi*

2.1 INTRODUCTION

The Emissions Trading System (ETS), one of the most discussed policies in the fight against climate change, was created within the European context as an instrument of control over overall greenhouse gas (GHG) stocks in the atmosphere, balancing protection aims and development needs.[1] A coexisting essential policy for environmental protection also exists in all EU member states. This is a system of energy taxation harmonized to a certain degree at EU level by Energy Taxation Directive No. 2003/96/EC, 27 October 2003.[2] Here we will briefly analyse the main steps that have brought the current situation into being.

Beginning from 2005, the European Union has unilaterally created its own GHG emissions trading system. On 8 March 2000, the legal framework for European emissions trading was anticipated by the Green Paper on GHG emissions trading within the European Union,[3] within the scope of the European Climate Change Programme and the Sixth Environment Action Programme. This step led directly to the adoption of Directive No. 2003/87/EC.[4] In 2005, with the upcoming Kyoto Protocol obligations in mind, learning-by-doing emissions trading testing started. After an initial 'trial period', from 2005 to 2007 (first phase), a second period of market practicality followed, from 2008 to 2012 (second phase). In January 2013 and lasting till 2020, the third phase began.

The current rules are the result of a stratification of measures on the early structure of Directive No. 2003/87/EC. Other significant modifications are worth mentioning. First, Directive No. 2004/101/EC of 27 October 2004[5] (the so-called 'Linking Directive') connected the Emissions Trading System to the Joint Implementation and Clean Development mechanisms of the Kyoto Protocol, making it possible for European installations to use the Certified Emission Reduction (CER) and Emission Reduction Unit

(ERU) credits that derive from such systems, as long as qualitative and quantitative limits are respected. Second, with Directive No. 2008/101/EC[6] aircraft emissions became part of the European system.[7] Last, Directive No. 2009/29/E[8] included new productive sectors and gas within the scope of the ETS, and also modified emission allocation criteria. It then fixed a European emission maximum cap and provided for its yearly reduction.

Concurrently, moving onto the analysis of the fundamental elements of Directive No. 2003/96/EC[9] – the Energy Taxation Directive – we may see how it sets out common rules establishing what should be taxed and by how much, by fixing minimum rates based mainly on consumed volumes of energy. The Energy Taxation Directive (ETD) also provides for the possibility of a total or partial exemption for electricity and fuels derived from renewable energy.

In 2011, the European Commission presented its proposal to overhaul such an outdated set of rules, in order to remove current imbalances and take into account both CO_2 emissions of energy products and their energy content. The Commission also observed a lack of coordination between the ETD and the EU ETS, as the purpose of both is to allow for cost-efficient reductions in GHGs for specific sets of activities. However, CO_2 taxation, on the basis of the ETD, is applied by member states in an uncoordinated manner – some operators consuming energy are covered by both instruments (e.g., paper mills), whilst others are left outside the scope of both regulatory frameworks (e.g., small installations using energy in certain industrial processes). Both situations can lead to lack of cost efficiency and can distort the EU internal market by undermining the very logic of the EU ETS.

Undoubtedly, the two frameworks need to be coordinated, and the EU Commission identified such a means of coordination in the exemption instrument. This chapter, with reference to the ETS framework and its legal nature, will try to demonstrate the limits of such a hypothesis and to explore another path to reach the same goal through a more environmentally efficient solution. In the last part of the study in fact, the proposal of a tax credit as a method of coordination will be analysed.

2.2   A STEP BACK: EU ETS

The ETS model, which limits exploitation of natural resources belonging to the community by creating emission trading rights, combines a 'command-and-control' regulation – which has a prominent public power role – with trading and economic instruments – mainly based on private choices and behaviours. In the European Court of Justice's words:

[T]he economic logic of the allowance trading scheme consists in ensuring that the reductions of greenhouse gas emissions required to achieve a predetermined environmental outcome take place at the lowest cost. By allowing the allowances that have been allocated to be sold, the scheme is intended to encourage a participant in the scheme to emit quantities of greenhouse gases that are less than the allowances originally allocated him, in order to sell the surplus to another participant who has emitted more than his allowance.[10]

The ETS mechanism is based on the 'cap-and-trade' principle, that is, the determination of harmful emission maximum caps. A central authority allocates or sells a limited number of permits to discharge specific quantities of a specific pollutant per time period. Polluters are required to hold permits in amounts equal to their emissions. Polluters that want to increase their emissions must buy permits from others willing to sell them. Cap and trade is meant to provide the private sector with the flexibility required to reduce emissions while stimulating technological innovation and economic growth.

At first, under the subsidiarity principle, the decision to fix the cap and the reduction obligations among the various productive sectors was left to the member states through a national plan. Since 2013, however, national plans have been substituted for a Commission decision that establishes the cap according to the total number of allowances issued by member states in the second phase (2008–12). Concisely, a maximum cap is placed at European level and the overall GHGs that factories, installations and plants are allowed to emit must not transcend such a level. Thus, the overall numbers imputed to each member state are further distributed among its operators. This mechanism affects the environmental behaviour of the operator: plants are able to choose whether to make their productive processes more efficient, by reducing polluting emissions and selling the excess allowances, or to overstep the cap and buy the number of allowances corresponding to the excess emissions from other operators. Each allowance gives the holder the right to emit one tonne of CO_2, or the equivalent in other GHGs, according to Article 3, paragraph 1(a) of Directive No. 2003/87/EC. Every year the cap decreases in order to guarantee that at an aggregated level the predetermined goals are reached; the cap is expressed in numbers of allowances to emit (European Union Allowance Units – EUAs), which are allocated by auction or are grandfathered to the plants. National authorities must present a list of national installations covered by the ETS; the Commission controls such lists and determines the benchmark in order to fix the number of allowances to allocate for free. A progressive reduction of the allowances is provided in such a way as to reach the overall goal of a 20 per cent reduction by 2020. The allowances are divided into two kinds: those for fixed installations (EUAs) and those for aircraft operators (European Union Allowances Aviation – EUA-A).

To conclude, the ETS is applied to the following gases: carbon dioxide (CO_2), methane (CH_4), nitrous oxide (N_2O), hydrofluorocarbons (HFCs), perfluorocarbons (PFCs) and sulphur hexafluoride (SF_6). With regard to categories of activities, it is applied to combustion installations, mineral oil refineries, carbon dioxide coke ovens, metal ore, roasting or sintering installations, installations for the production of pig iron or steel, cement clinker, glass, ceramics, pulp and paper, and finally, the aircraft sector.

2.2.1   From Grandfathering to Auction

Over the years, the allocation system has changed and its evolution can be divided into three phases. In the first two phases free allocation was adopted,[11] while the third phase – from 2013 to 2020 – is based on allocation auctioning.[12]

The original criterion of free allocation was justified in the step-by-step logics of Directive 2003/87. This was possible due to the fact that the first phase of the scheme between 2005 and the end of 2007 preceded the Kyoto Protocol's commitment period and there were no legally binding targets limiting the emissions of GHGs of member states. Indeed, the allowance price was not yet known.[13]

Currently, there are some free allocation exemptions: from electricity generators to installations for the capture of CO_2, pipelines for transport of CO_2 or CO_2 storage sites (Directive 2009/29/EC, Article 10a, paragraph 3). Instead, free allowances are allocated to district heating as well as to high-efficiency co-generation (Directive 2009/29/EC, Article 10a, paragraph 4). Further derogations from the general rule of auction are provided for 'new entrants' and sectors deemed to be exposed to a significant risk of carbon leakage. Even in the aircraft sector, most allowances are grandfathered (Directive 2008/101/EC, Article 3, paragraph 5). It is clear that installations that get free allowances can produce further emissions by buying other allowances from the market.

Free allocation – by now, a marginal criterion – is subject to a harmonization process in order to guarantee the aim of GHG emission reduction and the proper functioning of the internal market.[14] The identification of which allowances to give for free is based on a benchmark that is different for every kind of product, harmonized at European level and determined on the basis of the average performance of the 10 per cent most efficient installations per sector or subsector in 2007–08.

Allowances that have not been allocated for free must be auctioned. To this end, EU Regulation No. 1031/2010[15] provides a common auctioning infrastructure in order to avoid any internal market distortions. With respect to European environmental principles, it is evident that only auction-allocated allowances are in line with the polluter-pays-principle (PPP), which – as is well known – also favours competition.[16] The cap represents the acceptable risk at European level: the amount of emissions included in the cap follows the PPP as economic compensation for the emitted tonnes of CO_2. Beyond such a limit, according to the prevention principle, further allowances cannot be emitted and, as a consequence, no further emissions are tolerable. The cap itself is the measure identified ex ante to reduce the risk of environmental damage.

2.3   IS ETS A TAX?

As previously mentioned, the unique nature of ETS is based on the fact that on one hand it is an instrument of administrative regulation, and on the other the expression of a market-based approach. This 'dual' nature makes the question 'Is ETS a tax?' difficult to answer. As a matter of fact, at neither European nor national level is there unanimous consent: the legal status of allowances has not been harmonized, leaving the issue to the discretionary power of member states. Notwithstanding the above problems, let us try to answer the question at any rate.

First of all, it is clearly necessary to delineate the scope of our question by underlining the difference between intangible 'allowances' and the obligation to buy a certain number of allowances corresponding to polluting emissions. Our question is relevant only to the latter and concerns in particular the payment imposed in order to buy allowances.

We can now summarize the European-context dominant definition of tax as: a compulsory patrimonial performance, characterized by the feasibility of contributing to public expenditure. The element of contributing to public expenditure has certainly always been the essence of taxes, while the element of compulsoriness has progressively lost status. In order to define the concept of tax, the current focus of the debate has been switched from its compulsory profile to the authoritative regime (or more correctly, the public law regime) that rules it.[17] In other words, what we are discussing is the evolution of relationships and performances, from compulsoriness at source – in contrast with individual choice – to public regulation, which is instead perfectly compatible with it.

Within this theoretical background, para-commutative taxation[18] is gaining ground concurrently with the traditional concept of tax. It is a wide and heterogeneous category that includes fees and special contributions. It is characterized on the one hand by the traditional profile (common in tax's strictest sense) of a public law unilaterally imposed monetary contribution used to finance public expenditure and, on the other hand, by the legally relevant specific correlation that exists between a public activity or public good and taxpayers' virtual benefit, which lacks reference to a relationship that is really commutative.

In this respect, it is worth remembering that both the European Court of Justice and the California Superior Court excluded the 'tax nature' of market instruments.[19] In particular, with reference to the EU ETS, the European Court of Justice stated that:

> . . . unlike a duty, tax, fee or charge on fuel consumption, the scheme introduced by Directive 2003/87 as amended by Directive 2008/101, apart from the fact that it is not intended to generate revenue for the public authorities, does not in any way enable the establishment, applying a basis of assessment and a rate defined in advance, of an amount that must be payable per tonne of fuel consumed for all the flights carried out in a calendar year.[20]

So, the ETS does not 'involve a form of obligatory levy in favour of the public authorities that might be regarded as constituting a customs duty, tax, fee or charge on fuel held or consumed'.[21] Thus, the Court excludes the ETS's 'tax nature' based on two features: the lack of revenue functionalization to public expenditure and the lack of a direct link to specific polluting substances (fuel). On the one hand, however, analysing the Court's first argument, although the fact that the operators can buy allowances from public authorities is considered irrelevant,[22] such an aspect is actually crucial, as allocating revenue to public expenditure funding is, indeed, the main requirement of the notion of tax.

On first sight, the allowances bought through auction from public authorities satisfy the condition of revenue functionalization to public expenditure, especially considering the fact that the Directive leaves the member states free to determine the destination of revenues generated from auctioning. However, it recommends allocating at least 50 per cent of such revenues to environmental purposes listed in Article 10, paragraph 3 of the Directive itself.[23] Moreover, although all states diligently assign the said 50 per cent to environmental purposes,[24] the majority choose to assign close to 100 per cent.[25] Indeed, projects to fight climate change, such as the 'NER 300 Programme'[26] are funded using the 'New Entrants Reserve'. In the 2014 Progress Report, while communicating the data related to ETS auction revenues, the Commission talks about 'fiscal revenues': 'for the first time, the 2014 Progress Report provides data on the use of fiscal revenues from auctioning allowances in the EU Emission Trading System (ETS). This new source of revenues for member states amounted in total to €3.6 billion in 2013.'[27] Therefore, even if it is informal and a statement 'in passing', it is, at the same time, a sort of endorsement of the tax nature of auction revenues.

Against this backdrop, the Court of Justice's opinion – which considers auctions ruled by public powers and revenue functionalization to public expenditure irrelevant – is not persuasive. The nature of ETS tax is 'silent' until the moment of revenue destination, when it appears together with this functionalization, especially considering its prominent environmental purpose. In substance, even though environmental destination is distinct from general tax flow destination, the public nature of environmental expenditure still exists and represents a crucial element to support the tax function thesis.

On the other hand, the Court's second objection could be considered more valid in the passage where it states the lack of an assessment basis and a rate defined in advance.[28] As a matter of fact, ETS operators, as long as they need to emit one tonne of CO_2, suffer a patrimonial curtailment strictly linked to the polluting substance; however, the quantum is left to market forces.

This quantum seems to be an ordinary payment for allowance purchases: the public side of the market, in fact, appears only if and when such a price is notably lower than the current price in the secondary market, because in that case the platform withdraws the auction.[29] Predetermination involves only the number of allowances placed on the market, but the price has no limits in the bid-up.

Nevertheless, although the quantum is not defined in advance but becomes definable as the European Legislator settles rules and criteria to identify the price there is a causal connection between the levy and environmental degradation. Furthermore, the tax basis is a physical unit of a substance that has been scientifically proven to negatively affect the environment when used. It is also important to add that a basis of assessment and a rate defined in advance are not essential features of the notion of tax. Thus, European judges' exceptions can be easily surmountable.

A further argument, usually stated to exclude the ETS's tax nature, is the adoption of the ETS Directive through the co-decision procedure[30] instead of the unanimity ruled for tax matters.[31] Of course, this is a serious and valid topic but it is a formality, because the adoption procedure does not affect the legal substance of the phenomenon. Moreover, as we will clarify later, the co-decision procedure is perfectly compliant with the hybrid and multipurpose nature of ETS.

At this stage, the ETS can be defined as a hybrid and multipurpose mechanism, with a tax function in the broad sense, combined with the main environmental function. After all, its nature seems to be closer to the classification of a 'fee', traditionally characterized by the fact that it gives benefits back to payers.[32] Nevertheless, it has been recognized that charges deriving from market instruments do not fit squarely within any traditional fee classification, although they share some attributes with several of them. At the same time, charges have some traditional attributes of taxes: first, they are not entirely voluntary; second, an allowance has no value outside the regulatory scheme; third, the amount charged is determined, at least in part, by government fiat; last, the allowance proceeds could be used for general government purposes.[33]

Moreover, its multipurpose function is outlined even by the Court of Justice in a passage where the Court recognizes that:

> ... the principal objective of Directive 2003/87 is to reduce greenhouse gas emissions substantially. That objective must be attained in compliance with a series of sub-objectives and through recourse to certain instruments. The principal instrument for that purpose is the EU scheme for greenhouse gas emissions trading. As indicated in recitals 5 and 7 to Directive 2003/87, among the other sub-objectives to be fulfilled by the scheme are the safeguarding of economic development and employment and the preservation of the integrity of the internal market and of conditions of competition.[34]

In conclusion, to answer the question 'Is ETS a tax?', let us assume that it cannot be considered as such (in the strict sense), but that its function is comparable. This becomes obvious at its inception (compulsory obligation imposed on the economic operator to pay to receive the 'benefit to pollute'), while it is hidden in its circulation phase, and when determining the quantum to be paid by operators it finally it reappears at the revenue destination.

2.4   THE EU COMMISSION'S PROPOSAL: COORDINATION VIA TAX EXEMPTION

As noted earlier, answering calls for coordination that have arisen both among scholars[35] and in practice,[36] the European Commission proposed to modify Directive 2003/96/EC, 27 October 2003. One of the actions proposed by the Commission on 13 April 2011 was the coordination of energy taxation and ETS via tax exemption. Although such a proposal has recently been withdrawn due to the unsuccessful negotiations between the EU member states, it still represents the key project in existence for coordinating energy taxation and ETS. It is therefore the reference point for testing goal achievement feasibility of the 'exemption instrument'. In particular, wanting to assure ETD and ETS complementarity, the Commission worked in two directions: extending the scope of ETD to energy products already covered by the ETS and consequently, introducing a compulsory exemption from CO_2 taxation for activities included in the ETS.

What is important to underline in this respect, is that, since the Commission felt the need to coordinate it with CO_2 taxation, such a proposal implicitly admitted ETS's tax function, highlighting the thesis that energy tax and ETS have the same objective.[37] Both of them are aimed at reducing CO_2 emissions, at promoting energy efficiency and – as widely demonstrated – at collecting revenue for the government.

Against this backdrop, let us evaluate whether the exemption proposed is environmentally efficient. In this respect, free allocation seems to be a derogation from the levy on polluting activities as it reduces the ordinary burden that consists in the obligation to buy, that is to say, the disbursement of a quantum determined by market rules.

Therefore, free allocation can be seen as an exemption from the obligation to buy allowances, which is justified by the purpose of protecting new entrants or of facing competition from industries in third countries that are not subject to comparable GHG emission restrictions.[38] The purpose is to protect 'weak' agents in the internal market and to safeguard the internal market from extra-EU competition, deterring operators, working in sectors exposed to strong international competition, from moving to extra-EU states where the emission restraints are less strict. Of course, these are extra-fiscal purposes, different from the compulsory obligations ratio compliant to the PPP, the overriding principle in European environmental policies. Consequently, the coordination of CO_2 energy taxation and ETS through tax exemption seems to be 'critical' for free allowances, as a sort of double exemption: CO_2 energy taxation exemption is summed to free allowances allocation, which can be defined as a sort of *sui generis* exemption. A shareable need for coordination is transformed into a de facto double exemption.

Is the exemption option compliant with overriding environmental taxation principles? Above all, free allocations run against the PPP, as they imply a mitigation of the levy for polluting operators. This is clearly confirmed by the state aid proceedings against Sweden and Denmark, as the Commission stated that 'Exempting all companies participating in the EU ETS from such a CO_2 tax might not be justifiable, since it could run against the "polluter pays principle" to exempt companies which received emission allowances for free.'[39] This exemption, in fact, gives us a glimpse of the weakening of the PPP, which is an expression both of environmental purposes and of competition protection. On the one hand, the principle is proclaimed as a cornerstone of European environmental policies; on the other, it is actually downgraded as a 'second-class' principle.

In this respect, the free allocation hypothesis is justified in most cases by the need to avoid the risk of carbon leakage, that is, the transfer of European installations to extra-EU countries in which environmental restraints are less strict. Therefore, we can deduce that both PPP and internal market competition can be sacrificed because of a 'higher' aim to protect European companies from external competition. This makes it possible to tolerate free allocation criteria although it does not reward virtuous operators (e.g., the ones who have invested in reducing polluting emissions): what prevails is a mere conservative logic to protect European companies from external competition.

Consequently, it is evident that free allocation – combined with the exemption mechanism – runs against the prevention principle, as it neither affects the entrepreneurial option for healthier activities nor does it encourage innovation. At the same time, even the 'correction-at-source' principle is broken, as free allocation favours operators who behave harmfully towards the environment: free allocation 'rewards', indeed, are not appointed according to merit parameters that take into account the investments made to reduce pollution. As a result, the benefit of free allocation cumulated with exemption causes a double benefit for operators who have not carried out any activity to reduce their emissions or indeed, have polluted more on account of their competitive advantage.

Moreover, the mechanism is inadequate from the environmental point of view, even in the case of allocation by auction: relieving from this CO_2 tax those companies that have to buy additional allowances because they need to cover their extra pollution might go against environmental logic – it could amount to granting a benefit to those who did not make investments and did not lower their pollution or indeed polluted more.

2.5   WHAT ARE THE PROSPECTS?

Concluding, ETS and CO_2 taxation coordination via tax exemption can actually be considered a double exemption, as operators, in the case of free allocation, are exonerated from both levies. Therefore, violations against the fundamental principles in European environmental policies are undeniable. As demonstrated above, there is no doubt that the double exemption phenomenon runs against not only the PPP but also prevention and correction-at-source principles.

So, what are the potential options for better EU ETS and ETD coordination? Tax credit could represent a more suitable environment-oriented solution. Structure and operation of this 'means of coordination' are, of course, expressions of industrial and economic policies rather than legal choices. As a matter of fact, environmental principles, internal market protection, and risk of carbon leakage, must always be balanced. However, even if such a mechanism would undoubtedly be more complex than exemption, some guidelines can be drafted:

- Tax credit should be proportional to the maximum amount of CO_2 taxes imposed on the operator.
- Should CO_2 taxes exceed the amount paid in ETS, the operator must pay the difference.
- Should the amount paid in ETS exceed CO_2 taxes, there would neither be any extra credit to bank on for the following years nor to sell to other operators. The difference would be charged to the operator.
- The existence of such credit could be certified at EU level through common auctioning platforms and then used at national level to reduce the burden deriving from energy taxation.

These simple guidelines could be the base on which build a better structured and coordinated framework compliant with internal market competition and environmental principles.

NOTES

*   The authors would like to thank Professor Marta Villar Ezcurra for including them in the Erasmus+ Jean Monnet Project entitled 'Energy Taxation and State Aid Control: Looking for a Better Coordination and Efficiency' (ETSA-CE), funded by the European Commission and managed by the IDEE–CEU San Pablo University (Madrid, Spain). This chapter stems from the research being conducted by both the authors in the project. In particular, sections 2.1 and 2.3 were written by L. del Federico and sections 2.2, 2.4 and 2.5 by S. Giorgi.
1.   Bohm P. (1999), *International Greenhouse Gas Emission Trading – With Special Reference to the Kyoto Protocol*, Copenhagen: TemaNord, p. 506.
2.   Directive 2003/96/EC of the Council of 27 October 2003 restructuring the Community framework for the taxation of energy products and electricity.
3.   COM(2000) 87, 8 March 2000, Green Paper on greenhouse gas emissions trading within the European Union (presented by the EU Commission).
4.   Directive 2003/87/EC of the European Parliament and of the Council of 13 October 2003 establishing a scheme for greenhouse gas emission allowance trading within the Community and amending Council Directive 96/61/EC. See Poncelet, C. (2011), 'The Emission Trading Scheme Directive: analysis of some contentious points', *European Energy and Environmental Law Review*, **20**(6), 245–54.
5.   Directive 2004/101/EC of the European Parliament and of the Council of 27 October 2004 amending Directive 2003/87/EC establishing a scheme for greenhouse gas emission allowance trading within the Community, in respect of the Kyoto Protocol's project mechanisms.
6.   Directive 2008/101/EC of the European Parliament and of the Council of 19 November 2008 amending Directive 2003/87/EC so as to include aviation activities in the scheme for greenhouse gas emission allowance trading within the Community.
7.   Schwarze, G. (2007), 'Including aviation into the European Union's Emission Trading Scheme', *European Energy and Environmental Law Review*, **16**(1), 10–22.

8. Directive 2009/29/EC of the European Parliament and of the Council of 23 April 2009 amending Directive 2003/87/EC so as to improve and extend the greenhouse gas emission allowance trading scheme of the Community.
9. Bilbao Estrada, I. and P. Pistone (2013), 'Global CO_2 taxes', *Intertax*, **41**(1), 2–14.
10. European Court of Justice, *Société Arcelor Atlantique et Lorraine and others* v. *Premier ministre, Ministre de l'Ecologie et du Développement durable et Ministre de l'Economie, des Finances et de l'Industrie*, Case C-127/07, 16 December 2008, paragraph 32, accessed 7 April 2016 at http://curia.europa.eu/juris/liste.jsf?language=en&num=C-127/07.
11. Article 10 of the Directive stated that 'For the three-year period beginning 1 January 2005 member states shall allocate at least 95% of the allowances free of charge. For the five-year period beginning 1 January 2008, member states shall allocate at least 90% of the allowances free of charge.'
12. Tenbakk, B., F. Sinner and J. Nysæther (eds) (2009), *EU Emission Trading – Economical Effects of Emission Auctions*, Copenhagen: TemaNord.
13. COM(2001) 581, Proposal for a Directive of the European Parliament and of the Council establishing a scheme for greenhouse gas emission allowance trading within the Community and amending Council Directive 96/61/EC, General Remarks 1.2, p. 3, accessed 7 April 2016 at http://ec.europa.eu/transparency/regdoc/rep/1/2001/EN/1-2001-581-EN-F1-1.Pdf.
14. See Commission's Decision 27 April 2011, first whereas clause.
15. Commission Regulation (EU) No. 1031/2010 of 12 November 2010 on the timing, administration and other aspects of auctioning of greenhouse gas emission allowances pursuant to Directive 2003/87/EC of the European Parliament and of the Council establishing a scheme for greenhouse gas emission allowances trading within the Community.
16. Bugge, H.C. (2009), 'The polluter pays principle: dilemma of justice in national and international contexts', in J. Ebbesson and P. Okowa (eds), *Environmental Law and Justice in Context*, New York: Cambridge University Press; Herrera Molina, P.M. (2008), 'El principio "quien contamina, paga"' [The 'polluter pays' principle], in F. Becker Zuazua et al. (eds), *Tratado de tributación medioambiental*, Navarra, Spain: Aranzadi, p. 184; Verrigni, C. (2003), 'La rilevanza del principio comunitario "chi inquina paga" nei tributi ambientali' [The relevance of the Community's 'polluter pays' principle' in environmental taxes], *Rassegna Tributaria*, **5**, 1617.
17. Del Federico, L. (2005), 'The notion of tax and the different types of taxes', in B. Peeters et al. (eds), *The Concept of Tax*, Amsterdam: IBFD, p. 75.
18. Taxes imposed to have a public service or to enjoy a public good. The notion of 'fees' is perhaps the most similar to the notion of 'commutative/para-commutative taxation'.
19. *California Chamber of Commerce* v. *California Air Resources Board*, Case No. 34-2012-80001313, consolidated with *Morning Star Packing Company* v. *California Air Resources Board*, Case No. 34-203-80001464. 'The Court recognizes that such charges do not bear any of the "traditional attributes of a tax, in that (1) the charges were imposed for regulatory purposes and not for unrelated revenue purposes; (2) those who purchase allowances acquire a valuable benefit not enjoyed by others; (3) the charges are not compulsory; (4) the amount charged is determined by the market and not by government fiat; (5) the proceeds will be used to further the regulatory purposes of AB 32 and cannot be used for the general support of the government.' Accessed 7 April 2016 at http://advocacy.calchamber.com/wp-content/uploads/2015/10/Joint_Ruling_on_Submitted_Matters.pdf.
20. *European Court of Justice, Air Transport Association of America and Others/Secretary of State of Energy and Climate Change*, Case C-366/10, 21 December 2011, paragraph 143.
21. Ibid., paragraph 145.
22. Ibid., paragraph 146.
23. To summarize paragraph 3: to reduce greenhouse gas emissions; to develop renewable energy and measures to avoid deforestation and increase afforestation and reforestation in developing countries; forestry sequestration; the environmentally safe capture

and geological storage of CO_2; to encourage a shift to low-emission and public forms of transport; to finance research and development in energy efficiency and clean technologies in the sectors covered by the Directive; measures intended to increase energy efficiency and insulation; to cover administrative expenses of the management of the Community scheme.

24. Italy, for example, has provided an ad hoc fund, Fondo nazionale per l'efficienza energetica (National Fund for Energy Efficiency), instituted by the Economic Development Ministry. The national authority (GSE) deposits auction revenues in a current account, then the revenues are transferred into a State Treasury account as a State Budget entry, with a compulsory destination, as they derive from European commitments.

25. See *Report from the European Commission to the European Parliament and the Council on 28 October 2014, on Progress towards achieving the Kyoto and EU 2020 objectives* (COM(2014) 689 (Progress Report). In particular, the revenues used for climate and energy-related purposes are 100 per cent in Germany, Spain, UK, France, Netherlands, Greece, Portugal, Slovakia, Ireland, Lithuania and Latvia, with an overall average of 87 per cent of the revenue used for environmental purposes.

26. European Commission's press release on 8 July 2014, accessed 6 April 2016 at http://europa.eu/rapid/press-release_IP-14-780_en.htm. Through the NER (New Entrants Reserve) 300 funding programme, 1 billion euros were used to finance 19 projects that will be hosted in 12 EU member states: Croatia, Cyprus, Denmark, Estonia, France, Ireland, Italy, Latvia, Portugal, Spain, Sweden and the United Kingdom.

27. European Commission (2014), 'EU greenhouse gas emissions and targets', *Global Sustain Newsletter*, 31 October, accessed 7 April 2016 at http://globalsustain.org/en/story/10205. See also *Report from the European Commission to the European Parliament and the Council on 28 October 2014*, cited above.

28. See on this point Milne, J.E. and M.S. Andersen (2012), 'Introduction to environmental taxation concept and research', in J.E. Milne and M.K. Andersen (eds), *Handbook of Research on Environmental Taxation*, Cheltenham, UK and Northampton, MA, USA, Edward Elgar Publishing, p. 29: 'taxes establish fixed costs for polluters, while the cost of traded allowances fluctuates according to the market demand'.

29. According to EU Regulation No. 1031/2010, Article 7, paragraph 6.

30. According to the Treaty on the Functioning of the European Union – TFEU (Article 294), the co-decision procedure is the ordinary legislative procedure. It is based on the principle of parity and means that neither institution (European Parliament or Council) may adopt legislation without the other's assent. Nevertheless, tax matters are subject to the unanimity rule (Articles 113–114). This denotes the obligation to reach a consensus among all the member states meeting within the EU Council so that a proposal can be adopted.

31. According to the Treaty on the Functioning of the European Union, tax measures must be adopted unanimously by the member states.

32. Milne, J.E. (2014), 'Environmental taxes and fees: wrestling with theory', in L. Kreiser, S. Lee and K. Ueta et al. (eds), *Environmental Taxation and Green Fiscal Reform*, Cheltenham, UK and Northampton, MA, USA, Edward Elgar Publishing, p. 8.

33. *California Chamber of Commerce* v. *California Air Resources Board*, cited above, which concludes that 'not all revenue-producing measures fit into the traditional fee classifications. This does not mean such charges are invalid. Revenue measures may be valid despite having attributes of more than one classification.'

34. European Court of Justice, *Iberdrola and others* v. *Administración del Estado*, paragraph 43, accessed 8 April 2016 at http://eur-lex.europa.eu/legal-content/EN/TXT/?uri=CELEX%3A62011CJ0566.

35. Antón, A. and I. Bilbao Estrada (2010), 'State aid and the EU Council Directive 2003/96/EC: the case for augmenting the environmental component', in C. Dias Soares, J.E. Milne and H. Ashiabor et al. (eds), *Critical Issues in Environmental Taxation. International and Comparative Perspectives, Volume VIII*, Oxford: Oxford University

Press, p. 448; M. Villar Ezcurra (2013), 'State aids and energy taxes: towards a coherent reference framework', *Intertax*, **41**(6/7), 341.

36. Denmark, Sweden, Norway, Finland and Iceland have introduced CO_2 taxation, which is the reason why the Scandinavian countries were the first to feel the need for coordination.
37. Even in ETS, energy efficiency is promoted: the most efficient operators can buy fewer allowances or they can bank the excess ones.
38. Clò, S. (2011), *European Emission Trading in Practice*, Cheltenham, UK and Northampton, MA, USA: Edward Elgar Publishing, p. 122.
39. State aid – Sweden – State aid No. C 46/2006 (ex N 347/2006) – Relief from CO_2 tax on fuels consumed in installations covered by the EU Emission Trading Scheme – Invitation to submit comments pursuant to Article 88(2) of the EC Treaty, 2 Preliminary Assessment and the Commission's Doubts, section 2.2, accessed 8 April 2016 at http://eur-lex.europa.eu/legal-content/EN/TXT/?uri=uriserv:OJ.C_.2006.297.01.0027.01. ENG.

3. Carbon policy in Australia – a political history

Evgeny Guglyuvatyy and Natalie P. Stoianoff

3.1 INTRODUCTION

In June 1992 at the Rio Earth Summit, 154 countries joined the United Nations Framework Convention on Climate Change (UNFCCC).[1] The UNFCCC set the goal for industrialized countries to limit greenhouse gas (GHG) emissions to 1990 levels in the year 2000. However, since the targets were voluntary, only some countries introduced legally binding policies to reduce GHG emissions and achieve the goal.[2] Australia had actively participated in the Rio Earth Summit in 1992, endorsing the Summit goals that were formed by the desire for sustainable development. Australia also joined the UNFCCC[3] and later signed the Kyoto Protocol[4] supporting GHG reduction.

However, even before the Rio Summit, climate change was on the agenda in Australia. In 1989, in the lead-up to the 1990 Australian federal election, both leading political parties discussed the introduction of GHG reduction policy. The Labor Party in particular considered a GHG emissions reduction target of 20 per cent by 2005.[5] Simultaneously, the Liberal Party was developing similar policies and the Liberal shadow environment minister at the time argued during the 1990 election campaign that the Liberal Party was ahead of Labor on climate change, and on many other environmental issues.[6] However, interest in climate change issues diminished during the 1990s. Environmental issues were gradually dropped from the political agenda and did not appear in the 1993 election campaign. According to some commentators, the 1990s' recession, increasing dominance of neoliberalism among Labor ministers and ascendancy of the energy and coal lobby were amongst the factors leading to declining interest in environmental issues.[7]

3.2   HOWARD GOVERNMENT (MARCH 1996–DECEMBER 2007)

Despite the reduced attention given to environmental issues in the early 1990s, a range of measures aimed at reducing Australia's greenhouse gas emissions have been on the federal- and state-level agendas for the last two decades. Successive Australian governments have been committed to the introduction of either a carbon tax or an emissions trading scheme (ETS) designed to mitigate climate change.[8] Some Australian state and local governments have introduced pollution and waste management charges – for example, landfill levies. There has been some experience with the deployment of ETSs in Australia. At a subnational level, that is, state level, for instance, the NSW Greenhouse Gas Abatement Scheme (GGAS) began in 1997 and became mandatory in 2003, imposing obligations on all electricity retailers in New South Wales.[9] This was the world's first mandatory GHG ETS.[10]

At the federal level, support for a national ETS followed long-standing support at the state government level. According to Senator Birmingham, the Howard government considered climate change issues and acted upon them from the moment of election in 1996.[11] For example, in 1997 Prime Minister Howard announced a AU$180 million package to reduce GHG, established the Australian Greenhouse Office in 1998 together with a AU$555 million package to develop systems for measuring and monitoring GHG emissions as well as energy performance standards for a range of appliances and equipment.[12] In 2000 the Howard government introduced the Renewable Energy (Electricity) Act 2000, which established the mandatory renewable energy target scheme aimed to boost the development of renewable energy sources across Australia.

However, in 2004, the Howard government produced an Energy White Paper that rejected an ETS, refused to adopt a mandatory renewable energy target of 20 per cent by the year 2020 and confirmed its 2002 decision not to ratify the Kyoto Protocol.[13] Two years later, in 2006, 'doing something' about global warming gathered strong political momentum in Australia.[14] In particular, the Labor Opposition called for the ratification of Kyoto, demonstrating a deeper commitment to action on global warming.[15]

In order to 'do something' the Howard government responded by accepting the recommendation of a joint business/government taskforce to introduce an ETS that would protect export-exposed sectors and the mining industry.[16] Additionally, the government indicated that Australia would support a new international agreement to limit the growth of GHG emissions, provided that it bound all nations.[17]

In December 2006, Prime Minister Howard announced that Australia would move towards a domestic ETS, to start no later than 2012.[18] The

Prime Ministerial Task Group on Emissions Trading was established to develop an ETS considering the following terms of reference: (1) 'Australia enjoys major competitive advantages through the possession of large reserves of fossil fuels and uranium. In assessing Australia's further contribution to reducing greenhouse gas emissions, these advantages must be preserved.' (2) 'Against this background the Task Group is asked to advise on the nature and design of a workable global emissions trading system in which Australia would be able to participate. The Task Group will advise and report on additional steps that might be taken, in Australia, consistent with the goal of establishing such a system.'[19]

The Task Group reported that 'the most efficient and effective way to manage risk is through market mechanisms' and that accordingly an ETS is the preferable emission reduction mechanism for Australia.[20] This firm belief was based on the view that it is far better to enable the market to 'decide which new or existing technologies will reduce emissions at least cost' rather than leaving it to the government to 'pick winners'.[21] The main design features of the Task Group's proposed ETS were based on a 'cap-and-trade' system and included the following:

- a long-term aspirational emissions abatement goal and associated pathways to provide an explicit guide for business investment and community engagement;
- an overall emissions reduction trajectory that commences moderately, progressively stabilizes, and then results in deeper emissions reductions over time, and:
  - is sufficiently flexible that it can be periodically recalibrated by government to changing international and domestic circumstances through regular and transparent reviews;
  - provides markets with the ability to develop a forward carbon price path to guide business investment decisions and help drive longer-term technology development – markets would be expected to establish a low initial carbon price and a forward price curve that rises over time;
- maximum practical coverage of all sources and sinks, and of all greenhouse gases:
  - with permit liability placed on direct emissions from large facilities and on upstream fuel suppliers for other energy emissions;
  - with those sectors initially excluded from the emissions trading scheme subject to other policies designed to deliver abatement;

- initial exclusion of agriculture and land use from the scheme:

  - though agricultural emissions should be brought into the scheme as practical issues are resolved;

- a mixture of free allocation and auctioning of single-year dated emissions permits that:

  - provides an up-front, once-and-for-all, free allocation of permits as compensation to existing businesses identified as likely to suffer a disproportionate loss of value due to the introduction of a carbon price;
  - ameliorates, through free allocation, the carbon-related exposures of existing and new investments in trade-exposed, emissions-intensive industries while key international competitors do not face similar carbon constraints, but which also provides ongoing incentives for abatement and adoption of industry best practice;
  - allows for the periodic auctioning of remaining permits;

- a 'safety valve' emissions fee designed to limit unanticipated costs to the economy and to business, particularly in the early years of the scheme, while ensuring an ongoing incentive to abate;
- recognition of a wide range of credible carbon offset regimes, domestically and internationally;
- capacity, over time, to link to other comparable national and regional schemes in order to provide the building blocks of a truly global emissions trading scheme;
- incentives for firms to undertake abatement in the lead-up to the start of the scheme, including through the purchase of offset credits from carbon plantations, and potentially from other accredited activities;
- revenue from permits and fees to be used, in the first instance, to support emergence of low-emissions technologies and energy efficiency initiatives:

  - the focus might shift more toward households and business as the scheme matures.[22]

In addition to these design features, the Task Group noted the necessity for the ETS to be flexible, technology neutral and operating nationally. It was made clear in the report that complementary measures addressing market failures not corrected by the ETS would need to be adopted, including informational or educational and voluntary strategies,[23] as well as subsidies for the development of new technologies.[24]

In September 2007, the National Greenhouse and Energy Reporting Bill was introduced as a first step towards emissions trading. This bill established an emissions reporting scheme that would cover around 75 per cent of total emissions in Australia.[25] The coverage of the scheme incorporated transport and other fuels as well as including all six gases identified by the Kyoto Protocol. The scheme's reporting requirements covered about 700 Australian companies and provided a uniform, national reporting framework that removed duplicative arrangements developed by state and territory governments.[26] The legislation passed both Houses of Parliament and received Royal Assent by the end of the month.[27] The next federal election was called and 24 November 2007 saw the demise of the Howard government.[28]

3.3 RUDD GOVERNMENT (DECEMBER 2007–JUNE 2010)

In the lead-up to the 2007 Federal Election, Opposition Leader Kevin Rudd declared Labor's intention to 'tackle'[29] climate change as a crucial point distinguishing Labor from the Liberal–National Coalition (Coalition).[30] In particular, Labor indicated its intention to ratify the Kyoto Protocol, supported the Garnaut Review[31] commissioned by the Labor state premiers and confirmed the introduction of an ETS that included a set of targets aligned with a 60 per cent reduction of GHG emissions below 2000 levels by 2050.[32] It appeared that Labor would act determinedly on climate change.

Indeed, soon after the election, the Rudd government ratified the Kyoto Protocol[33] and, by the middle of its first year in office, proposed the Australian Carbon Pollution Reduction Scheme (ACPRS). The proposed ACPRS had two objectives: first, to meet Australia's emissions reduction targets in the 'most flexible and cost-effective way'; and second, to sustain a global response to climate change.[34] In July 2008 the Rudd government issued a Green Paper that outlined the preferred design of the ACPRS and identified the parameters that needed to be considered further.[35] Then a White Paper was made public in December 2008,[36] including a third objective of 'adapting to the impacts of climate change that we cannot avoid'[37] (which will not be considered in this chapter), followed by the proposed legislation in May 2009.

According to the proposed legislation, a series of short-term annual caps for overall emissions were to be established from 2011, consistent with meeting the long-term goal to reduce Australia's emissions by 60 per cent by 2050.[38] The emissions cap would be progressively reduced over time, which should result in a higher GHG price, enhanced investment in low-emissions technologies and a decline in overall emissions. Participants in the scheme would need to hold enough emissions permits to account for their annual emissions. Permits would be allocated through auctioning, though some would be grandfathered in order to assist emissions-intensive trade-exposed (EITE) industries in adjusting to a carbon-constrained economy.[39]

The Rudd government was committed to reducing emissions by 5 per cent of 2000 emissions levels by 2020.[40] This reduction level was expected to increase to as much as 25 per cent of 2000 levels by 2020, conditional on an international agreement.[41] Originally, however, the reduction target was 5 per cent on 2000 levels by 2020 and 15 per cent if an international agreement was reached. As a result of industry pressure, the Rudd government delayed the start of the scheme (initially until 2010, then 2011) until 2012, kept the 5 per cent goal and enlarged the conditional 15 per cent to 25 per cent.[42] In addition, the compromise included a relatively low, fixed initial price for permits of AU$10 per tonne, and even more permits were to be grandfathered.[43]

The ACPRS covered the same GHGs as the Kyoto Protocol – those emitted by stationary energy, transport, fugitive emissions (such as methane emissions from black coal mining), industrial processes, imports, production and use of synthetic GHGs, and wastes.[44] The proposed ACPRS expected to cover around 1000 large emitters estimated to be responsible for/account for 75 per cent of Australia's emissions.[45] It was also expected to be broader in coverage and scope than any other ETS proposed or operating in Australia or overseas, including the EU ETS, and the proposal put forward by the Australian states and territories in 2006.

The development of the ACPRS from its conception in the Green Paper to the draft legislation was a movable feast. For example, in relation to the international offset credit arrangements, the Green Paper proposed restricted linkage, explicitly stating that only a limited number of international offset credits could be surrendered for compliance.[46] Meanwhile, the exposure draft legislation later provided unrestricted linkage – participants would be able to use an unlimited number of Kyoto units[47] on top of GHG permits. Unlimited use of Kyoto units could have potentially jeopardized the achievement of Australia's national reduction target. It would have been reasonable for the Rudd government to set a limit on the number of international offset units that could be surrendered by businesses, as is provided, for example, in the EU ETS. This relaxing of restrictions demonstrated the need to address the intense political environment brewing around the attempt to introduce the ACPRS.

There are further examples of where the Rudd government needed to placate a variety of industry sectors, such as the EITE industries. The

Rudd government proposed to allocate more than 30 per cent of annual permits free of charge in order to assist EITE industries to meet their obligations under ACPRS. EITE activities that would generate more than 1500 tonnes of CO_2 for each million Australian dollars of revenue would receive free permits to cover up to 66 per cent of their emissions; meanwhile, EITE activities that would generate more than 2000 tonnes of CO_2 for each million Australian dollars of revenue would receive free permits to cover up to 94.5 per cent of their emissions.[48] However, the expectation was that the level of assistance to EITE sectors would decline over time.

In addition, special attention was given to industries expected to be strongly affected by the ACPRS but not eligible for EITE assistance. The proposed legislation indicated that coal-fired electricity generators were likely to be included in this category. Thus, additional assistance was to be provided to the coal-fired electricity generation industry, such as support for carbon capture and storage technology development, and structural adjustment for affected workers, communities and regions.[49] Direct cash payments to these coal-fired electricity generators were to be provided as well.[50]

It should be noted that more than 50 per cent of Australia's GHG is emitted by electricity generators and 77 per cent of Australia's electricity is generated from coal. Consequently, any serious climate change solution must target the electricity sector directly.[51] A price on GHG through the ACPRS would provide some incentive for the energy generation sector to reduce its GHG intensity. However, the significant compensation to EITE sectors and to the coal-fired electricity generation industry proposed by the then Rudd government would have almost certainly given businesses the wrong signal, and distorted the ultimate target of mitigating climate change. Substantial compensation can wipe out, or at least seriously diminish, the projected incentives for developing new energy-efficient production processes or shifting to renewable energy sources.[52] Furthermore, if external costs are not internalized by the producers, the environmental impact of such a climate change mitigation instrument would be neutralized.

Since the ACPRS was expected to cover approximately 1000 businesses, a relatively small number of entities would receive valuable free permits. This was expected to result in considerable extra costs to non-EITE industries and to those EITE businesses falling outside the eligibility thresholds.[53] Assistance to EITE industries and the energy-generating sector would effectively provide a subsidy to the worst carbon emitters, leaving the burden of the ACPRS to less polluting industries and reducing the opportunities for cleaner energy alternatives.[54] Instead of compensating designated businesses, the revenue from the ACPRS would have been put to better use by providing additional assistance for the implementation of low-emissions technologies.

In order to eliminate the negative impact of the ACPRS on the cost of living of households, the Rudd government proposed to increase payments to people receiving social allowance benefits above automatic indexation.[55] In addition to that, targeted assistance was to be provided to low-income households through the tax and welfare systems.[56]

Further, with the inclusion of petrol in the proposed scheme, the cost of fuel would increase and that increase would be passed on to consumers. In order to compensate the initial price increase caused by the ACPRS, the government indicated that the excise tax on petrol would be reduced on a 'cent-for-cent' basis.[57] However, as a result of this measure, petrol consumers would not notice the price effect of the ACPRS and would not see an emissions cost included in the petrol price. Consequently, an incentive to reduce petrol consumption would be eliminated as the preferential fuel prices regime would not pass a correct price signal on to consumers.

Like the EU ETS, the Rudd government prioritized an international harmonization of emissions trading. Many analysts agree that an ETS is much easier to harmonize with other countries' carbon mitigation programmes.[58] Indeed, an ETS generates a natural unit of exchange for harmonization: permits denominated in units of GHG emissions. If emissions reductions are cheaper to make in China than in Australia, emissions ought to be reduced first in the former where costs are lower.[59] Another key consideration of the Rudd government was international competitiveness. In other words, Australian industries subject to the proposed ACPRS would be disadvantaged in international markets compared to their competitors from countries that did not impose a price on carbon. To address this issue the Rudd government proposed that exposed industries would receive free permits to diminish this concern.[60] Unlike the EU ETS, the ACPRS extensively addresses distributional issues associated with it.[61]

Despite the numerous concessions and preferential treatment incorporated in the design of the ACPRS, industry pressure led to the Rudd government deciding to delay the start of the proposed scheme as mentioned above. However, in the end, the ACPRS legislation was twice defeated in the Australian Parliament in 2009 despite extensive political negotiations with the Liberal–National Coalition Opposition led by Malcolm Turnbull, who was then deposed by Tony Abbott as leader while the legislation was in play. The defeat occurred in the upper house, the Senate, with Green Party members voting with the Coalition against the ACPRS legislation.[62] An unlikely alliance, the Greens voted against the legislation on the basis that the scheme did not do enough while the Coalition voted against the legislation due to a strong objection to an emissions trading scheme on the basis that it was just another tax.[63] As a result, in April 2010 the Rudd government put the ACPRS on hold.

3.4 GILLARD GOVERNMENT (JUNE 2010–JUNE 2013)

Later in 2010, there was a change of leadership in the Labor Party and the deputy to Kevin Rudd, Julia Gillard, became Australia's first female prime minister. She led the government into the next election with an election promise of no carbon tax, but, due to a significant swing toward the Coalition Opposition, found that she could only form government with the assistance of the Greens and three independent Members of Parliament. In order to maintain this alliance to form a government, Prime Minister Gillard announced the new government's intention to propose a temporary carbon pricing scheme[64] as well as to establish the Multi-Party Climate Change Committee (the Committee)[65] consisting of members of the federal government and senators.[66]

The Committee's intention was to establish a climate change framework outlining the broad architecture for a carbon price. The Committee issued 11 policy principles designed to provide a consistent basis for the deliberations on a carbon price.[67] The principles were as follows:

- environmental effectiveness;
- economic efficiency;
- budget neutrality;
- competitiveness of Australian industries;
- energy security;
- investment certainty;
- fairness;
- flexibility;
- administrative simplicity;
- clear accountabilities; and
- to support Australia's international objectives and obligations.[68]

The Multi-Party Climate Change Committee stated that the 11 principles would guide the design decisions of the pricing mechanism.

The Committee released draft legislation on 28 July 2011. In October 2011, the Australian House of Representatives passed the carbon pricing legislation, which was also passed by the Australian Senate in November. The carbon pricing scheme (the scheme), forming part of the Clean Energy Future regime, operated from 1 July 2012 as a temporary measure designed to reduce GHGs. The carbon price was AU$23 for the 2012–13 financial year and was designed to increase by 2.5 per cent in each of the following two years.[69] Under the scheme, liable entities were to buy and surrender carbon units equal to their direct emissions (based on historic levels) of carbon dioxide equivalents (CO_2e). Failure to surrender necessary carbon units would result in a fine. After the transitional period, the carbon pricing mechanism was to convert to a cap-and-trade ETS supplying a flexible carbon price.[70] From 1 July 2015, the carbon units were intended to be auctioned. Hence, even though the carbon pricing mechanism is some-times labelled a 'carbon tax', the Australian government was committed to emissions trading.

The carbon pricing scheme covered four of the six GHGs counted under the Kyoto Protocol, those being: carbon dioxide (CO_2), methane (CH_4), nitrous oxide (N_2O) and perfluorocarbon (PFC),[71] and had broad coverage of the following emissions sources:

- the stationary energy sector;
- industrial processes sector;
- fugitive emissions (other than from decommissioned coal mines); and
- emissions from non-legacy waste.[72]

The scheme covered around 500 entities emitting 25 000 tonnes of CO_2 per year or more and certain waste facilities emitting more than 10 000 tonnes per year, constituting about 50 per cent of Australia's GHGs.[73] Agriculture and transport fuels were excluded from the scheme, although transport fuels used by off-road heavy vehicles (except for agriculture, fishing and forestry) were covered indirectly by a reduction in existing fuel tax concessions.[74] To transfer a carbon price signal to rail, domestic shipping and domestic aviation, fuel tax excises were increased. The treatment of fuel was to be reviewed in 2014. During the fixed price transitional period under the scheme, liable parties could not use international emissions reduction units for compliance. However, during the flexible price period, it was intended that internationally recognized permits might be used to acquit up to 50 per cent of a party's liability.[75]

There was no cap on emissions during the fixed price period and the number of carbon units was unlimited. However, starting from 2015–16, it was intended that the Climate Change Authority[76] would set a cap on emissions taking into consideration international and Australian emissions reduction targets. During the Gillard government, Australia was commit-ted to reducing emissions by 5 per cent of 2000 emissions levels by 2020, and by 80 per cent of 2000 levels by 2050.[77]

It was projected that the carbon price scheme would raise AU\$24.5 billion over its first four years. However, the scheme would not be revenue neutral; the budget deficit was expected to be around AU\$4 billion.[78] The explanation was an extensive spending plan to compensate industries and households and to invest in renewable energy including the provision of significant income tax cuts and increases in allowances, payments and benefits. In particular, the tax-free threshold on incomes was more than tripled from the previous AU\$6000 to AU\$18 200 from 1 July 2012, and then set to increase to AU\$19 400 from 1 July 2015. The consequence of these changes was that all taxpayers with an income below AU\$80 000 effectively received tax cuts from 1 July 2012.[79]

Further, an assistance package of AU\$9.2 billion was allocated over the first three years to Australian industries to eliminate competitiveness issues associated with the carbon price scheme.[80] Most affected industries such as steel, aluminium, zinc, pulp and paper-makers will acquire free permits covering about 94.5 per cent of industry's average carbon costs. In addition, AU\$300 million was to be assigned to the steel industry's shift to clean energy. A coal sector jobs package of AU\$1.3 billion was dedicated for mines most affected by the carbon price.[81]

Consideration was also given to complementary measures that supported research, development and commercialization of green technologies. In particular, an AU\$10 billion Clean Energy Finance Corporation was created to invest in new technologies, and AU\$3.2 billion was allocated to the Australian Renewable Energy Agency.[82] Additionally, small grants were made available for community-based energy efficiency programmes. On top of that, the Gillard government was committed to the closure of 2000 megawatts of the dirtiest power generators by 2020.[83]

Since agricultural and land sector emissions were not covered under the carbon pricing mechanism the Gillard government introduced the Carbon Farming Initiative (CFI). The CFI is a carbon offsets scheme that provides new economic opportunities for farmers, forest growers and landholders to help the environment by reducing carbon pollution.[84] Farmers and land managers are able to generate credits that could then be sold to other businesses wanting to offset their own carbon pollution. In particular, the CFI enables land managers to earn credits for actions including:

- reforestation and revegetation;
- reduced methane emissions from livestock digestion;
- reduced fertilizer pollution;
- reduced pollution or increased carbon storage in agricultural soils (soil carbon);
- savannah fire management;

- native forest protection;
- forest management;
- reduced pollution from rice cultivation;
- reduced pollution from legacy landfill waste.

Liable entities covered by the carbon pricing scheme were allowed to surrender Kyoto-compliant CFI credits for up to 5 per cent of their liability in the fixed price period and, during the flexible price period there would be no quantitative restrictions on surrender of Kyoto-compliant CFI credits. Kyoto-compliant CFI credits were tradable between entities.

Overall, the broad architecture of the Clean Energy Future regime, and in particular the carbon pricing scheme, seemed to resemble in some aspects the design of the proposed ACPRS.[85] However, the carbon price, in some respects, was a substantial improvement on the heavily compromised ACPRS. Generous compensation for affected industry was a temporary measure and based on historic emissions levels: thus the incentive to reduce emissions was not eroded. The assistance package for households was designed to compensate low- and medium-income earners rather than high-income earners. Raising the income tax threshold removed about a million low-income taxpayers from the income tax system.[86] Further, the range of supporting measures designed to encourage carbon farming, energy efficiency and green innovation provided a significant improvement over the ACPRS.

3.5   ABBOTT GOVERNMENT (SEPTEMBER 2013–SEPTEMBER 2015)

In September 2013, the Coalition, led by Tony Abbott, won the federal election. The attitude to climate change was quite different from that of the previous two prime ministers. The Gillard government's carbon pricing legislation was repealed by the Abbott government in July 2014 and replaced by the Direct Action Plan by the end of that year.

The Abbott government indicated the Direct Action Plan was introduced to 'efficiently and effectively source low cost emissions reductions that will contribute towards our 2020 target'.[87] The Direct Action Plan includes as a centrepiece the Emissions Reduction Fund (ERF) designed to provide incentives for GHG reduction activities across the entire Australian economy. Under the ERF the government pays for projects that will reduce CO_2 emissions at minimal cost. Funding from the ERF is allocated through auctions. A range of possible projects for CO_2 reduction include: energy efficiency, cleaning up power stations, reafforestation and re-vegetation and/or improvement of soil carbon.[88]

There has been very little detailed public or economic analysis of the Emissions Reduction Fund and its design.[89] However, there are numerous in-built design problems with the Emissions Reduction Fund. According to various commentators, the major design issues that will impact on the ERF's ability to reduce Australia's greenhouse gas emissions include:

- additionality;[90]
- difficulties in setting baselines;
- compliance mechanisms and penalties;
- overall limits on emissions;
- the need for longer time frames, including funding and planning beyond 2020;
- future scalability of the ERF; and
- access to international permits.[91]

Evidently, any policy to reduce Australia's GHG emissions requires a limit or 'cap' on overall emissions, and mechanisms preventing polluters from exceeding emissions limits.[92] However, at present there are no emissions caps or instruments that would insure that the polluters are limiting their GHG emissions. The government issued a Consultation Paper on a safeguard mechanism that will apply to facilities with direct emissions in excess of 100 000 tonnes of CO_2-e per year.[93] According to the Consultation Paper, the safeguard mechanism would cover around 140 businesses (emissions-intensive generators) that emit around 57 per cent of GHGs from the electricity sector.[94] The safeguard mechanism obliges polluters to avoid net emissions from their facility from exceeding the baseline emissions levels throughout a monitoring period (a financial year).

Nevertheless, the Consultation Paper does not present details on how individual baselines will be designated or how emissions-intensive generators will be identified. It is also unclear whether all generators, irrespective of fuel source, will be treated similarly or if there will be allowances for businesses that are expected to produce higher emissions. The Consultation Paper proposes a number of enforcement options for entities that exceed an emissions limit, including: infringement notices, enforceable undertakings, injunctions to rectify an emissions exceedance, and civil penalties to be imposed by a court. The amount of civil penalty for an emissions exceedance is not specified. The government indicated that the safeguard mechanism, which is absolutely critical to the scheme, will not be in place until July 2016 at the earliest.[95]

The important feature of the Direct Action Plan is its voluntary nature. Numerous commentators argue that a voluntary carbon mechanism does not provide an incentive for businesses to participate and compete for participation in the ERF.[96] The Australian Senate inquiry on the Direct Action Plan provided the following comment: 'The committee is persuaded that the government's Direct Action Plan and the proposed Emissions Reduction Fund are fundamentally flawed. They ignore the well-established principle of "polluter pays", and instead propose that the Australian taxpayer should effectively subsidize big polluters.'[97] Overall, the Direct Action Plan has been significantly criticized and it is labelled as a step backwards for Australian climate change policy.

The Abbott government also sought to abolish the Climate Change Authority, which was established by the previous government to provide independent assessment and advice on carbon policy. Should the Authority be abolished, there will be no independent assessment of policy and targets and no requirement for the government to respond to independent review, which would further reduce transparency and accountability of carbon policy-making. In this light, it is difficult to consider the climate change law-making process of the present government (now led by Malcolm Turnbull after Tony Abbott's leadership as prime minister was successfully challenged in October 2015) as adequate and comprehensive. Thus, the Abbott government's policy-making practice raised even more questions, and as one may note, the climate change policy-making process in Australia deteriorated over the last two years, falling far short of that of the previous Coalition government in 2007.

3.6 ANALYSIS

From the discussion above it is noteworthy that, starting from the Howard government, federal governments considered climate change and acted on it. Conversely, the efforts of the governments vary significantly with markedly different resultant policies. The obvious explanation for such a different approach is complex political games of the leading Australian political parties. This analysis attempts to shed some light on what is influencing climate-related policies in Australia and how specific climate change polices are developed.

As highlighted above, the Howard government started to act on climate change soon after the election in 1996. The range of packages and programmes introduced by the Howard government arguably provided some basis for future GHG reduction efforts. Nevertheless, if we will look closer at the reasons behind some of the introduced policies, for example, the AU$400 million GHG abatement programme that reinforced large-scale cost-effective abatement focusing on the first commitment period of the Kyoto Protocol (2008–12), was, according to the former treasurer

Peter Costello, a trade-off for the support of the Australian Democrats (who held the balance of powers in the Senate at time) in relation to the introduction of Goods and Services Tax.[98] A further statement by Peter Costello illustrates the 'concerns' of the Howard government about climate change at that time: 'This was 1999. Neither Howard nor I had much of an idea of what a greenhouse gas was, let alone how to abate it.'[99]

In June 2002, despite international pressure especially from European countries, the Howard government announced that Australia would not ratify the Kyoto Protocol.[100] The justification for this was that: the treaty covers less than 70 per cent of global emissions; developing countries were excluded from emission limitations; and the then largest GHG emitter, the United States, did not ratified the treaty. Nonetheless, the Howard government declared that Australia would meet its Kyoto target, but without ratification.[101]

The Howard government undeniably introduced some of the most innovative climate change policies such as the establishment of the first national agency in the world to tackle GHG emissions. However, the Howard government has been considered to have acted rather erratically on environmental issues. Some commentators argue that John Howard 'has misread the trend – witness the rising concern about climate change'.[102] Realistically, it appears that Prime Minister Howard had no specific vision and/or ideas regarding the environment and as a result, his government's actions in prioritizing issues and/or allocating expenditure in relation to climate change were not considered the most effective.[103] This point is better expressed by John Howard himself: 'I have always been something of an agnostic on global warming. I have never rejected, totally, the multiple expressions of concern from many eminent scientists but the history of mankind has told me of his infinite capacity to adapt to the changing circumstances of the environment in which he lives.'[104]

The ACPRS scheme introduced by the Rudd government was a significant improvement in terms of policy development in comparison with the Howard government approach to climate change policy. The ACPRS legislation took into consideration work of the Prime Minister Howard's Task Group on Emissions Trading, National Emissions Trading Taskforce, the Garnaut Climate Change Review and Treasury modelling.[105] As a result of this methodical approach the proposed legislation provided a number of measures addressing various issues associated with carbon market instruments. One of the key considerations was the competitiveness issue. The ACPRS provided that internationally exposed industries receive free permits to diminish this concern. Additionally, the ACPRS extensively addressed distributional issues associated with it.

As mentioned above there was an intensive industry pressure that forced the Rudd government to adjust the initial design of the scheme.

Specifically, restricted international linkage of the scheme was changed to unrestricted linkage and even more free permits were to be allocated to industries. As one of the commentators notes: 'the carbon lobby and EITEI put significant pressures on the newly elected Labor government to delay the CPRS and pursue a scheme as favourable to industry as the one proposed by the Howard government'.[106]

The concessions provided by the Rudd government to polluting industries did not help to achieve passage of the legislation but considerably influenced the ACPRS design to the point where the scheme's capacity to combat climate change was greatly corrupted.[107] As a result, as noted above, the start of the scheme was delayed and later the government put the ACPRS on hold.

The Gillard government continued the efforts of the Rudd government regarding the introduction of emissions trading but chose a different approach. Instead of introducing a straightforward emission trading scheme, the government, supported by the Greens, introduced the Clean Energy Future regime, which included an initial temporary carbon pricing scheme to be followed by an ETS from 2015. This designed was as a result of the deliberation of the Multi-Party Climate Change Committee (the Committee)[108] established by the Gillard government soon after forming government in September 2010. The Committee added extra strength to the policy development process by utilizing explicit policy principles designed to provide a consistent basis for the considerations of a carbon price. This process was also a departure from the usual approach to policy development led by the relevant government department. It is arguable that by charging the Committee (consisting of Labor, Greens and Independent members of the federal government and senators) with the task of developing a climate change policy is what led to successfully introducing the Clean Energy Future regime. Even though the architecture of the carbon pricing scheme resembled in some aspects the design of the ACPRS, some features of the Gillard carbon pricing scheme provided significant enhancements compared to the ACPRS. Further, the Clean Energy Future package as a whole provided a number of novel and advanced policies and measures in addition to the carbon pricing component.

Although the Rudd government was unable to resist the industry lobby, the Gillard government utilized the vehicle of the Committee, with the support of the Greens, and effectively overcame industry pressure. Overall, that resulted in a successful introduction of the Clean Energy Future climate change policy by the Gillard government, even though it was short-lived.

The Abbott government's attitudes towards climate change were radically different from the past two Labor governments as demonstrated above. After the federal election in September 2013, there was some scepticism concerning the election promise by Tony Abbott to repeal the carbon pricing scheme.[109] Nonetheless, the carbon pricing legislation was indeed repealed by the Abbott government soon after the election. According to some commentators Abbott 'reinstate[d] industry influence over policy'.[110] The Direct Action Plan proposed by the government instead of carbon pricing was heavily criticized from the start. The Abbott government stated that the Direct Action Plan was introduced to 'efficiently and effectively source low cost emissions reductions'.[111] Unfortunately, the Abbott government did not provide details concerning the development of the Direct Action Plan. It is not clear what the basis for the introduced policy was. Successive Australian governments attempting to introduce climate change-related policies took into consideration policy developments and proposals of previous governments. However, the policy introduced by the Abbott government is strikingly different to carbon pricing and/or emissions trading mechanisms favoured by former Australian governments. In the same vein, the Abbott government neither disclosed which criteria were used to develop the Direct Action Plan, if any, nor which criteria or principles were prioritized to establish the new regime. Now that Australia has a new Coalition Prime Minister, Malcolm Turnbull, there is an expectation that climate change policy will be addressed in the new term if he is successful in retaining government. And even if Turnbull and the Coalition lose the upcoming election, the Labor Opposition has vowed to reintroduce carbon pricing in that next term should they form a government.[112]

3.7 CONCLUSION

What this chapter demonstrates is the significance of political influence on the development of policy and design of market-based instruments in the quest to deal with the issue of climate change. Whether the motivation is to placate the business and industry sectors, as did the Howard, Rudd and Abbott governments, or to ensure the Gillard government remained in power by placating parliamentary power brokers who hold the balance of power, it is clear that actually dealing with climate change has been a secondary consideration. The Howard government engaged with climate change in exchange for support of the Goods and Services Tax. The Rudd government tried to satisfy all the players and thereby satisfied none. The Gillard government was trying to form a government after having gone into an election promising no carbon tax. However, her approach to climate change policy was the most successful, having engaged with the relevant political power brokers to create a regime by consensus. And even though the carbon pricing mechanism was repealed by the Abbott government, not all aspects of the Clean Energy Future regime have been dismantled. Although there has been no change to the current government's climate change policy since the ascension of the new Coalition Prime Minister, Malcolm Turnbull, there is hope that the use of market-based instruments to tackle climate change will have their time again in the near future.

NOTES

1. *United Nations Sustainable Development: Agenda 21*, accessed 8 April 2016 at https://sustainabledevelopment.un.org/content/documents/Agenda21.pdf.
2. In particular, Scandinavian and some other European countries have implemented policies to reduce GHG emissions since 1990.
3. Australia signed the Convention on 4 June 1992, ratified it on 30 December 1992, with entry into force on 21 March 1994.
4. On 29 April 1998, but did not ratify it until 12 December 2007, with entry into force on 11 March 2008.
5. Staples, J. (2009), 'Australian government action in the 1980s', in H. Sykes (ed.), *Climate Change: On for Young and Old, Future Leaders*, Melbourne: Future Leaders.
6. Ibid.
7. Ibid.
8. Wilder, M. and L. Fitz-Gerald (2008), 'Overview of policy and regulatory emissions trading frameworks in Australia', *Australian Resources and Energy Law Journal*, **27**(1), 1–22.
9. Independent Pricing & Regulatory Tribunal (IPART) (2013), *NSW Greenhouse Gas Reduction Scheme – Strengths, Weaknesses and Lessons Learned*, p. 1, accessed 8 April 2016 at http://www.ipart.nsw.gov.au/Home/Industries/Greenhouse_Gas_Reduction_Scheme/NSW_Greenhouse_Gas_Reduction_Scheme_-_Strengths_weaknesses_and_lessons_learned_-_Final_Report_-_July_2013.
10. IPART (undated), 'Greenhouse Gas Reduction Scheme', accessed 28 January 2015 at http://www.ipart.nsw.gov.au/Home/Industries/Electricity/Greenhouse_Gas_Reduction_Scheme.
11. See Senator Birmingham's speech in the Australian Senate Thursday, 20 September 2007, accessed 8 April 2016 at http://parlinfo.aph.gov.au/parlInfo/search/display/display.w3p;query=Id%3A%22chamber%2Fhansards%2F2007-09-20%2F0379%22.
12. Ibid.
13. Zahar, A., J. Peel and L. Godden (2013), *Australian Climate Law in Global Context*, New York: Cambridge University Press, p. 156.
14. Howard, J. (2013), 'One religion is enough', *The Global Warming Policy Foundation Annual Lecture*, The Institution of Mechanical Engineers, 5 November, London.
15. Staples, 'Australian government action in the 1980s'.
16. Howard, 'One religion is enough'.
17. Staples, 'Australian government action in the 1980s'.
18. Ibid. Note, however, that in 2005, the Australian states and territories issued a discussion paper concerning a national emissions trading scheme that would cover the power generation sector.
19. Howard, J. (2006), 'Prime Ministerial Task Group on Emissions Trading' (press release), 10 December.
20. Prime Ministerial Task Group on Emissions Trading (2007), *Report of the Task Group on Emissions Trading*, p. 13, accessed 8 April 2016 at http://www.cramton.umd.edu/papers2005-2009/australia-nett-emissions-trading-report.pdf.

21. Ibid.
22. Ibid., pp. 18–19.
23. Gumley, W. and N. Stoianoff (2011), 'Carbon pricing options for a post-Kyoto response to climate change in Australia', *Federal Law Review*, **39**(1), 131.
24. Prime Ministerial Task Group on Emissions Trading, *Report of the Task Group on Emissions Trading*.
25. Australian Government, Department of the Environment (2016), 'National greenhouse and energy reporting', accessed 8 April 2016 at http://www.environment.gov.au/climate-change/greenhouse-gas-measurement/nger.
26. Ibid.
27. Federal Register of Legislation (2007), *National Greenhouse and Energy Reporting Act 2007*, section 2, accessed 8 April 2016 at https://www.legislation.gov.au/Details/C2007A00175.
28. ABC Elections (2007), 'Australia votes 2007', accessed 28 December 2015 at http://www.abc.net.au/elections/federal/2007/.
29. Gartrell, T. (2007), 'Labor won the campaign outright' speech to the National Press Club, Canberra, 4 December, accessed 8 April 2016 at http://parlinfo.aph.gov.au/parlInfo/search/display/display.w3p;query=Id%3A%22media%2Fpressrel%2FTB6P6%22.
30. In Australia, the Coalition is an alliance of centre-right political parties. The partners in the alliance are the Liberal Party, the National Party and others.
31. The Garnaut Climate Change Review was commissioned in 2007 and the final report was released on 30 September 2008.
32. Gartrell, 'Labor won the campaign outright'.
33. 12 December 2007.
34. Parliament of Australia, 'Carbon Pollution Reduction Scheme', accessed 8 April 2016 at http://www.aph.gov.au/About_Parliament/Parliamentary_Departments/Parliamentary_Library/Browse_by_Topic/ClimateChangeold/governance/domestic/national/cprs.
35. Ibid.
36. Ibid.
37. Ibid.
38. Ibid.
39. Ibid.
40. Beder, S. (2009), 'Token environmental policy continues in Australia', *Pacific Ecologist*, **18**, 45–8.
41. Parliament of Australia, 'Carbon Pollution Reduction Scheme'.
42. Beder, 'Token environmental policy continues in Australia'.
43. Parliament of Australia, 'Carbon Pollution Reduction Scheme'.
44. Ibid.
45. Ibid.
46. See Australian Government (2008), *Carbon Pollution Reduction Scheme Green Paper*, accessed 8 April 2016 at http://pca.org.au/application/files/9614/3795/7350/00563.pdf and Australian Government (2010), *Carbon Pollution Reduction Scheme Bill 2010*, accessed 8 April 2016 at http://www.aph.gov.au/Parliamentary_Business/Bills_Legislation/Bills_Search_Results/Result?bId=r4281.
47. Kyoto units are the units that were created by means of the Kyoto Protocol mechanisms.
48. Parliament of Australia, 'Carbon Pollution Reduction Scheme'.
49. Ibid.
50. Ibid.
51. Ibid.
52. Parry, I.W. and W. Pizer (2007), 'Emissions trading versus CO_2 taxes versus standards', *Resources for the Future, Issue Brief 5*, Washington, DC.
53. Beder, 'Token environmental policy continues in Australia'.
54. Ibid.

55. Parliament of Australia, 'Carbon Pollution Reduction Scheme'.
56. Ibid.
57. Australian Government, Department of Climate Change (2008), *Carbon Pollution Reduction Scheme: Australia's Low Pollution Future: White Paper*, 15 December 2008, accessed 8 April 2016 at http://pandora.nla.gov.au/pan/102841/20090728-0000/www.climatechange.gov.au/whitepaper/report/index.html.
58. Green, K.P., S.F. Hayward and K.A. Hassett (2007), 'Climate change: caps vs. taxes', *Environmental Policy Outlook*, No. 2, June, accessed 8 April 2016 at https://www.aei.org/wp-content/uploads/2011/10/20070601_EPOg.pdf; Garnaut, R. (2008). *Garnaut Climate Change Review* (2008), accessed 8 April 2016 at http://www.garnautreview.org.au/2008-review.html.
59. Stavins, R. (2007), 'Proposal for a U.S. cap-and-trade system to address global climate change: a sensible and practical approach to reduce greenhouse gas emissions', *Hamilton Project Discussion Paper, 1007-13*, Washington, DC: The Brookings Institution.
60. Australian Government, *Carbon Pollution Reduction Scheme: Australia's Low Pollution Future: White Paper*.
61. For detailed discussion see Guglyuvatyy, E. (2012), 'Australia's carbon policy – a retreat from core principles?', *eJournal of Tax Research*, **10**(3), 552–72.
62. Beder, 'Token environmental policy continues in Australia'; Kelly, T. (2009), 'Carbon tax or cap-and-trade? The debate we never had', *Brave New Climate* (blog by Dr Barry W. Brook), accessed 18 January 2016 at http://bravenewclimate.com/2009/02/14/carbon-tax-or-cap-and-trade-the-debate-we-never-had/.
63. AAP and Davis, M. (2009), 'Dead ETS to rise again', *Sydney Morning Herald*, 2 December, accessed 18 January 2016 at http://www.smh.com.au/national/dead--ets-to-rise-again-20091201-k4c1.html.
64. The Australian carbon pricing scheme is often called a 'tax' because during the fixed price period the liable parties are obliged to purchase fixed price carbon units, which is similar to paying tax. However, they cannot trade the units on the market, as under an emissions trading scheme.
65. Guglyuvatyy, 'Australia's carbon policy'.
66. The Committee includes: the Prime Minister, the Hon. Julia Gillard MP, the Deputy Prime Minister, the Hon. Wayne Swan MP and the Minister for Climate Change and Energy Efficiency, the Hon. Greg Combet AM MP, joined by co-deputy chair of the Committee, Australian Greens Deputy Leader Senator Christine Milne, Australian Greens Leader Senator Bob Brown, Mr Tony Windsor MP, and Mr Rob Oakeshott MP. The Committee is assisted by the Parliamentary Secretary for Climate Change and Energy Efficiency, Mr Mark Dreyfus QC MP and Mr Adam Bandt MP, and by expert advisors Professor Ross Garnaut, Professor Will Steffen, and Mr Rod Sims.
67. Zahar, A., J. Peel and L. Godden (2012), *Australian Climate Law in Global Context*, Melbourne: Cambridge University Press.
68. It is important to note that the principles are not stated in any order of priority.
69. Zahar et al., *Australian Climate Law in Global Context*.
70. Ibid.
71. Hydrofluorocarbons (HFCs) and sulphur hexafluoride (SH_6) will face an equivalent carbon price, which will be applied through existing synthetic greenhouse gas legislation.
72. Stationary energy includes emissions from fuel consumption for electricity generation, fuels consumed in the manufacturing, construction and commercial sectors, and other sources like domestic heating. Industrial processes emissions are side-effects of production from non-energy sources, for example, it includes emissions from cement production, metal production, chemical production, and consumption of HFCs and SF_6 gases. The fugitive emissions relate to the energy sector and cover emissions that are linked with the production, processing, transport, storage, transmission and distri-

bution of fossil fuels such as black coal, oil and natural gas. The waste emissions relate to waste dumped at landfills.

73. Zahar et al., *Australian Climate Law in Global Context.*
74. Australian Government, Department of Climate Change (2008), *Carbon Pollution Reduction Scheme: Australia's Low Pollution Future: White Paper.*
75. The Commentary on the provisions also states that international linking with the European Union scheme and New Zealand Schemes is desirable and if agreed, EU allowances and NZ units would be prescribed under the Clean Energy Bill (Zahar et al., *Australian Climate Law in Global Context*). However, a detailed discussion of this international aspect is beyond the scope of this chapter.
76. The Climate Change Authority is an independent statutory body that was established in July 2012.
77. The Australian government has been criticized for these low GHG reduction targets. For example, Professor Garnaut (the federal government's climate change adviser) recommended a 25 per cent reduction, while many other commentators suggest that an even more ambitious GHG reduction target is needed. See, for example, Garnaut, R. (2008), 'Australia counts itself out', accessed 17 January 2016 at http://www.the age.com.au/national/australia-counts-itself-out-20081219-72ei.html?page=-1; Kelly, 'Carbon tax or cap-and-trade?'
78. Zahar et al., *Australian Climate Law in Global Context.*
79. However, the individual income tax rates for higher income earners were raised. For example: 19 per cent for income over AU$18 200 (was 15 per cent) and 32.5 per cent for income over AU$37 000 (was 30 per cent). See Australian Government, Taxation Office (2016), 'Individual income tax rates', accessed 8 April 2016 at https://www.ato. gov.au/rates/individual-income-tax-rates/.
80. Zahar et al., *Australian Climate Law in Global Context.*
81. For details see: Parliament of Australia 'Carbon Pollution Reduction Scheme' above; Clean Energy Regulator (2015), 'About the Mechanism', accessed 21 April 2016 at http://www.cleanenergyregulator.gov.au/Infohub/CPM/About-the-mechanism.
82. Environmental Defense Fund and International Emissions Trading Association (2012), *Australia: A Case Study*, p. 7, accessed 8 April 2016 at https://www.edf.org/ sites/default/files/Australia_ETS_Case_Study.pdf.
83. Australian Government, *Carbon Pollution Reduction Scheme: Australia's Low Pollution Future: White Paper.*
84. Ibid.
85. Parliament of Australia, 'Carbon Pollution Reduction Scheme'.
86. Australian Government, *Carbon Pollution Reduction Scheme: Australia's Low Pollution Future: White Paper.*
87. Australian Government, Department of the Environment (2016), 'About the Emissions Reduction Fund', accessed 20 January 2016 at http://www.environment. gov.au/climate-change/emissions-reduction-fund/about.
88. Ibid.
89. The Australian Senate, Environment and Communications References Committee (2014), *Direct Action: Paying Polluters to Halt Global Warming*, 26 March 2014, accessed 8 April 2016 at http://www.aph.gov.au/Parliamentary_Business/Committees/ Senate/Environment_and_Communications/Direct_Action_Plan/Report/index.
90. An additionality assesses whether a project or activity creates 'additional' emissions reductions that would not have occurred in the absence of the incentive.
91. Ibid.
92. Ibid.
93. Australian Government, Department of the Environment (2016), 'Emissions Reduction Fund: safeguard mechanism: public consultation – emissions intensity benchmark guidelines', accessed 20 January 2016 at http://www.environment.gov.au/ climate-change/emissions-reduction-fund/about/safeguard-mechanism.
94. Ibid.

95. Ibid.
96. See, for example, Australian Government, Department of Environment (2013), *Emissions Reduction Fund – Green Paper*, public submission of Professor David Karoly, Professor Ross Garnaut, WWF-Australia and others, accessed 20 January 2016 at http://www.environment.gov.au/climate-change/emissions-reduction-fund/green-paper.
97. The Australian Senate, Environment and Communications References Committee (2014), *Direct Action: Paying Polluters to Halt Global Warming*.
98. Hartcher, P. (2011), *The Sweet Spot: How Australia Made Its Own Luck – And Could Now Throw It All Away*, Melbourne: Black Inc.
99. Ibid.
100. Bamsey, H. and K. Rowley (2015), 'Australia and climate change negotiations: at the table, or on the menu?', Lowy Institute, accessed 9 April 2016 at http://www.lowyinstitute.org/files/australia-and-climate-change-negotiations_1.pdf.
101. Staples, 'Australian government action in the 1980s'.
102. Kelly, P. (2008), 'The Howard decade – separating fact from fiction', *The Howard Decade*, Issue 7, May 2008, accessed 18 January 2016 at http://www.ias.uwa.edu.au/new-critic/seven/howarddecade.
103. Ibid.
104. Howard, 'One religion is enough'.
105. Australian Government, *Carbon Pollution Reduction Scheme: Australia's Low Pollution Future: White Paper*.
106. Crowley, K. (2013). 'Irresistible force? Achieving carbon pricing in Australia', *Australian Journal of Politics and History*, **59**(3), 368–81.
107. Beder, 'Token environmental policy continues in Australia'; Kelly, 'Carbon tax or cap-and-trade?'
108. Ecogeneration (2010), 'Multi-Party Climate Change Committee announced', 29 September, accessed 18 January 2016 at http://ecogeneration.com.au/news/multi-party_climate_change_committee_announced/043970/.
109. Crowley, 'Irresistible force? Achieving carbon pricing in Australia'.
110. Priest, M. (2013), 'Coalition eyes $20bn carbon cuts', *Australian Business Intelligence*, 10 March.
111. Australian Government, 'About the Emissions Reduction Fund'.
112. Whinnett, E. (2014), 'CARBON COPY: Labor leader Bill Shorten vows to bring back policy', *The Mercury*, 17 July, accessed 18 January 2016 at http://www.themercury.com.au/news/tasmania/carbon-copy-labor-leader-bill-shorten-vows-to-bring-back-policy/news-story/93626d14e1a1a2b7b10c9e9215521582?nk=f69abe4548bcf4b5dcc95eb7a89f871e-1453092764.

4. Trends in the greening of energy and vehicle tax systems – Japan and the EU

Aya Naito and Yuko Motoki

4.1 INTRODUCTION

Japan's CO_2 emissions from energy use reached a record 1.224 billion tonnes in FY2013 due to increased fossil fuel consumption as a result of the shutdown of nuclear power plants after the Great East Japan Earthquake.[1] At the same time, the *Fifth Assessment Report* of the Intergovernmental Panel on Climate Change (IPCC) showed a strong likelihood that climate change was caused by human activities, and renewed its warning to the countries of the world that they must take immediate action to drastically reduce emissions.[2]

The Japanese government must mobilize every possible means in order to achieve significant reduction of CO_2 emissions while 'easing the dependency on nuclear power to the extent possible'.[3] Taxation policy is one of the tools effective for this purpose. Japan has implemented various measures by adopting environmental viewpoints, including a tax to be used to introduce climate change mitigation measures (Tax for Climate Change Mitigation) and greening vehicle taxation. The Committee for the Promotion of Greening the Whole Tax System[4] was established by the Ministry of the Environment in FY2012 in response to the adoption of the 'promotion of greening the whole tax system'[5] into the Fourth Environmental Master Plan (endorsed by Cabinet in 2012). The Committee, which is organized by experts in the areas of taxation, finance and the environmental economy, is discussing a taxation system that is environmentally desirable from the perspective of promoting a sustainable society.

From a global viewpoint, numerous reports have indicated that economic instruments to promote a low-carbon society, such as carbon taxes and emission trading, would lead to economic growth and innovation.[6] In particular, leading the world's climate change negotiations with its ambitious goals for CO_2 emission reduction, the European Union (EU) has been mapping out a clear direction in its *Annual Growth Survey* 2015,[7] showing priority issues required for annual economic growth. This survey indicates the necessity of shifting the tax burden away from labour towards other types of taxes that are less economically distortional, such as environment and consumption taxes, in view of green growth and fiscal discipline.

In order to understand the most recent trends in Europe, we visited the EU administration as well as Finland, Denmark, the UK and Germany, which were implementing advanced approaches, and carried out interview surveys of the experts such as administrators of each country to learn how the carbon tax was adopted, the latest information with regard to environmentally related taxation (e.g., tax rates, revenue and revenue recycling, tax relief measures, etc.) and policy adjustment among different instruments (policy mix). This chapter summarizes and compares the trends in the greening of tax systems in Japan and Europe based on our survey findings, and presents our views on the future direction of action for the greening of the tax system in Japan.

4.2   WHAT IS THE GREENING OF THE TAX SYSTEM?

First, we should define what is meant by the 'greening of tax system'. It means reorganizing a tax system according to the environmental load to create economic incentives aimed at diminishing that load with a view to building a sustainable society.[8] It is an attempt to establish an environmentally desirable society (the greening of society) through the taxation of acts and goods considered to influence the environment.

According to the Organisation for Economic Co-operation and Development (OECD), environmentally related taxes are categorized into 'energy taxes' levied on energy goods, such as gasoline and electricity, 'vehicle taxes' levied on acquisition and ownership of automobiles and other transportation equipment, and 'other environmental taxes' levied on waste, natural resources and so on.[9]

What is the size of revenues from environmentally related taxes in percentage of GDP for each country? Figure 4.1 presents the 2012 figures for OECD members. Japan's ratio, approximately 1.6 per cent, is higher than the United States and Canada, but lower than European countries. Denmark's ratio of 4 per cent is 2.5 times higher than that of Japan. In some countries, including Japan, energy and vehicle taxes account for almost all of the revenues, while some other countries, such as Denmark and the Netherlands, which have a water tax and a packaging tax that have

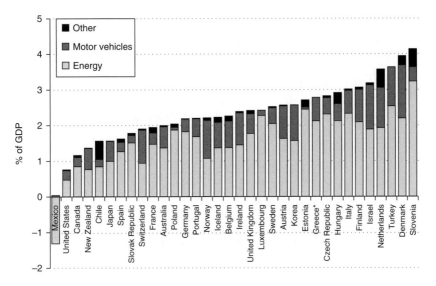

Note: * 2011 figure.

Source: OECD, *Database on Instruments Used for Environmental Policy*, accessed 10 April 2016 at http://www2.oecd.org/ecoinst/queries/.

Figure 4.1   Revenue from environmentally related taxes in percentage of GDP (2012)

yet to be adopted by Japan, have 'other environmental taxes' accounting for a certain percentage of environmentally related taxes.

In the latter part of this chapter, we shall examine the approaches taken by Japan and Europe for the greening of tax system.

4.3   THE LATEST TRENDS IN THE GREENING OF THE TAX SYSTEM IN JAPAN

This section takes a look at the trends in Japan. The environmentally related tax revenue in the fiscal year 2015 (initial budget) presented in Figure 4.2 indicates that energy and vehicles taxes amounted to 7.2 trillion JPY, or 8 per cent of total tax revenue. Although other environmentally related taxes, such as the forest conservation tax, industrial waste tax and hunting tax, are levied mainly by regional administrations, revenues from these taxes account for less than 1 per cent[10] of the environmentally related taxes in Japan. Therefore, we shall focus our explanation on the energy taxes and vehicle taxes.

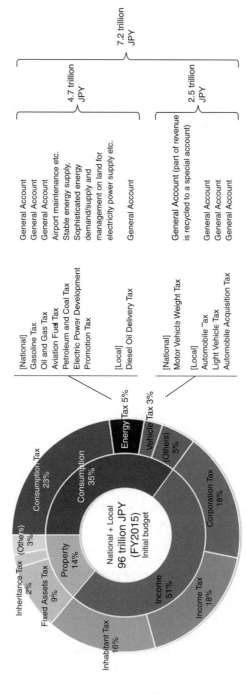

[National]
Gasoline Tax — General Account
Oil and Gas Tax — General Account
Aviation Fuel Tax — General Account
Petroleum and Coal Tax — Airport maintenance etc. Stable energy supply, Sophisticated energy demand/supply and management on land for electricity power supply etc.
Electric Power Development Promotion Tax

[Local]
Diesel Oil Delivery Tax — General Account

4.7 trillion JPY

[National]
Motor Vehicle Weight Tax — General Account (part of revenue is recycled to a special account)

[Local]
Automobile Tax — General Account
Light Vehicle Tax — General Account
Automobile Acquisition Tax — General Account

2.5 trillion JPY

7.2 trillion JPY

Energy Tax 5%
Vehicle Tax 3%

Consumption Tax 23%
Consumption 35%

Inheritance Tax 2%
(Others) 3%
Fixed Assets Tax 9%
Property 14%

National + Local
96 trillion JPY
(FY2015)
Initial budget

Inhabitant Tax 16%
Income 51%
Income Tax 18%

(Others) 5%
Corporation Tax 18%

Source: Ministry of Finance, 'Tax and stamp revenues'; Ministry of Internal Affairs and Communications 'Local tax revenues'.

Figure 4.2   Revenue from environmental taxes in Japan (2015)

4.3.1   Energy Taxes

There are a total of seven such taxes: petroleum and coal tax levied on the importation and extraction of fossil fuels, gasoline tax, local gasoline excise tax, oil and gas tax, diesel oil delivery tax, and aviation fuel tax, which are levied on different fuels throughout their distribution, and the Electric Power Development Promotion Tax levied on electricity sold. The combined revenue from these taxes was 4.7 trillion JPY in 2015, accounting for 5 per cent of the total tax revenue in Japan.

The energy taxes were identified initially as a source of revenue for the funding of road and airport constructions. The tax revenue earmarked for road construction was released and transferred to the general budget in 2009. When the petroleum tax was changed to the petroleum and coal tax in 2005, a new tax was introduced for coal that had higher emissions per energy content. At the same time, a portion of its revenue was transferred from the general account to a special account earmarked for a fund for measures to reduce CO_2 emissions. In 2010, the government decided to maintain the provisional rates for gasoline tax indefinitely for the time being in consideration of the impact on the environment and the difficult fiscal situation. Japan has gradually started to take steps to reorganize its tax system to take environmental aspects into consideration.

In October 2012, the Tax for Climate Change Mitigation was introduced as an add-on to the petroleum and coal tax after almost two decades of discussions. This tax is a so-called 'carbon tax', which imposes tax on all fossil fuels at the same rate according to their CO_2 emissions, as shown in Figure 4.3. The rate is to be increased gradually over three and a half years to 289 JPY (approximately 2 EUR) per tonne of CO_2 emission (or 760 JPY per kilolitre for crude oil and petroleum products, 780 JPY per tonne for gaseous hydrocarbons, and 670 JPY per tonne for coal) and the final rate will be imposed from April 2016. After that the tax rate will be frozen and there is no plan for a further increase of the carbon tax rate at this time. After the last increase in FY2016, the revenue is expected to be in the range of 260 billion JPY. The entire revenue is placed in the Special Account for Energy Policy to be used for the introduction of renewable energy and enhancement of energy-saving measures, and so on.[11]

While the industry has been a strong critic of the Tax for Climate Change Mitigation, stating the need for a drastic review of the tax including possible abolition of the tax itself,[12] it is strongly expected that the tax will contribute to the growth strategy being promoted by the Japanese government. The Committee for the Promotion of Greening the Whole

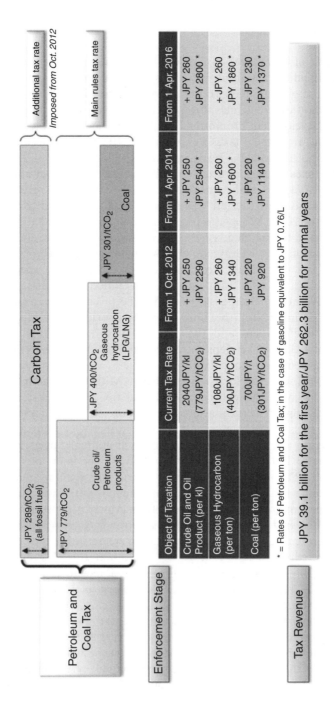

The table shown in the figure:

Object of Taxation	Current Tax Rate	From 1 Oct. 2012	From 1 Apr. 2014	From 1 Apr. 2016
Crude Oil and Oil Product (per kl)	2040JPY/kl (779JPY/tCO$_2$)	+ JPY 250 JPY 2290	+ JPY 250 JPY 2540 *	+ JPY 260 JPY 2800 *
Gaseous Hydrocarbon (per ton)	1080JPY/kl (400JPY/tCO$_2$)	+ JPY 260 JPY 1340	+ JPY 260 JPY 1600 *	+ JPY 260 JPY 1860 *
Coal (per ton)	700JPY/t (301JPY/tCO$_2$)	+ JPY 220 JPY 920	+ JPY 220 JPY 1140 *	+ JPY 230 JPY 1370 *

Labels in figure:

Petroleum and Coal Tax

Carbon Tax

JPY 289/tCO$_2$ (all fossil fuel)

JPY 779/tCO$_2$

Crude oil/ Petroleum products

JPY 400/tCO$_2$ Gaseous hydrocarbon (LPG/LNG)

JPY 301/tCO$_2$ Coal

Additional tax rate Imposed from Oct. 2012

Main rules tax rate

Enforcement Stage

Tax Revenue

JPY 39.1 billion for the first year/JPY 262.3 billion for normal years

* = Rates of Petroleum and Coal Tax; in the case of gasoline equivalent to JPY 0.76/L

Source: Ministry of Environment, 'Details of Carbon Tax (Tax for Climate Change Mitigation)', accessed 10 April 2016 at https://www.env.go.jp/en/policy/tax/env-tax/20121001a_dct.pdf.

Figure 4.3 *Overview of the Tax for Climate Change Mitigation*

Tax System, which is administered by the Ministry of the Environment, suggested that further efforts should be considered with respect to the energy taxes, including the contemplation of a means to maximize the effect of the Tax for Climate Change Mitigation on the reduction of CO_2 emissions.[13]

4.3.2 Vehicle Taxes

There are a total of four taxes: the automobile acquisition tax levied on the acquisition of automobiles, and the motor vehicle weight tax, automobile tax and light vehicle tax that are levied on ownership. The combined revenue from these taxes was 2.5 trillion JPY in 2015, accounting for 3 per cent of the total tax revenue in Japan. Although almost all the revenues are incorporated into the general budget as the result of the 2009 abolition of the tax revenues earmarked for road construction, a portion of the motor vehicle weight tax is used to fund the compensation expense pollution-related health damage under the Pollution-Related Health Damage Compensation Law (enacted in 1973).

Under the current system, taxes are based on the acquisition price (for the automobile acquisition tax), the weight of vehicle (for the motor vehicle weight tax), cylinder capacity (for the automobile tax) and a fixed amount (for the light vehicle tax) with no inclusion of eco-friendly performance factors, such as fuel efficiency and CO_2 emissions. Starting with the introduction of special exemption for the automobile tax in 2001, however, the government began to introduce exceptional measures with a focus on fuel efficiency, such as the Eco-Car Tax Incentives for automobile acquisition tax and motor vehicle weight tax, and setting of multiple tax rates for the motor vehicle weight tax, which apply reduced tax rates on energy efficient cars.

With respect to vehicle taxes, the 'government's large package of tax revisions for the fiscal year 2014' and that of 2015[14] expressly mention the implementation of 'taxation methods in accordance with eco-friendly performance for the automobile tax in the year of vehicle acquisition' in conjunction with a consumption tax hike to 10 per cent, which is planned to be conducted in April 2017. Also, a rate increase for light vehicle tax in FY2015 is mentioned. Thus, changes are expected to shift the focus more toward greening the vehicle tax system. In the new standard of Eco-Car Tax Incentive in 2015, the required emissions efficiency is increased from the 2014 standard and the new standard is equivalent to the target standard that all car companies have to comply with by 2020.

4.4   COMPARISON OF THE ENVIRONMENTALLY RELATED TAX SYSTEM IN JAPAN AND EUROPE AND SUGGESTED FUTURE DIRECTION FOR THE GREENING OF THE TAX SYSTEM IN JAPAN

In this section, we will compare Japan and Europe based on the efforts towards the greening of taxation. In this chapter, four EU countries are selected as reference countries to be compared with Japan. Nordic countries that implement advanced policies about climate change mitigation (Denmark and Finland), the UK as an advanced country in its introduction of a variety of economic instruments, and Germany as economically resembling Japan. As mentioned in section 4.3, environmental tax revenue in Japan is raised mostly by energy taxes and vehicle taxes, thus in this section we compare environmental taxes in light of energy taxes and vehicle taxes. After the comparisons, we will discuss the direction that Japan could take to make its tax system greener. Most of the information about the tax system in each subject country is based on our interview surveys of EU administrators and experts in each country and we also referred to official documents of the European Commission and Eurostat such as *Taxation Trends in the European Union*[15] and *Excise Duty Tables* to know overall trends of environmental taxation in European countries. Please refer to Table 4.1 for each country's environmental tax list.

4.4.1   Comparison of Energy Taxes

We start by comparing energy taxes between Japan and the four European countries. Figure 4.4 is a comparison of tax rates per tonne of CO_2 emissions on energy products. It shows that rates are lower in Japan than in the four European countries. Differences in tax rates for coal and natural gas for commercial use are noticeable among these countries. Denmark has the highest rate at more than 30 times that of Japan. The taxes on gasoline and diesel oil for transportation use are two to three times higher in Europe than in Japan although the differences are small.

In EU countries, tax rates on energy products have been raised many times but in Japan petroleum-related tax rates have not been increased for many years. For example, the gasoline tax rate has not been increased since 1993. In terms of carbon tax rates between EU and Japan, similarly to energy tax rates, EU countries have raised their tax rates gradually while there has not been a drastic rise in the carbon tax rate in Japan. For example, in Finland, the carbon tax rate has been raised dramatically from 1.12 EUR/tCO_2 (1990) to 58 EUR/tCO_2 (2015, for transport fuels) while

Table 4.1 Overview of environmentally related taxation in four European countries

Countries	Tax Types	Tax Name	Targeted Products[a]	Revenue[b] (billion JPY)	Share	Account
Finland	Energy	Carbon tax	Fuels, electricity	5401	67%	General Account
		Energy contents tax	Fuels, electricity			
		Stockpile duties	Fuels, electricity			
	Vehicle	Car tax	Vehicles	2568	32%	
		Annual vehicle tax	Vehicles			
	Other	Excise duties on beverage packages	Beverage packages	81	1%	
		Waste tax	Wastes			
Denmark	Energy	CO_2 tax	Fuels, electricity	683	5%	General Account
		Gasoline tax	Gasoline	7100	51%	
		Tax on petroleum products	Oil products			
		Gas tax	Gases			
		Tax on coal	Coal			
		Duty on electricity	Electricity			

Table 4.1 (continued)

Countries	Tax Types	Tax Name	Targeted Products[a]	Revenue from Environmental Taxes		
				Revenue[b] (billion JPY)	Share	Account
	Vehicle	Tax on registration	Vehicles	5240	38%	
		Tax on ownership	Vehicles			
		Tax on vehicle insurance	Vehicles			
		Road use charge	Heavy vans			
	Other	Water tax	Water	808	6%	
		Packaging tax	Packaging			
		Nitrogen oxides tax	Nitrogen oxides			
		Pesticide tax	Pesticides			
		Waste tax	Wastes			
		Tax on wastewater	Wastewater			
		Sulphur tax	Fuels			
		Other environmental taxes	–			

United Kingdom	Energy	Climate change levy	Coal, gas, electricity	2839	4%	General Account
		Fuel duties	Oil, biofuels	48256	69%	
	Vehicle	Vehicle excise duties	Vehicles	10467	15%	
		Company car tax	Company cars			
	Other	Air passenger duty	Passenger transport	8338	12%	
		Other HMRC taxes	–			
Germany	Energy	Energy duty	Fuels	65152	82%	General Account
		Electricity duty	Electricity			
	Vehicle	Motor vehicle tax	Vehicles	11938	15%	
	Other	Aviation tax	Passenger transport	2384	3%	
		Nuclear fuel duty	Nuclear fuels			

Notes:
a. Fuels means oil, coal and gas.
b. Only national/federal taxes are included. Tax revenue is 2014 data. Exchange rates are 140.4 JPY/EUR, 177.4 JPY/GBP and 18.9 JPY/DKK, from Mizuho Bank Ltd (third and fourth quarters 2014).

Sources: Statistics Finland, Statistics Finland PX-Web databases; Danish Ministry of Taxation, *Fees – the Proceeds of Taxes and VAT 2007–15*; Federal Ministry of Finance Germany (2015), Abstract of the Federal Ministry of Finance's Monthly Report; HM Treasury (2015), *Budget 2015*.

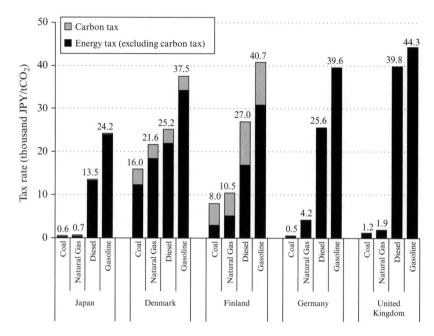

Note: Only business use of coal and natural gas and non-leaded gasoline and diesel (for transport) are used in this calculation. Tax rates are as at April 2015 (note: Japan's tax rate is as at April 2016 when the rate is increased to the maximum rate). Emission factors and energy contents used are from the Ministerial Ordinance on Calculation of Greenhouse Gas Emissions Emitted by Specified Emitters (the METI and the MOE Ordinance No. 3 of 2006) (e.g., the Finnish carbon tax rate can be calculated from these figures but the number would be higher than the actual rate in Finland due to the difference of emission factors). Exchange rates are 140.4 JPY/EUR, 177.4 JPY/GBP and 18.9 JPY/DKK, from Mizuho Bank Ltd (third and fourth quarters 2014).

Source: Calculated by Mizuho Information & Research Institute based on each government's reports etc.

Figure 4.4 Comparison of rates of energy taxes per tonne of CO₂ emissions

when it comes to the Tax for Climate Change Mitigation (so-called carbon tax) in Japan, although its tax rate will be raised in three steps and the final rate will be introduced from April 2016 to 289 JPY/tCO₂, there is no plan for a further increase of the tax rate after that.

There is another obvious difference in revenue recycling between EU countries and Japan. In Europe, the tax revenues are placed in general budgets and used primarily for the reduction in social security cost for companies and income tax for businesses according to the financial demands of the government in each country. Contrastingly, Japan places a portion of the petroleum and coal tax revenue (including the whole revenue from the Tax for Climate Change Mitigation) in the Special Account for Energy Policy, and uses it for projects such as the promotion of stabilization of the oil and coal supply, energy conservation and adoption of renewable energy.

For Japan's carbon tax, effects of carbon tax on reducing CO_2 emissions can be divided into two categories: 'price effect' and 'budget effect'. Price effect means the effect of the fuel price increase by the newly introduced carbon tax on reducing CO_2 emissions, and budget effect means the effect delivered by using carbon tax revenue to reduce CO_2 emissions. Due to the above-mentioned features of Japan's energy taxes, the price effect of the carbon tax in 2020 is lower than the budget effect in Japan, these being −0.2 per cent and −0.4 to −2.1 per cent respectively.[17]

4.4.2 Comparison of Vehicle Taxes

Next, the vehicle taxes are compared between Japan and the four European countries. Figure 4.5 presents estimated burdens of vehicle acquisition tax and vehicle ownership taxes if one owns a standard gasoline-powered passenger vehicle with a fuel efficiency that meets Japan's 2015 emission standards for 12 years as compared with the tax systems of the other four countries. The tax systems of these countries are outlined in Table 4.2 for reference.

Figure 4.5 shows that Japan has the smallest tax burden (about 43 000 JPY) among all countries that have adopted a tax on acquisition (Japan, Finland and Denmark). The burden is about ten times and 50 times larger than Japan in Finland and Denmark respectively. In addition to the Nordic social system of high welfare with high taxes, the absence of a large domestic automobile manufacturing industry seems to be a factor that accounts for Denmark's large tax burden. It should be noted that a value-added tax (VAT) is added to sale price of an automobile at a rate of around 20 per cent in Germany and the UK where no automobile acquisition tax has been adopted. An ownership-based vehicle tax, on the other hand, has been adopted by all countries, with Japan's burden being the second largest next to Denmark. These findings indicate that the vehicle taxation system in Japan is weighted more on ownership than acquisition.

Furthermore, we compared the degree of changes in the user's tax burden at different fuel efficiencies of gasoline-powered automobiles based on the above comparisons of the energy and vehicle taxes. Figure 4.6 shows the results of our estimation of changes in the total amount of tax burden on acquisition (vehicle acquisition tax plus VAT on vehicle purchase), ownership (vehicle ownership tax for 12 years) and motoring (energy tax

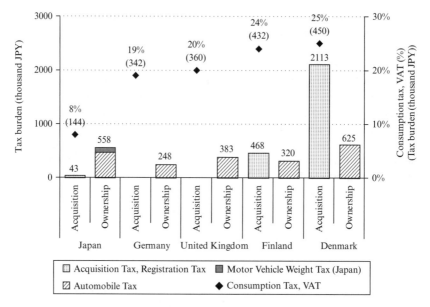

Note: Given definitions in this calculation are as follows: vehicle price: 1.8 million JPY (without VAT), engine size: 1800 cc, weight: 1.5 tons, energy efficiency: 15.4 km/L (JC08 mode), CO_2 emission factor: 2.32 $kgCO_2$/L, annual travel distance: 10 000 km, and life durability: 12 years. Tax burden is calculated with these given definitions and each country's tax rate (as of April 2015). Tax on vehicle insurance in Denmark is not included here. Exchange rates are 140. 4 JPY/EUR, 177.4 JPY/GBP and 18.9 JPY/DKK, from Mizuho Bank Ltd (third and fourth quarters 2014).

Source: Calculated by Mizuho Information & Research Institute based on each government's reports etc.

Figure 4.5   Comparison of tax burden of vehicle taxes per automobile

for 12 years plus VAT on energy price for 12 years) with better or worse fuel efficiency when compared to the standard automobile used in Figure 4.5 for each country. Based on the fact that the CO_2 emission target for 2021 (95 gCO_2/km) in EU demands on each member country is approximately a 30 per cent improvement over the current level (equivalent to the 2015 target of 130 gCO_2/km),[18] our estimation assumed the rate of changes from the baseline to be 30 per cent for both better and worse fuel efficiency. The graph on the left represents changes in tax burden from the baseline, and the graph on the right breaks down the total value of the magnitudes of change into categories of acquisition, ownership and motoring.

The results indicate that the changes in tax burden are larger in Europe than in Japan in all categories. The total of the magnitudes of change is

Table 4.2   Outline of taxation of gasoline-powered passenger cars in four EU countries and Japan

Countries	Tax Types	Overview of Environmental Taxes	Other
Finland	Acquisition	Car tax (tax rate: 5–50% according to CO_2/km)	VAT (24%)
	Ownership	Annual vehicle tax (tax rate: 69.71–617.94 EUR/year according to CO_2/km)	–
	Motoring	Energy tax (0.50 EUR/L), carbon tax (0.16 EUR/L), stockpile duty (0.01 EUR/L)	VAT (24%)
Denmark	Acquisition	Tax on registration (81 700 DKK or less: 105%, more than that: 180%), tax reduction and fines ((petrol cars) more than 16 km/L: 4000 DKK reduction per km/L, less than 16 km/L: 1000 DKK fine per 1 km/L it exceeds) Tax on vehicle insurance (42.9%)	VAT (25%)
	Ownership	Tax on ownership ((petrol) 580~20 160 DKK/year according to km/L)	–
	Motoring	Gasoline tax (4.21 DKK/L), CO_2 tax (0.41 DKK/L), NO_x tax (0.04 DKK/L)	VAT (25%)
United Kingdom	Acquisition	–	VAT (20%)
	Ownership	Vehicle excise duties (first year rate: 0–1100 GBP, from second year: 0–505 GBP/year according to CO_2/km)	–
	Motoring	Fuel duties (0.58 GBP/L)	VAT (20%)
Germany	Acquisition	–	VAT (19%)
	Ownership	Motor vehicle tax ((CO$_2$ base) more than 95 gCO_2/km: 2 EUR/year per CO_2/km it exceeds. (Engine size) 2 EUR/100cc/year)	–
	Motoring	Energy duty (0.66 EUR/L)	VAT (19%)

Table 4.2 (continued)

Countries	Tax Types	Overview of Environmental Taxes	Other
Japan	Acquisition	Automobile acquisition tax (3%), the Eco-Car Tax Incentives (20–100% tax reduction according to the CO_2/km)	VAT (8%)
	Ownership	Motor vehicle weight tax (2500–5000 JPY/0.5t/year), the Eco-Car Tax Incentives (25–100% reduction for three years (in the case of total exemption, five years) according to CO_2/km) Automobile tax (29 500~111 000 JPY/year according to cylinder capacity), special treatment of the vehicle acquisition (in the following year 50~75% tax reduction according to CO_2/km)	–
	Motoring	Gasoline tax (53.8 JPY/L), Tax for Climate Change Mitigation (0.76 JPY/L)	VAT (8%)

Note: Each country's tax rates as of April 2015.

Source: Calculated by Mizuho Information & Research Institute based on each government' reports etc.

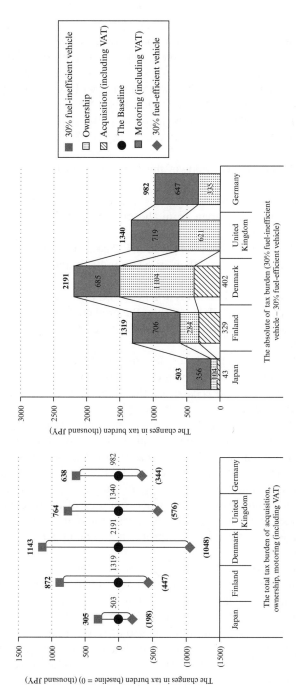

Note: Gasoline price (without VAT): Japan: 95.35 JPY/L, Finland: 0.60 EUR/L, Denmark: 4.96 DKK/L, UK: 0.47GBP/L, Germany: 0.62 EUR/L. Given definitions are the same as Figure 4.5.

Source: IEA, *Energy Prices and Taxes, Volume 2015, Issue 2*, average prices of third and fourth quarters 2014. Calculated by Mizuho Information & Research Institute based on each government's reports etc.

Figure 4.6   Changes in tax burden per automobile at different fuel efficiencies

two to four times that of Japan (approximately 500 000 JPY). As can be seen on the graph on the right, the largest changes are in tax on owner-ship, with Europe being 2–11 times larger than Japan (approximately 100 000 JPY). In other words, our findings indicate that these European countries are encouraging the diffusion of automobiles with superior eco-friendly performance by using the CO_2 emission-based tax system. Taxes on motoring also show similar trends, with the magnitude of change in Europe being twice that of Japan (approximately 360 000 JPY).

4.4.3 Future Direction for the Greening of the Tax System in Japan

Last, we present our opinion regarding the direction of action for the greening of the tax system in Japan from the perspectives of taxes on energy and vehicles.

According to the comparison between the four EU countries and Japan, energy tax rates in Japan are lower than in EU countries and the same thing can be applied to carbon tax rates. In one study, it is predicted that the carbon tax rate will be 33 EUR/tCO_2 in 2030[19] and from this perspec-tive, Japan's carbon tax rate is much lower than the predicted price of CO_2 and even the total amount of carbon tax and energy taxes do not reach the level of the predicted price.

Therefore, with respect to energy taxes, Japan should step up its taxa-tion. The OECD also recommends that the Japanese government raises carbon tax rates year by year.[20] It is expected that people's behaviour can be shifted to low-carbon lifestyles by higher energy tax rates. Furthermore, the emissions reduction effect by putting a price on carbon (price effect), which is lower than that of tax revenue use (budget effect) could be larger if the carbon tax rate in Japan is raised. In an effort to strengthen taxation on energy, however, the government should consider fine-tuning a system of tax exemptions and refunds according to energy usage (e.g., retaining the current tax rates for commercial use) and incorporation of tax revenues into the general budget, as is the case in Europe, from the point of view of mitigating the burden on households and protecting the competitiveness of businesses.

As discussed in section 4.4.2 above, the changes in tax burden based on eco-friendly performance, including fuel efficiency and CO_2 emissions, are relatively small under the Japanese tax system compared to the four European countries. Accordingly, Japan should reconsider its tax system from the point of view of vehicle taxes relating to acquisition and owner-ship in order to develop a more adaptable tax system that changes tax burdens according to eco-friendly performance levels, as is the case in Europe. Although special tax measures based on fuel efficiency, such as the Eco-Car Tax Incentives, have been already implemented in Japan, their effects on the tax burden are smaller than is the case in Europe, suggesting there is room for developing a tax system that better reflects eco-friendly performance. Future discussion in reviewing vehicle taxes should not be limited to temporary measures, such as a tightening of the eligibility for the Eco-Car Tax Incentives. It should also consider the adoption of a permanent framework using fuel efficiency and CO_2 emissions as tax bases, particularly with respect to the tax on ownership, as is the case in Europe

4.5   CONCLUSION

In this chapter, we summarized the latest trends in the greening of tax systems in Japan and four European countries (Finland, Denmark, the United Kingdom and Germany). Our findings indicate that the greening of the tax system is making progress, although the degree of such progress varies from country to country. However, Japan shows the worst performance compared to these four European countries. In terms of energy taxes, tax rates on fuels and carbon could be higher and a revenue recycling system of the carbon tax, which is allocated only to the fund for energy-saving activities in Japan, can be used for a wider variety of uses such as reduction of corporation tax rates. In terms of vehicle taxes, the current tax system could be altered to an environmental performance basis such as fuel efficiency and CO_2 emissions so that the vehicle taxes can work as incentives for consumers to purchase more environmentally friendly cars.

In addition to the practices in the countries we examined in this chapter, there are a number of other cases that should be examined. With respect to energy taxes, many countries, such as Sweden, Norway, Switzerland, Ireland, France and Portugal among others, have adopted a carbon tax. There are some examples of regional or local carbon taxes in North America, such as those adopted by British Columbia (Canada) and the city of Boulder (USA). The carbon tax approach is not limited to advanced countries if the countries that are contemplating its adoption, such as the Republic of South Africa, are included.

Furthermore, international organizations, such as the World Bank and OECD, have issued a number of reports recommending the adoption of carbon tax or raising its rates and it will be interesting to see how the countries around the world will respond to these recommendations. With respect to vehicle taxes, the EU countries are expected to strengthen their taxation based on eco-friendly performance in order to meet the targets set by the Regulation 443/2009. Attention should also be paid to the movement toward expanding the scope of taxation based on eco-friendly performance to include trucks. In addition, there are many environmentally related taxes that have been adopted by many countries or regions but are yet to be introduced in Japan. They include a water tax, chlorofluorocarbon tax, packaging tax and logging tax. In addition to the four European countries examined in this chapter, further research is needed on a wider variety of countries including other European countries, North American countries, Australia and so on. We will further our study of measures by which to promote the greening of tax system from multiple perspectives such as tax rates, tax base and a revenue recycling system in Japan while keeping our eye on these global movements.

NOTES

1. Ministry of Economy, Trade and Industry Japan (2014), 'Energy demand and supply in FY2013 (preliminary figures)', accessed 22 April 2016 at http://www.meti.go.jp/press/20 14/11/20141114001/20141114001.html [in Japanese].
2. IPCC (2014), *Climate Change 2014: Synthesis Report. Contribution of Working Groups I, II and III to the Fifth Assessment Report of the Intergovernmental Panel on Climate Change.*
3. Ministry of Economy, Trade and Industry Japan (2014), 'Basic energy plan', accessed 22 April 2016 at http://www.meti.go.jp/press/2014/04/20140411001/20140411001-1.pdf [in Japanese].
4. Ministry of the Environment Japan (undated), 'The Committee for the Promotion of Greening the Whole Tax System', accessed 22 April 2016 at http://www.env.go.jp/policy/tax/conf01.html [in Japanese].
5. Ministry of the Environment Japan (2012), 'Basic environment plan', accessed 22 April 2016 at http://www.env.go.jp/policy/kihon_keikaku/plan/plan_4/attach/ca_app.pdf [in Japanese].
6. Global Commission on the Economy and Climate (2014), *Better Growth, Better Climate: The New Climate Economy Synthesis Report*, accessed 10 April 2016 at http://newclimateeconomy.report/TheNewClimateEconomyReport.pdf; World Bank (2014), *State and Trends of Carbon Pricing 2014*, accessed 10 April 2016 at http://www-wds.worldbank.org/external/default/WDSContentServer/WDSP/IB/2014/05/27/000456286_20140527095323/Rendered/PDF/882840AR0REPLA00EPI2102680Box385232.pdf.
7. European Commission (2014), *Annual Growth Survey 2015*, accessed 10 April 2016 at http://ec.europa.eu/europe2020/pdf/2015/ags2015_en.pdf.
8. The Committee for the Promotion of Greening the Whole Tax System (2012), 'Discussions so far on the promotion of greening the whole tax system (mid-term report)', accessed 22 April 2016 at http://www.env.go.jp/press/files/jp/20610.pdf [in Japanese].
9. OECD (2010), *Taxation, Innovation and the Environment*, accessed 10 April 2015 at http://www.keepeek.com/Digital-Asset-Management/oecd/environment/taxation-innovation-and-the-environment_9789264087637-en#page1.
10. Ministry of the Environment Japan (undated), 'Progress of greening the whole tax system in Japan', accessed 22 April 2016 at http://www.env.go.jp/policy/tax/conf/conf01-08/mat03.pdf [in Japanese].
11. Ministry of the Environment Japan (undated), 'Introduction of the Tax for Climate Change Mitigation', accessed 22 April 2016 at http://www.env.go.jp/policy/tax/about.html [in Japanese].
12. Japan Business Federation (Keidanren) (2014), 'Opinion on the 2015 tax reform',

accessed 22 April 2016 at http://www.keidanren.or.jp/policy/2014/074_honbun.html [in Japanese].

13. The Committee for the Promotion of Greening the Whole Tax System, 'Discussions so far on the promotion of greening the whole tax system' [in Japanese].

14. Liberal Democratic Party of Japan and Komeito (2013), 'Outline of the 2014 tax reform proposals', accessed 22 April 2016 at http://jimin.ncss.nifty.com/pdf/zeisei2013/pdf128_1.pdf and Liberal Democratic Party of Japan and Komeito (2014), 'Outline of the 2015 tax reform proposals', accessed 22 April 2016 at http://jimin.ncss.nifty.com/pdf/news/policy/126806_1.pdf [in Japanese].

15. Eurostat Taxation and Custom Union (2014), *Taxation Trends in the European Union: Data for the EU Member States, Iceland and Norway*, accessed 10 April 2016 at http://ec.europa.eu/taxation_customs/resources/documents/taxation/gen_info/economic_analysis/tax_structures/2014/report.pdf.

16. European Commission (various years), *Excise Duty Tables: Part II Energy Products and Electricity*, accessed 24 August 2015 at http://ec.europa.eu/taxation_customs.

17. Ministry of the Environment (2012), 'Details on the Carbon Tax (Tax for Climate Change Mitigation)', accessed 10 April 2016 at https://www.env.go.jp/en/policy/tax/env-tax/20121001a_dct.pdf.

18. European Environment Agency (2014), 'Monitoring CO_2 emissions from passenger cars and vans in 2013', accessed 10 April 2016 at http://www.eea.europa.eu/publications/monitoring-co2-emissions-from-passenger.

19. Thomson Reuters Point Carbon (2014), *Carbon Market Analyst*.

20. OECD (2015), *OECD Economic Surveys: Japan 2015*, accessed 10 April 2016 at http://www.oecd.org/eco/surveys/Japan-2015-overview.pdf.

PART II

Trade, taxation and sustainability

5. CO_2 in goods

Agime Gerbeti*

5.1   INTRODUCTION

The EU Emissions Trading Scheme (EU ETS), launched in 2005, has not achieved its goals. It has not been attractive to other geographic areas and global emissions have increased (business as usual). Leaving aside the recession, Europe did not consume less but produced less, importing goods from emerging countries with high carbon intensity. EU is delocalizing its production and consumption. In addition, CO_2 permits reached a price level that has been insufficient to encourage research and investment. So, the ETS has become a kind of (low) negotiable energy tax burden on EU business competitiveness in a global market. The World Trade Organization (WTO) (and international policy opportunities) does not allow the imposition of an unjustified carbon border tax.

For trading within the European market, the proposal in this chapter is to consider CO_2 as a raw material used in the production of goods, regardless of where they are produced and enhance it (i.e., give it an economic value) in the quantity 'contained' in a single product as a result of the energy mix. The CO_2 cost would be administered as a charge converging in value-added tax (VAT). This approach allows an enhancement of CO_2, to be free from market fluctuations and from recession, if the CO_2 cost is set at an appropriate level to encourage research and low-carbon investments in EU and non-EU territories. Because of the greater efficiency of the European energy mix it would also create competitiveness in the energy costs of production. This approach – adopted unilaterally by Europe – complies with WTO rules, as long as it allows industries outside the EU to demonstrate their production energy mix. If European standards are respected, industries would be exempted from the additional charge on emissions within the VAT.

In the extremely complicated context of energy and industry – the United States moving towards energy independence thanks to shale gas; China and India increasing their market shares; Organization of the Petroleum Exporting Countries (OPEC) countries adopting 'strong' international policies on the cost of crude oil – Europe needs to take advantage of the low carbon intensity of its industrial system, especially now that the abandonment of free CO_2 permits will inevitably increase production costs. This could be a way to create conditions for lower global emissions and increase environmental benefits faster than any global agreement. The aim is not to lower EU environmental objectives but to urge the rest of the world to follow Europe.

5.2 HISTORICAL AND METHODOLOGICAL FRAMEWORK

5.2.1 Environmental Markets

With the growing of awareness at European and international levels that emissions in the air, water and soil affect the overall balance of the planet, there has been the need for a public type of environmental protection by imposing industrial and domestic limits on emissions. During the years when traditional measures, called 'command and control', for environmental protection were effective and implemented through permits, technical regulations, taxation of maximum emissions, and so on, flexible mechanisms have been developed as well. Recent environmental protection interventions might be classified as 'in the market' and 'through the market'.[1]

'In the market' intervention concerns the environmental certifications given to certain companies that allow them to take advantage of their competitors in terms of image among consumers. Another type is the eco-label, also regulated at a European level, such as the carbon footprint label and ISO standards.

Legislation has also enacted 'through the market' protection, creating environmental markets with an induced demand sustained by growing or renewing objectives. These markets are structured for curbing emissions through the negotiation of permits representing directly or indirectly 'negative externalities' of energy supplies or industrial processes.

An early example of this approach was introduced in the United States with Title IV of the Clean Air Act Amendments of 1990. US Congress aimed at reducing, in 20 years, 2 million tons of NO_x and 10 million tons SO_2 compared to 1980 levels. Together with the Acid Rain Program, for NO_x a traditional approach was adopted by imposing limits. On the other hand, for SO_2 tradable pollution rights were introduced. Participating installations annually received (for free) a number of permits (for 1 ton of SO_2 each) from the US Environmental Protection Agency, representing the limit to be maintained during a year. Such permits could be used directly by companies or be sold on the market, allowing individuals to choose how and when to achieve the binding targets on emissions. This approach characterizes the main environmental market resulting from the Kyoto Protocol: the EU ETS.

5.2.2 Kyoto Protocol (KP)

The carbon market is the most important environmental market: it aims at reducing greenhouse gases (GHGs) through the exchange of emission permits. It was adopted in Article 17 of the KP, which foresees the assignment of tradable permits to the Annex I countries – called Assigned Amount Units equal to 1 ton CO_2 each – based on emissions targets for 2008–12. If a country manages to emit less than the assigned limit, it could sell the excess permits on the market. On the other hand, it could buy or generate them through off-set projects.

The credits are generated by: (1) the Clean Development Mechanism (CDM), Article 12, which allows the implementation of projects (technology transfer) aimed at reducing GHGs in developing countries and gaining Certified Emission Reductions (CERs); and (2) Joint Implementation (JI), Article 6, which allows generation of Emission Reduction Units (ERUs) also in industrialized countries. The difference between the actual emissions and what would have been emitted without the project implementation (baseline), is considered emission reduction and certified as carbon credits.

5.2.3 EU ETS

Europe has adopted the KP objectives by structuring an independent cap-and-trade mechanism called the EU ETS, which continues even without an agreement replacing the KP. Directive 2003/87/EC defines ETS in two periods: (1) 2005–07, the pilot phase, and (2) the 2008–12 phase coinciding with the KP. Directive 2009/29/EC regulated ETS for 2013–20, introducing significant amendments to the previous regime. With reference to the years 2008–12, an EU total amount of permits was established. To that applies a yearly linear reduction factor of 1.74 per cent, leading to a reduction of emissions of 21 per cent by 2020 as compared 2005 levels. In so doing, companies should improve their environmental performance in goods production by 1.74 per cent.

The general principle of auctioning of Emission Allowance Units (EUAs) was then introduced (Article 10). Free allocation remains an exception, albeit large, to the general rule. Due to the inclusion of new industrial sectors such as chemicals, aluminium production, carbon capture and storage and aviation, other GHGs were included in the ETS.

Despite the regulatory changes, the ETS market suffered from oversupply caused by the reduction of industrial production. The surplus of EUAs at the beginning of 2013 was 2.1 billion and the EU Commission estimated (in the absence of legal changes) that the surplus would remain constant by 2020. In January 2015, therefore, back-loading[2] (postponement of auctioning) of a significant number of CO_2 permits (400 million in 2014, 300 million in 2015 and 200 million in 2016) was implemented. An assessment showed that back-loading can rebalance supply and demand in the short term and reduce price volatility,[3] and thus, after several years, the price went up to €7.34/tonCO_2 in January 2015.

The lower price of EUAs, the main driver of the international carbon market, and the limited possibility of using CER/ERUs within the ETS have influenced the worldwide price of the CO_2, discouraging low-carbon investments. Nonetheless, the ETS represents an extraordinary experiment even though it proved to be an inadequate tool for the purpose. The reasons for the failure are both economic and environmental.

Limitations of the EU ETS
The major criticisms of the EU ETS are the following:

- It failed to become an attractive market due to the low economic added value. This market has adopted a territorial approach in a globalized market without involving other international players. The result was that Europe imports high-carbon goods from developing countries and relocates its companies in countries that have light environmental obligations.
- It was unable to keep the CO_2 price high, which was insufficient to encourage research and investments. CO_2 permits turned into a 'negotiable tax' borne by European enterprises. The adoption of the back-loading and the market stability reserve[4] confirm the difficulty of achieving price efficiency.
- It has not reduced the overall emissions. The total impact of the ETS is equivalent to a decrease of approximately 0.04 per cent of global emissions, which continue to grow, business as usual, by 3 per cent annually. The EU has reached the KP target and will easily reach all of its unilateral 2020 goals. Whether this results from the ETS is debatable: other factors such as industry delocalization, the recession and especially consumption delocalization have decisively contributed. The economic situation suggests that the EU has delocalized emissions, showing a net negative trade balance with third countries such as China.

However, the European Council (23–24 October 2014) considered ETS as the 'main instrument for achieving the 2030 goals', albeit with a provision for reform. It was agreed to continue (partly) with free allocation of CO_2 permits also for the 2020–30 phase in order to prevent delocalization of plants outside the EU and, '[i]n order to maintain international competitiveness, the most efficient installations in these sectors should not face undue carbon costs leading to carbon leakage'.[5]

Europe not only continues to fear the risk of carbon leakage but also seeks to protect businesses from the loss of competitiveness. The latter, however, comes from a combination of causes such as environmental and social dumping, energy costs and economic crisis.

5.2.4 Carbon Border Tax

World Trade Organization (WTO)
Each country is free to adopt binding commitments for GHG reduction. Countries can choose to do so both through market mechanisms and administered prices. There would be no violation of international trade rules if a country adopted domestic taxes. The complication arises when these are imposed on imported products or on companies located abroad.

The recent debate has focused on a border carbon tax to protect industrial competitiveness, to prevent the delocalization of companies, to increase the national tax revenue and, of course, to contribute to overall emissions reduction.

The WTO aims to reduce or eliminate obstacles to trade (import tariffs and other barriers). The basic principle of the General Agreement on Tariffs and Trade, under effect of the WTO framework (GATT/WTO) is Article I, paragraph 1, 'General Most-Favoured-Nation Treatment', and states:

> With respect to customs duties and charges of any kind imposed on or in connection with importation or exportation . . . any advantage, favour, privilege or immunity granted by any contracting party to any product originating in or destined for any other country shall be accorded immediately and unconditionally to the like product originating in or destined for the territories of all other contracting parties.

Therefore, fees, taxes in general recognized for a product from one contractor party, for example, to its historical economic partner, immediately and unconditionally apply to all the other contracting parties – a de facto ban on imposing import generic taxes on countries that are major emitters participating in the GATT/WTO.[7]

Pigouvian taxes

Pigouvian taxes are taxes levied on any market activity that generate negative externalities (costs not internalized in the market price), such as industrial processes. Externalities in an industrial process occur when the action of one subject results in consequences, positive or negative, in another's sphere (such as pollution), without corresponding compensation in monetary terms. Thus, there is a need to assume and impose a cost per pollution unit that is considered additional damage if compared to the level of pollution detected before the industrial action occurred. The revenue should be returned to those who are direct victims of the impoverishing externalities or perhaps to an entire population within a specific fund (e.g., for the remediation of polluted aquifers).

Companies must perceive the pollution as one of the production factors, as if it were a raw material to which to assign a price. This price, in the absence of a tax, is zero. If a tax gives a value to this raw material, the producer will try to use it less. This tax has the advantage of redirecting the parameterization of individual utility or, in simpler terms, if the tax is the appropriate one, the subject who pollutes will pursue its economic interests through production with low emissions. Subsidies in the form of a tax might change the approach of businesses (in fact, they could be supportive of those who generate positive externalities, such as absorbing CO_2 or producing energy from renewables) and determine a greater investment in these technologies.

The approach is very simple and should work by taxing those who produce pollution and giving subsidies to those who remove it. Pollution has an annoying habit of ignoring borders and if national regulations do not prevent its entry into a territory, then it is appropriate to put externalities on goods produced and fiscalize the CO_2.

Carbon-added tax (2008) – Courchene, Allan and McLure[8]

In 2008, Canada entered into a debate that profiled the carbon-added tax (CAT), and subsequently implemented it at local level.[9] The CAT was based on the payment of a premium rate on the VAT proportional to the amount of carbon emitted during the production process of a good. The various hypotheses examined envisaged that internal taxation was exactly the same as that imposed on the import, to comply with the GATT/WTO. Nevertheless, the emissions calculation methodology per product could not be applied to the extraterritorial production goods. As a consequence, there would always be a disparity in taxation between local and imported products. Even the possibility of a mixed system for carbon pricing, similar to the French proposal (see below), included a methodology of counting CO_2 that does not comply with the GATT/WTO.

Climate & Energy study (2013) – Jennifer Hillman[10]
The possibility that a border carbon tax may be in conflict with the
WTO rules depends on how you structure it. That is what a US study by
Jennifer Hillman on 'carbon tax to imports' states, providing a comprehen-
sive legal analysis of many cases in order to consider this tax in terms of
compliance with the WTO.[11]

According to the study, using both Article XX of the GATT/WTO[12]
and Article II[13] in conjunction with Article III,[14] would configure the same
tax either for local companies and importers. Moreover, this border tax on
imports would be supported by a tax deduction only for US companies in
amounts equal to the carbon tax that they previously paid. The amount
of money for the reimbursement would come from a fund established to
collect and manage the revenues of the tax and to devote a percentage
of the revenues to the reduction of emissions and climate adaptation for
developing countries, in particular for the least developed countries. It
sounds like the old Pigouvian tax . . .

However, this extremely accurate study has two major inconsistencies.
(1) Even if the tax were equivalent for both local and imported products,
the opportunity given to local businesses for tax relief on exports of these
same goods overshadows a clear protection of local companies and their
competitiveness, violating Article I of the GATT/WTO, and making it discriminatory. (2) In this case, the tax does not lead to a global environmental
benefit, and it would become a source of taxation, adding to those already
collected, and a mere economic benefit.

Carbon Inclusion Mechanism (CIM)
A similar proposal for a border tax was advanced at an international level
(before the United Nations Framework Convention on Climate Change,
COP15, 2009) by France[15] to balance products emissions coming from
third countries. The Carbon Inclusion Mechanism (CIM) was the most
concrete proposal to change the ETS. The mechanism was based on the
purchase and the restitution by the importer of the CO_2 allowances in an
amount equal to the amount of carbon existing in the imported products.

The obligation, placed on the importer, was related to the purchase of
flat-rate emission permits, the quantity of which had to be equal to the difference between the average EU emissions and the level of the European
parameters (product benchmarks), similar to the obligations imposed on
European producers. Alternatively, the importer could demonstrate that
the products they intend to import inside the EU have a carbon intensity
that is equal (or lower) to the EU benchmarks and therefore must be
exempted from the purchase of the CO_2 allowances.

France submitted the CIM proposal after the adoption of Directive

2009/29/EC modifying the ETS, foreseeing Article 10b of the Directive entitled: 'Measures to support certain energy-intensive industries in the event of carbon leakage' that listed possible measures to be adopted in case of failure of the international negotiations. Among them is paragraph 1(b) 'inclusion in the Community scheme of importers of products which are produced by the sectors or subsectors determined in accordance with Article 10a'.

This mechanism, although interesting, has three flaws:

- The burden weighs on importers which is not in line with the 'polluter-pays-principle', since an importer is not an emitter.
- Foreign producers do not have any incentive to reduce emissions because they do not pay the border tax directly. On the contrary, they would emit more (using cheap energy) to maintain competitive prices of the final products. For the EU such a tax would only become an economic advantage based on the mandatory purchase of allowances without any positive impact on emissions reduction.
- It is worth investigating its compatibility with the GATT/WTO. The CIM relies on Article XX of the GATT/WTO, 'General exception', and recalls precisely points (b) and (g):

> Subject to the requirement that such measures are not applied in a manner which would constitute a means of arbitrary or unjustifiable discrimination between Countries . . . nothing in this Agreement shall be construed to prevent the adoption or enforcement by any contracting party of measures: . . . (b) necessary to protect human, animal or plant life or health; . . . (g) relating to the conservation of exhaustible natural resources if such measures are made effective in conjunction with restrictions on domestic production or consumption.

It seems to comply with the regulation from Article XX, but from a more careful reading, the proposal seems to conflict with the WTO. To support a carbon border tax based on the above-mentioned point (g) means imposing it only on importers. In this way it turns out to be discriminatory because it becomes a tax on imports; in the absence of data on actual emissions, the level of taxation cannot be considered exactly the same as that imposed on European producers.

The proposal was incomplete because it is unlikely that imported products have an energy mix, that is, an amount of CO_2 emissions, similar to average EU emissions. It may be lower or probably much higher. As a consequence, taking into consideration only the difference between EU average emissions and the European benchmarks for imported products appears to be, paradoxically, a preferential treatment for the 'polluting' industries.

In the end, it is worth adding that countries have often evoked Article XX, but only in two cases have they met its requirements (European Communities – Asbestos[16] and US – Shrimp[17]).

5.3   A DIFFERENT APPROACH

5.3.1   Charge on Additional Emissions

European consumers, especially at this stage, have to choose between products with similar characteristics, but with different final prices. (EU products, due to the higher energy cost and stricter environmental limits, excluding the social dumping and the transport cost, are more expensive.) It is highly likely that European consumers, lacking information about products' carbon intensity, although conscious of the environmental issues, will choose the cheapest product. This will set the stage for a range of economic and environmental consequences:

● Loss of competitiveness for local low-carbon products in the internal market.
● In order to maximize profits, producers from countries with light environmental limits will increase the use of dirty energy because is cheaper.
● The global average emissions per product unit will increase due to the use of a less clean energy mix if compared to Europe.
● EU plants will delocalize production to 'pollution havens'.

The EU has become an absorption market and is funding the growth of developing countries at the expense of its low-carbon production. In addition, we must stress that the EU is bound by the international rules of free trade. If the pollution is global, not local, and its circulation cannot be prevented by the adoption of national rules, then we must put externalities on goods and fiscalize[18] CO_2 within VAT.

Europe can set limits on CO_2 production only by considering it not as an input for the energy used in production, as defined by Pigou, but as a real output, a by-product associated with the property of the good, as if it were contained in a shoe or a kitchen utensil, or, more correctly, as the CO_2 produced during the manufacturing process of goods becomes an intrinsic characteristic of the product.

We must structure a solution that simultaneously achieves the following three objectives:

(a)   Promotion of low-carbon products through an incentive that reduces global emissions;
(b)   Clarity and simplicity based on pre-established objective criteria;
(c)   Compatibility with the GATT/WTO.

(a)   An incentive that reduces global emissions

The first objective is fulfilled if the CO_2 is perceived, evaluated, counted and indexed on products. If CO_2 becomes an unavoidable feature of a good, that is, if it is considered in the same way as the material composing the good and treated as such, the perspective and the emissive geography change, as do economic and environmental policy.

(b)   Clarity and simplicity

To meet the second objective a charge on additional emissions must be designed in a clear and simple way:

● On one hand, the cost of 1 ton of CO_2 must be quantified (from a fiscal point of view) that is adequate to the environmental cost and, therefore, convenient for the producer in order for them to invest in making their plants efficient and using renewables. That is to say, the producer or the supplier of services must find it convenient to invest in low-carbon industrial processes instead of accepting being less competitive and paying higher taxation (VAT) imposed for the high content of CO_2 in their products. We have to carefully pre-establish a standardization of emission limits by setting parameters.
● On the other hand, we must rebalance the added fiscal revenue related to high-carbon products by reducing the taxation for low-carbon products, thus avoiding the dreaded inflation. Therefore, the mechanism will operate in fiscal neutrality.
● Last, a linear and non-discriminatory methodology to quantify the right amount of CO_2 embodied in goods produced by a specific factory must be adopted. It is also necessary to create advantages on a worldwide scale for those who produce with low emissions, in order to export products to Europe without paying higher taxes.

(c)   Compatibility with GATT/WTO

Regarding the third objective, the legal basis may be found in Article II, paragraph 2 of the GATT/WTO, entitled 'Schedules of concessions', which reads:

Nothing in this Article shall prevent any contracting party from imposing at any time on the importation of any product: (a) a charge equivalent to an internal tax imposed consistently with the provisions of paragraph 2 of Article III in respect of the like domestic product or in respect of an article from which the imported product has been manufactured or produced in whole or in part; (b) any anti-dumping or countervailing duty applied consistently with the provisions of Article VI.

With regard to point (b) it would be difficult to prove that any enterprise is involved in environmental dumping and this would be, probably, just linked to single cases. On the contrary, point (a) is very clear: 'a charge equivalent to an internal tax imposed . . . in respect of the like domestic product or in respect of an article from which the imported product has been manufactured or produced in whole or in part'. If the good is associated with the CO_2 emitted during its production, why limit ourselves and not take into account the entire life cycle of the product until its disposal? It may make sense to impose a tax, an additional charge on products containing higher CO_2 levels than the predetermined ones.

Now, it is obvious that if we want to enhance the consumption of CO_2, the pollution externalities, VAT would be the ideal and suitable fiscal instrument to activate: it is flexible, has easy traceability and is charged on products when the goods enter the EU without falling within the general prohibition of unfavourable conditions imposed by the WTO. The best solution, therefore, is the use of VAT as a clearing house, that is, applying to the 'clean' products a lower value than the 'polluting' ones: a 'Charge on Additional Emissions' that is legitimate and does not break the free trade agreement, that is to say, setting an administered cost per ton of CO_2, adding it in the form of VAT, in relation to the content of CO_2 for each product. In this way, it would apply a very small percentage of VAT to a carbon-free product, while for a good made with high emissions the charge would be much higher. Such a system would have the advantage of not being discriminative. In fact, any enterprise producing goods according to predetermined standards would not be subject to an additional charge.

There are, however, two aspects that must be underlined. The first is that production processes and the energy mix have nothing to do with the long debated problem of the 'made in' label. We are not talking about deciding if a type of product must or must not have a label denoting whether it has been produced in Germany or Italy; the problem is evaluating the exact amount of CO_2 that was emitted in order to produce or dispose of it. The second aspect is that such a charge is not an import tax but a way to urge enterprises to optimize efficiency, regardless of where they operate. It does not deal with borders but with CO_2, which should be clearly labelled on every product. This approach would allow European products to compete equally with those of developing countries, at least from an energy and environmental point of view. Moreover, the fact that a company is obliged to pay CO_2 would increase consumer awareness about such topics.

Finally, checks on emissions should be voluntary. Companies all over the world will have a direct interest in seeking verifiers and asking for certified emissions.

5.3.2 Implementation

Obviously, the problem of implementation is very complicated for at least four valid reasons:

(a) defining emissions created by a complex good;
(b) ensuring information reliability about the productive process;
(c) the need for these two systems to operate in parallel, then replace the current ETS based on industrial plants;
(d) management leadership that will keep on studying and controlling the process.

(a) Defining emissions

The acronym ISO represents a series of technical standards or guidelines (created by the International Organization for Standardization) that define specific requirements or certification processes, most of them aimed at guaranteeing precise quality standards and improving customer satisfaction. Basically, the standardization of methodologies aimed at keeping score of the commitments and emissions makes an unvarying comparison among the organizations possible, and, as a consequence, enables a coherent, reliable and clear basis for the same comparison and facilitates trade permits. For organizations, the environmental reference standard is ISO 14064, whose goal is to guarantee the credibility and reliability of the monitoring, calculating and reporting of GHGs and the perspectives of the implementation processes aimed at reducing emissions. These certifications are extremely popular and reassuring because they are not particularly stringent, in fact, the EU Commission and the ETS Directive do not consider them as a legal basis, but only as a methodological reference.

Life Cycle Assessment (LCA) seems more interesting in terms of methodology. It is an analysis of energy costs in terms of emissions and environmental impact of a specific good and of the consequent production. It takes into consideration the different production phases, from the extraction of raw materials to their refinement through to its waste disposal and the end of the cycle.

LCA envisages a systematic, uniform and comparable collection of data referring to the production of a good, allowing traceability of the materials and of the processes. It also helps the producer who, after monitoring consumption, emissions and the whole environmental performance, is able to identify inefficiencies and can intervene in order to reduce energy and raw material consumption.

Perhaps LCA 'wants to prove too much', meaning that the analysis is so ramified that its application on all products at a worldwide level is likely to create many instances of double counting. Probably a light version of the LCA would be more useful for this purpose.

(b)   Ensuring information reliability

We should envision the implementation of a process whereby there would be a European–US accreditation body that gives to private companies the right to control all those factories that, on a voluntary basis, ask for verification and certification. Other than the costs of the European accreditation body and of the controls that this will necessarily have to randomly make on factories subject to verification (and apart from the costs of evaluating the performance of the verifier to ensure an activity without irregularities and opaque behaviour) it is an almost zero-cost system. In fact, it is in industries' interest to obtain accreditation and to avoid obstructing a process that rewards efficient producers that, in so doing, could pay cheaper VAT when selling their product on the EU–US market.

The objection that such a control is similar to that performed for the CDM has no basis. With the CDM there are two verification processes. The first is carried out before the implementation of the project and is aimed at evaluating whether the project meets the requirements for authorization (that is to say, if the project could be counted as an intervention that actually lowered the amount of CO_2 if compared to the amount in the same country if that specific intervention would not have occurred). The second is carried out after the plants are activated to ensure that the interventions actually implemented correspond to those designed, proposed and approved. And all this taking into account the country's baseline.

If the controls of the accreditation body were found to be effective, thanks to the charge on additional emissions the risks of fraud would be extremely low for two reasons. First, because the procedure to release certifications according to given parameters is much more straightforward and linear than the one conceived for the CDM/JI. As a consequence, the audit of the levels reported by the verifier for a specific factory can also be extremely rapid and transparent. The control is linear, that is, regardless of where a shoe is manufactured, in order to produce it, it must not have emitted more than a certain amount of CO_2 per kilo. The proposed control has almost 'arithmetic' and not algebraic features, and as a consequence unknowns are scarce and variables are very few.

Second, we have to consider that creating a need for accreditation by a European accreditation body would lead to a potentially lucrative business for private companies because, as already stressed, the requests for verification and certification would be endless. For this reason, the release of inaccurate or inappropriate certification, together with the risk of losing European accreditation, would be a serious blow, certainly more serious in terms of income than what would come from an illicit act. Fraud, ultimately, would never really offer any advantages.

(c) The need for the two systems to operate in parallel, then replace the current ETS

Attaching an well-defined emissions benchmark to products should occur gradually and, for a certain period of time, in a residual way in relation to the categories of production subjected to the ETS, then should expand and update itself and, in the medium term, replace the ETS. Revising emission benchmarks is necessary for the new products because every process that is not limited in a time frame must be kept up to date.

(d) Management leadership

Finally, it is necessary to have a team of experts that supervises the process. Paradoxically, this is one of the most difficult aspects for every mechanism that presents itself as new. If it is true that in Europe and all over the world there are 10 000–15 000 professionals and experts in this field, history teaches us that more often than not it is this group that opposes changes. In this specific case, it would be sterile opposition and it is not difficult to admit that the subject is so technical that it would prevent actors who are not already skilful and possessing strong know-how from entering the 'black magic' field of the ETS. It is, indeed, such a titanic task that it will not be possible to achieve it without the help and the expertise of environmental associations, economists and Life Cycle Assessment engineers.

5.4 CONCLUSION

Only a strategy of common growth, aimed at harmonizing the rules of the market and a sustainable production of goods, wherever this production is situated, could be seen as a success for Europe, the developing countries and the world. The need to limit emissions is not just a European prerogative. The moral obligation towards future generations to manage and defer the end of fossil fuels stocks not only belongs to Europeans but also to the whole world.

If Europe decides to establish appropriate efficiency levels for the production, for example, of a kitchen utensil, it must then be possible to ascribe the actual levels of emissions, higher or lower, regardless of where the good has been manufactured, either in Europe or in an African country.

We should prevent manufacturers from suffering an injustice by being exposed to prejudice. We should, in other terms, allow businesses to demonstrate that their production is implemented by maintaining efficient levels of emissions and, therefore, that the content of CO_2 per unit of product is in line with, or below the one established by the EU in order not to incur an increase in VAT on the product. We should allow manufacturers to be competitive in the market on the basis of their limitations or their virtues, without prejudice of origin.

For these reasons, the use of import markets as a tool to equalize emissions even in production outside the EU, and thus restore competitiveness to the European industry, may be a solution. Probably it will be a temporary advantage, since third countries will quickly adapt to the new standards, but it is worthy of investigation.

We must open up to the possibility of market competition not only for the quality of the products, and the purchase price, but also for improving the emission efficiency of production. CO_2 should become a new production parameter of industrial competitiveness.

NOTES

*   The content of this book does not necessarily represent the opinion of Gestore Servizi Energetici, with which the author is affiliated.
1.   Clarich, M. (2007), 'Environmental protection through the market', *Diritto pubblico*, March/April, 219–40.
2.   Commission Regulation (EU) No. 176/2014 of 25 February 2014 amending Regulation (EU) No. 1031/2010 in particular to determine the volumes of greenhouse gas emission allowances to be auctioned in 2013–20.
3.   European Commission (2012), *Proportionate Impact Assessment*, accessed 11 April 2016 at http://ec.europa.eu/clima/policies/ets/cap/auctioning/docs/swd_2012_xx2_en.pdf. See also European Commission (2016), 'Climate Action: Structural reform of the European carbon market', accessed 11 April 2016 at http://ec.europa.eu/clima/policies/ets/reform/index_en.htm.
4.   A long-term solution to be introduced as of 2016 to address the current surplus of allowances and improve the system's resilience to major shocks by adjusting the supply of allowances to be auctioned. See European Commission, 'Climate Action: Structural reform of the European carbon market'.
5.   European Council (2014), 'Conclusions on 2030 Climate and Energy Policy Framework', 23 October, accessed 11 April 2016 at http://www.consilium.europa.eu/uedocs/cms_data/docs/pressdata/en/ec/145356.pdf.
6.   GATT/WTO, Part I, Article I, 'General Most-Favoured-Nation Treatment', paragraph 1, accessed 11 April 2016 at https://www.wto.org/english/res_e/booksp_e/gatt_ai_e/art1_e.pdf.

7. In 2015, the GATT/WTO had 161 participating countries, including China and India, covering virtually all world trade and emissions.
8. The Courchene/Allan/McClure debate can be followed in the following articles: Courchene, T.J and J.R. Allen (2008), 'Climate change: the case for a carbon tariff/tax', accessed 11 April 2016 at http://irpp.org/wp-content/uploads/assets/po/obama-and-clinton/courchene.pdf; McLure, C.E. Jr (2010), 'The carbon-added tax: a CAT that won't hunt', *Policy Options Politique*, 1 October, accessed 11 April 2016 at http://policyoptions. irpp.org/magazines/obama-at-midterm/the-carbon-added-tax-a-cat-that-wont-hunt/; Courchene, T.J. and J.R. Allan (2011), 'Missing the bigger picture: a response to McClure's view of the carbon-added tax', *Policy Options Politique*, 1 February, accessed 11 April 2016 at http://policyoptions.irpp.org/magazines/from-climate-change-to-clean-energy/ missing-the-bigger-picture-a-response-to-mcclures-view-of-the-carbon-added-tax/.
9. British Columbia's carbon tax was implemented in 2008–12.
10. Hillman, J. (2013), 'Changing climate for carbon taxes: who's afraid of the WTO?', *Climate & Energy Paper Series 2013*, accessed 11 April 2016 at http://www.gmfus.org/ publications/changing-climate-carbon-taxes-whos-afraid-wto.
11. Ibid.
12. Article XX, 'General Exceptions', II, A, 3, paragraph (b): 'necessary to protect human, animal or plant life or health'; II, A, 6 paragraph (g) 'relating to the conservation of exhaustible natural resources' if such measures are 'made effective in conjunction with restrictions on domestic production or consumption' (II, A, paragraph 6 (g) (3)).
13. Article II, 'Schedules of Concessions', 2: 'Nothing in this Article shall prevent any contracting party from imposing at any time on the importation of any product: (a) a charge equivalent to an internal tax imposed consistently with the provisions of paragraph 2 of Article III in respect of the like domestic product or in respect of an article from which the imported product has been manufactured or produced in whole or in part'.
14. Article III, 'National Treatment on Internal Taxation and Regulation', 2: 'The products of the territory of any contracting party imported into the territory of any other contracting party shall not be subject, directly or indirectly, to internal taxes or other internal charges of any kind in excess of those applied, directly or indirectly, to like domestic products'.
15. This proposal, in 2009, was supported also by Germany.
16. World Trade Organization (2001), 'Environment: Disputes 9: European Communities – Asbestos'. The Panel and the Appellate Body in this case both rejected Canada's challenge to France's import ban on asbestos and asbestos-containing products, reinforcing the view that the WTO Agreements support members' ability to protect human health and safety at the level of protection they deem appropriate, accessed 11 April 2016 at https://www.wto.org/english/tratop_e/envir_e/edis09_e.htm.
17. World Trade Organization (2001), 'Dispute Settlement: Dispute D558: United States – Import prohibition of certain shrimp and shrimp products', accessed 11 April 2016 at https://www.wto.org/english/tratop_e/dispu_e/cases_e/ds58_e.htm.
18. Gerbeti, A. (2015), *A Symphony for Energy: CO$_2$ in Goods*, Milan: Editoriale Delfino.

6. The global natural resource consumption tax

Sally-Ann Joseph*

6.1 INTRODUCTION

It is now more than 20 years since the first call for action on climate change at the Earth Summit. The scale of progress to date has been uninspiring. Carbon emissions are still increasing, species and natural habitats are still being lost and poverty has not been eradicated. To these have been added two new crises: food security is a growing issue and financial instability means less resources for mitigation and adaptation programmes.

Numerous attempts have been made by the international community to negotiate a cooperative approach to tackling not only climate-related issues but also the funding to achieve these. It has been reiterated that this needs to be viewed as both fair and feasible while consistent with the principle of 'common but differentiated responsibilities and respective capacities'.[1] More recently it has been acknowledged that: 'An ideal burden-sharing formula ought to broaden participation to include all or at least the major greenhouse-gas-emitting countries, whether developed or developing. It should also support local economic development, achieve meaningful mitigation goals, and provide effective and self-enforcing compliance mechanisms.'[2]

The focus has remained solely and consistently on greenhouse gas emissions, particularly carbon related. Proposals to date have predominantly relied on pledges, that is, voluntary contributions (such as the Green Fund) or targets, which are also voluntary (such as the Kyoto Protocol). These are covered in more detail in the section on funding. Yet the issue is acknowledged to be broader than this, affecting ecosystems and biodiversity,[3] land use changes and land management activities.[4] Initiatives regarding international payments for ecosystem services are increasingly being adopted. The Reducing Emissions from Deforestation and Forest Degradation Programme (UN-REDD) scheme is an example of an incentivized system but its focus is nevertheless still on reducing emissions. The concept of a global natural resource consumption tax takes a holistic view of the environment and makes all nations accountable for their use of environmental resources.

Climate change and environmental degradation are global issues requiring a holistic solution on a global scale. Taking action is a global imperative. Increasing populations are placing ever more pressure on the world's available natural resources or biological capacity through ever increasing consumption levels. Over 60 per cent of the Earth's biological capacity is found in just ten countries.[5] This uneven distribution raises geopolitical and ethical questions regarding the sharing of the Earth's natural resources. To the extent that a country is able to consume more than its own biological capacity can provide, it is imposing a direct environmental cost on those countries that supply it with such means.

The next section canvasses the requirements of funding and types of models, noting their issues. Section 6.3 provides a broad outline of the concept of a global natural resource consumption tax that conforms to requirements of the Earth Summit. The requirements of a tax model, base, rate and liability, are noted in section 6.4. This is followed by the conclusion and consequences.

6.2   FUNDING

6.2.1   Requirements

Climate costs cannot be fully quantified because climate change destroys more than can simply be quantified or valued financially. In addition, too little adaptation has been done to provide robust cost assessments and many future impacts of climate change are still uncertain.[6] Nevertheless, funding is needed to finance climate change mitigation and adaptation.

There are a variety of funding options at the domestic level, including environmental taxes, market instruments, public national funding and private investment.[7] At a global level, the majority of international public finance is generated through voluntary contributions.[8] As at 2009, developed countries had pledged a total of US$41.8 billion over three to five years, US$38 billion for mitigation and US$3.8 billion for adaptation.[9] This equates to around US$8 to US$10 billion per annum, insufficient to meet the estimated US$80–140 billion needed annually by developing countries to mitigate and adapt to the effects of climate change.[10]

A revised approach was proposed in 2009 in the form of the Green Climate Fund.[11] It was established in 2011[12] to receive finance from developed countries according to their obligations under the Earth Summit and subsequent Conventions, and to disperse these funds for activities in developing countries.[13] The objective is to raise US$100 billion per year by 2020, with US$30 billion for the period 2010 to 2012. Yet, prior to the 2014 United Nations Climate Summit only US$2.3 billion had been pledged.[14] By November 2014, following a concerted effort by the United Nations, a further US$7 billion was pledged.[15]

Nevertheless it is still a system reliant on pledges. In the absence of an agreement on long-term sources of financing, the biggest challenge will be to secure funding that is both adequate and sustained.

6.2.2 Models

Explicit in the Earth Summit is that responsibility for dealing with the issue is not uniform but should be a function of culpability or responsibility (that is, a 'polluter-pays' perspective) and capacity or capability to pay.[16] This is described as 'common but differentiated responsibilities and respective capabilities'.[17] But funding for adapting to and mitigating climate change needs to be 'adequate, predictable and sustainable'[18] and in addition to a country's official development assistance.[19]

Thus, through the United Nations' summits, action plans and accords, developed countries have undertaken to provide developing countries with the financial and technical resources to mitigate, and adapt to, climate change. Yet there has been little impetus to determine each country's share of financing, largely due to a lack of consensus on the interpretation of burden sharing.[20]

Outside of the United Nations a few models have been suggested. None have been implemented. Measures of determining financial responsibility differ according to whether both culpability and capacity are considered, the time extent of emissions, the relative wealth of the nation and whether or not population is a factor.[21]

A key impediment to attaining agreement is the concern that policies that reduce greenhouse gas emissions may perpetuate inequalities in the distribution of wealth globally and impedes economic development. Recent empirical literature on climate policies validates this concern.[22] In particular, climate policies tend to reduce growth and welfare, inducing larger economic losses in developing countries than in developed countries. They are also generally regressive, having a greater (negative) impact on the poor. It has the potential to become a vicious circle, as developing countries are likely to suffer greater damage as a result of climate-driven natural disasters because they have less adaptive capacity. Addressing the nexus between fairness and development is therefore essential to achieving agreement.

6.2.3 Moving Forward

What is clearly evident from these models is that the environmental focus is solely on greenhouse gas emissions, particularly carbon emissions. Yet it is precisely because the focus is on carbon emissions that there has been no consensus. Further, relying on donations means relying on encouraging participation. To reduce opportunities for rebuttal, participation should be mandatory and subjective targets should be avoided and replaced with an objective measurement.

It is already acknowledged that activities involving land-use changes are expected to play an important role in future mitigation efforts and therefore should be taken into account when determining burden-sharing arrangements.[23]

Due to the scale of the issue, effective mitigation and adaptation will only be possible if it involves both developed and the larger developing countries as part of a global deal.[24] What is proposed here is a global funding model that is objective and difficult to confute.

6.3 A GLOBAL NATURAL RESOURCE CONSUMPTION TAX

6.3.1 The Concept

Climate change requires a global framework for international cooperation.[25] At an international level, the focus has been on trying to develop climate change agreements that impose significant costs on countries emitting carbon dioxide and other greenhouse gases. The proposal here is to impose an unrequited charge or tax not only on contamination of the atmosphere through emissions but also on renewable natural resource use. Further, because biological capacity (discussed below) is embodied in imports of raw materials and exports of manufactured products, a consumption model is proposed. All countries are familiar with the concept of consumption taxes, making this a familiar model. Such a tax can be viewed as compensatory transfers from resource-consuming countries to resource-producing countries irrespective of their level of development or wealth status.

Key attributes of this model are that it is principles based, transparent in its application and respects the right to development. That is, it does not infringe on the right of developing countries to economic and social development.[26] Not only is it consistent with being a function of responsibility and capability to pay, it also provides an adequate and sustainable source of revenue.

This is a concept that relies on global participation. It will therefore need to be enforceable. An option is an international environmental court, an idea that is gaining substantial support.

6.3.2 Responsibility

Biological capacity

Biological capacity is limited. Defined as the ability of the Earth to produce and/or regenerate natural resources and to absorb its wastes, predominantly pollution, it is determined by the area of 'designated' land available (consisting of cropland, grazing land, fishing grounds and forests) and how productive that land is. Low-income countries, in particular, are highly dependent on their natural resources where nearly 70 per cent of their natural wealth is cropland and grazing land.[27]

The populations of different countries differ greatly in their demands on the Earth's biological capacity, with those in higher income, more developed countries generally making higher demands.[28] The scale of the impact on biological capacity depends on three factors: (1) population, (2) the amount each person consumes (per capita demand) and (3) the efficiency with which natural resources are converted into goods and services.[29] Whenever demand for ecological goods and services exceeds supply (or biological capacity), not only is regenerated biological production being consumed but ecological capital that has accumulated over time is also being expended. This not only limits what can be regenerated but also depletes the capital reserves for future generations.

Countries also make demands on the Earth through carbon dioxide emissions. As these emissions disperse throughout the global atmosphere, biological capacity somewhere on the planet is required to sequester them. In addition, emissions are embodied in international trade. It is estimated that, for about 20 large economies, carbon dioxide emissions embodied in international trade may be 20 to 40 per cent of their domestic emissions.[30] Switching from a manufacturing to service economy does not necessarily decrease these emissions as import consumption generally increases. Similarly, manufacturing or resource-rich countries may 'export' significant quantities of emissions.

There is increasing awareness that the global commons provide 'public goods' (such as the absorptive capacity of the atmosphere) to which all human beings have an innately equal claim but are currently unequally used.[31] The term 'ecological debt' has been coined to refer to the ecological damage caused by the indiscriminate exploitation of resources and appropriation of the Earth's absorption capacity, essentially as a result of economic and trade relations.[32]

The ecological footprint

Whereas biological capacity represents the availability or supply of resources, the ecological footprint represents the demand. This is the area of land required to provide the food, energy and materials (or natural resources) people require, the areas occupied by infrastructure and the areas required for absorbing waste.[33] Thus the ecological footprint is a measure of the resources associated with the final consumption of goods, including imports and exports.

The ecological footprint can be described as a measure of the land required to produce a tonne of product. However, because different land types have different capacities to provide resources, land types are converted to a common currency of 'global hectares'.[34] This allows for international comparisons and facilitates the tracking of embodied biological capacity in international trade flows.[35]

The ecological footprint is divided into six major components: fishing grounds, cropland, grazing land, forests, sequestration land (or carbon footprint) and built-up land. Corresponding with similar categories of biologically productive land and water, a comparison can be made to ascertain whether a population group is consuming within its biological capacity or not. Because the size of the footprint is directly related to the size of the land appropriated to support consumption, the smaller the ecological footprint, the more sustainable that pattern of consumption is deemed to be.

The ecological footprint is not an economic measure of the amount of output produced; it does not consider labour and capital requirements. It is essentially an accounting tool that attempts to measure the extent to which human activities exceed two types of environmental limits: natural resource production and carbon dioxide absorption. Developed by scientists, the methodology is well established and consistently and uniformly applied.[36] It is used extensively throughout the world in both developed and developing countries.[37] It is objective and non-judgemental, respecting the rights of each country to determine its own optimal land allocation to different crops (food, biofuel, biomaterial and fibre), carbon storage and environmental conservation and thus its level and direction of development. Land competition is likely to be a greater challenge in the future than conventional wisdom suggests.[38]

Ecological overshoot

When demand (the ecological footprint) exceeds supply (biological capacity), the population is consuming renewable resources at a rate faster than ecosystems can regenerate them and/or releasing more carbon dioxide than ecosystems can absorb. This situation is called 'ecological overshoot'.

While the biological productivity of the planet changes each year, the net effect is that biological capacity is relatively stable.[39] Reclaiming degraded land, making marginal land more productive or increasing crop yield can increase biological productivity. Productivity can also decrease. This can be due to, for example, climatic events, increasing temperatures, salinity and pestilence. In addition, a number of factors influence land availability. Examples include competing claims such as food versus biofuel, water availability and land ownership and tenure especially with respect to indigenous people. The ecological footprint, on the other hand, is increasing rapidly. This is mainly due to the carbon footprint.

The carbon footprint of OECD countries is the largest of all regions, increasing ten-fold since 1961.[40] However, it has not increased the most rapidly. Over the same period, the carbon footprint of Brazil, Russia, India and China (BRIC) has increased 20-fold, African Union countries by 30-fold and Asian countries, as a region, by over 100 times.[41]

Population levels are also highly determinate of overshoot. For example, it is generally acknowledged that the higher income, more developed countries make higher demands on biological capacity. As a consequence, the average ecological footprint per person in OECD countries should be much larger than in BRIC countries. However, given the population size of BRIC countries, their per capita ecological footprint approaches that of OECD countries.[42]

Where ecological overshoot occurs, ecological debt arises. Such countries (debtor countries) ecologically fund their consumption from the resources of countries whose biological capacity exceeds their footprint (creditor countries). Globally, the total of ecological debt exceeds the total of ecological credit, meaning that ecological capital is being consumed. As each component of biological capacity and the ecological footprint can be separately calculated, this aids in policy development and decision-making with respect to land usage.

Measure of responsibility
The major threats to biological capacity arise from human demands for food, energy and materials and the corresponding need for infrastructure. The ecological footprint is an accounting framework that compares this demand on the biosphere to the regenerative capacity or biological capacity of the Earth. It reflects both the consumption of ecological resources and capital within a country, and the flows of biological capacity between countries.

A global tax, based on ecological footprint calculations, is proposed as a means of compensating low-consumption countries for their share of natural resources, including air contamination, consumed by high-consumption countries. Unlike other models it does not take into account accumulated emissions. It deals solely with current domestic consumption and current international trade. It is therefore a 'price' on current usage. This has three implications.

First, this 'price' is proposed to be the tax. Imposing a tax now on past emissions is akin to retrospective taxation. Retrospective tax law changes are those changes that have an effect before the actual change is made in relevant legislation.[43] Governments rarely legislate with retrospective effect, especially in the areas of penal and tax laws.[44] Whilst in some countries non-retroactivity is observed as a legally binding principle, most countries uphold it as a principle of tax policy.[45]

Second, this approach is not to be construed as denying that past emissions do not warrant attention. However, it is submitted that this is best achieved by compensation rather than taxation.

Finally, it allows countries to make decisions as to the level of development they wish to attain and/or maintain, as there is a positive correlation between industrialized development and ecological debt. This can be illustrated using forests. Emissions from deforestation account for around 17 per cent of global greenhouse gas emissions, more than the entire transport sector.[46] Forests are both a source and a sink for carbon emissions. Forests will therefore be an essential component of countries' efforts to combat climate change.[47] Indeed, countries may determine that maintaining forests for carbon sequestration is more economically viable than proceeds from timber.

However, it is important to recognize that footprint reduction efforts in one area could lead to footprint increases in another. Fossil fuel use is the most significant contributor to the ecological footprint. However, proposals to replace liquid fossil fuels with biofuel crops have the potential to increase pressure on land use and to increase problems caused by agriculture – a significant threat to biodiversity and a major footprint contributor.[48]

The approach advocated in this chapter determines responsibility based on consumption. The rationale for a consumption tax is that taxpayers should contribute in line with what they 'take out of the pot' rather than what they 'contribute to society'.[49] As a measure of current responsibility, the global natural resource consumption tax reflects current environmental decisions made by countries. Efforts to combat climate change will be reflected in decreased footprints and hence in lower tax payments.

6.3.3   Capability

Ability to pay (and to receive)
Ability to pay is usually associated with direct taxation generally and income taxation in particular.[50] It is viewed as reflecting fairness and

equity, being synonymous with justice in taxation.[51] Out of social considerations, those with incomes at or below the subsistence level arguably have no ability to pay. Complications often arise in determining the level of 'subsistence income' to be exempt.[52]

Income is generally considered a criterion of distributive fairness. However, because a just distribution of economic resources goes to standards of living, consumption may also be so considered.[53] Fairness, in this context, must involve distributional equity – the question of how environmental resources ought to be distributed in a globally fair society. This extends beyond consideration of who should pay, to include who should receive compensation.

Indicators

Historically a country's ability to pay has been premised on its economic activity, given by its GDP. However, a number of other indicators have been developed that can be used to the same effect. These are essentially measures of economic well-being, incorporating aspects of GDP, non-market activity, leisure and wealth.[54]

The more widely known and commonly referred to indicators that could stand proxy for an ability to pay include the Human Development Index, Happy Planet Index, Genuine Progress Indicator and Measure of Domestic Progress. Pursuing alternatives to GDP is still an area of development especially when seeking to incorporate quality of life, a broader concept than economic activity and living standards.[55]

Measure of capability

Two methodologies are discussed here. Both are premised on the fact that capability is not merely the ability to pay but also encompasses the need to receive. The first is threshold based whilst an indicator determines the second.

Using a threshold-based approach requires considering the two aspects of 'ability to pay' and 'need to receive' independently. First, there are ecological debtor countries that have limited financial resources such as Gambia and Haiti. As such, a capability threshold is required below which no country is required to pay the tax. Second, there are ecological creditor countries that arguably do not require financial assistance to adapt to, or mitigate, climate change effects. Examples include Australia and Canada. In this case, a capability threshold is required above which no country is entitled to receive the tax. Instead, the amount 'owing' to such countries for the 'use' of their biological capacity can be added to an adaptation or mitigation fund such as the Green Climate Fund. These thresholds may be based on the same criteria that are used for determining whether a country is considered to be 'developed', 'developing', or 'less developed'.

An alternative methodology for determining capability is by the indicator itself. Any indicator that has broad appeal can be used. If the Human Development Index is chosen, thresholds, determined to be equivalent to the United Nations Development Programme threshold for human development, may be used. Here, countries below the low or medium threshold are excluded from having to pay whilst those above the very high threshold are not permitted to receive.[56] If GDP is the chosen mechanism, the thresholds may be determined by the median (below which they do not pay) and the average (above which they do not receive).

6.4   TAX MODEL

6.4.1   Tax Base

A tax base is the measure upon which the assessment or determination of tax liability is based. It is, in essence, the source of the tax revenue.

The biologically productive land available to each country differs according to size and productivity. While differing productivity can be made comparable by converting available land into global hectares, this does not facilitate making size comparable. Comparing values among groups of different sizes can only be achieved by taking a per capita approach. And, as population density and consumption are positively related, a per capita approach is also in line with a consumption-based approach. The World Bank also advocates a per capita approach to welfare sustainability, its reason being that population is not static.[57]

The tax base is therefore net biological capacity (biological capacity less ecological footprint) per capita. The ecological overshoot determines that a tax debit (or tax liability) arises. Alternatively, where biological capacity exceeds the ecological footprint, a tax credit arises.

6.4.2   Tax Rate

Because different land types have different values, economic, environmental and social, these should be the de facto 'rate' and determine the 'price' or tax.

Valuing natural resources and ecosystem services has become a significant and rapidly evolving area of research, involving both market and non-market values.[58] Its innate complexity creates difficulties,[59] not least of which is determining the economic and ecological concepts of 'value'.[60]

While attempts are being made to include such values in GDP accounts, this is generally on the basis that ecosystem services are a stock of inputs that are depreciated or depleted over time.[61] A further constraint is that environmental assets are only considered if they have an identifiable owner who can benefit economically from the use of the asset.[62] This methodology is not suitable for a global natural resource consumption tax as it does not account for the productivity of ecological inputs, which are relied on in economic pursuits.[63] Nor does it include the significant ecosystem services for which no monetary value has been assigned.[64]

Ecosystem services are the benefits derived from ecosystems. These include provisioning such as food, water and fibre, regulating such as flood mitigation and disease control, cultural services such as recreation and spiritual benefits, and supporting services such as nutrient cycling and soil formation.[65]

The issue of valuation is inseparable from the choices and decisions governments must make about ecological systems and land usage.[66] Loss of environmental resources is not simply an environmental problem, it is also an economic problem because values are lost or eroded when these resources are destroyed or degraded.[67] Valuation methodologies are being increasingly utilized to quantify the benefits provided by natural environments.[68] However, no widely accepted standardized method has yet been developed.[69]

Notwithstanding multiple methodologies that are well documented,[70] very little attempt has been made to assign monetary values to land types and biocapacity. A team of researchers from North America, South America and Europe, led by Dr Robert Costanza, made one of the first attempts.[71] This was computed on the basis of a 'willingness to pay' for each land type, taking into account both direct and indirect ecosystem services.[72] More recently the World Bank has attempted to estimate the natural capital wealth of countries.[73] This methodology, however, includes non–biologically productive land, minerals and sub-soil resources, and excludes fishing grounds. This exclusion is significant given that the value of fishing is around US$78 billion annually with most export trading originating from developing countries.[74] As all elements included in the World Bank's proxy are estimated using market values, natural assets and ecosystem services that do not have market values are ignored.[75] As such this natural capital assessment approach is very limited.

6.4.3 Tax Liability

The term 'tax liability' refers to the amount of tax owed. It is calculated by applying the tax rate to the tax base.

Once a value (tax rate) has been ascertained this is applied to the net biological capacity per capita (tax base). A tax liability arises for debtor counties, that is, countries in ecological overshoot. This same formula determines the amount owing to creditor countries. At a global level the gross tax debt will exceed the gross tax credit, reflecting the use of natural or ecological capital as opposed to merely utilization of regenerated and regeneratable biological capacity. This 'surplus' tax can be paid into the adaptation and/or mitigation funds for further redistribution.

6.5 CONCLUSION AND CONSEQUENCES

The global natural resource consumption tax is a user-pays compensatory tax based on the current consumption of renewable natural resources and absorption of wastes. It does not directly conserve or preserve these resources or make any attempt to impose targets to do so. But, like any tax, it has the potential to change behaviour. However, its primary purpose is to raise revenue necessary to meet the costs of climate change mitigation and abatement programmes. It achieves this by applying a price on biological capacity. Being simple in calculation and transparent in application, it is difficult, both technically and ethically, for any country to deny liability.

Due to its inherent simplicity, the global natural resource consumption tax can aid in economic, environmental and social policy-making and decision-making. This tax ensures that the cost of resource consumption is measured. Once measured, natural resources can be monitored, thus more effectively managed. Indeed, properly managed, natural resources are capable of delivering economic profits. This, in itself, can be an important source of development for less developed and developing countries and should therefore be a key part of development strategies. Diverse land-use patterns generate and deliver different environmental outcomes.

It is incumbent upon each country to understand how much biological capacity they have as well as their rate of depletion. It is equally important for countries to understand their global ecological asset dependency associated with natural resource consumption. Such levels of understanding can only assist in identifying the current and future risks as well as the opportunities they present.

NOTES

*   Associate Member, Asia-Pacific Centre for Environmental Law, National University of Singapore.

1. *Rio Declaration on Environment and Development*, UN Doc. A/CONF.151/26 (Vol. 1), 12 June 1992, Principle 7; United Nations Framework Convention on Climate Change (UNFCCC) Articles 3(1) and 4(1).
2. Cao, J. (2010), 'Beyond Copenhagen: reconciling international fairness, economic development and climate protection', The Harvard Project on International Climate Agreements discussion paper, pp. 10–44.
3. Secretariat of the Convention on Biological Diversity (2010), *Global Diversity Outlook 3*, May 2010, p. 56; Bellard, C., C. Bertelsmeier, P. Leadley, W. Thuiller and F. Courchamp (2012), 'Impacts of climate change on the future of biodiversity', *Ecology Letters*, **15**(4), 365–77.
4. Houghton, R.A. (2003), 'Revised estimates of the annual net flux of carbon to the atmosphere from changes in land use and land management 1850–2000', *Tellus B*, **55**(2), 378–90; USEPA (2006), *Global Mitigation of Non-CO_2 Greenhouse Bases*, EPA 430-R-06-005, Washington, DC: United States Environmental Protection Agency.
5. World Wildlife Fund (2014), *Living Planet Report 2014: Species and Spaces, People and Places*, Gland, Switzerland: WWF, p. 41.
6. Oxfam International (2007), 'Adapting to climate change: what's needed in poor countries, and who should pay', *Oxfam Briefing Paper No. 104*, Oxford: Oxfam, p. 17.
7. World Wildlife Fund (2008), 'Finance and investment from developed to developing countries: a global financial architecture for climate change', WWF Global Climate Policy position paper, Gland, Switzerland: WWF; Parker, C. et al. (2009), *The Little Climate Finance Book: A Guide to Financing Options for Forests and Climate Change*, Oxford: Global Canopy Foundation; European Commission (2010), 'Climate change: who is going to pay?', *European Economy News No. 16*, January.
8. Parker et al., *The Little Climate Finance Book*, p. 34; Oxfam International, 'Adapting to climate change', p. 30; Spratt, S. (2009), *Assessing the Alternatives: Financing Climate Change Mitigation and Adaptation in Developing Countries*, a report for Stamp Out Poverty, London: New Economics Foundation, p. 19.
9. Parker et al., *The Little Climate Finance Book*, p. 24.
10. Parker et al., *The Little Climate Finance Book*, p. 7; World Bank (2010), *Economics of Adaptation to Climate Change Synthesis Report*, Washington, DC: World Bank, p. 19. For a critique of the estimates see Parry, M. et al. (2009), *Assessing the Costs of Adaptation to Climate Change: A Review of the UNFCCC and Other Recent Estimates*, London: International Institute for Environment and Development and the Grantham Institute for Climate Change, Imperial College.
11. United Nations, *Copenhagen Accord* (Draft decision -/CP.15, Framework Convention on Climate Change, FCCC/CP/2009/L.7, 18 December 2009), Agenda item 10(c).
12. Annexed to Decision 3/CP.17 presented in UNFCCC document FCCC/CP/2011/9/Add.1, Durban, South Africa.
13. See generally 'Green Climate Fund', accessed 4 August 2015 at http://news.gcfund.org/.
14. Department of Climate Change (2014), 'Pledges made towards GCF at the United Nations Climate Summit 2014', accessed 21 April 2016 at http://www.camclimate.org.kh/en/documents-and-media/climate-change-in-the-news/245-pledges-made-towards-gcf-at-the-united-nations-climate-summit-2014.html.
15. United Nations (2015), 'Ban welcomes $9 billion in pledges to Green Climate Fund at Berlin conference', *UN News Centre*, accessed 4 August 2015 at http://www.un.org/apps/news/story.asp?NewsID=49395#.VcA5_fmqpBc.
16. Spratt, *Assessing the Alternatives*, p. 19.
17. United Nations General Assembly (1992), *Rio Declaration on Environment and Development (Report of the United Nations Conference on Environment and Development, Rio de Janeiro, 3–14 June 1992, Principle 7)*.
18. UNFCCC (2007), *Part Two: Action Taken by the Conference of the Parties at its Thirteenth Session (Report of the Conference of the Parties on its Thirteenth Session, held in Bali from 3 to 15 December 2007, FCCC/CP/2007/6/Add.1*, 14 March 2008)*, Decision 1/CP.13, item 1(e)(i), (iii).

19.   Spratt, *Assessing the Alternatives*, p. 11; Klein, R.J.T. (2007), 'Links between adaptation to and mitigation of climate change. Dialogue on long-term cooperative action to address climate change by enhancing implementation of the Convention' (third workshop, session 3: 'Addressing action on adaptation', Bonn, Germany, 17 May 2007).
20.   Oxfam International, 'Adapting to climate change', p. 23; Parker et al., *The Little Climate Finance Book*.
21.   For example, the Stern Review: Stern, N. (2006), *Stern Review on the Economics of Climate Change*, Cambridge, UK: Cambridge University Press. See also Oxfam International, 'Adapting to climate change', Annex 1.
22.   Cline, W.R. (1999), *Global Warming and Agriculture: Impact Estimates by Country*, London: Center for Global Development; Bernstein, P., W. Montgomery and T. Rutherford (1999), 'Global impacts of the Kyoto agreement: results from the MS-MRT model', *Resource and Energy Economics*, **21**(4), 375–413; Cao, J. (2013) 'The incidence of carbon tax in China', in J.Y. Man (ed.), *China's Environmental Policy and Urban Development*, Cambridge, MA: Lincoln Institute of Land Policy.
23.   Cao, 'Beyond Copenhagen'.
24.   Spratt, *Assessing the Alternatives*, p. 18; Parker et al., *The Little Climate Finance Book*.
25.   UNFCCC (2007), *Climate Change: Impacts, Vulnerabilities and Adaptation in Developing Countries*, Bonn: UNFCCC.
26.   As contained in UNFCCC Article 4(7); *Convention on Biological Diversity*, Article 20(4).
27.   World Bank (2006), *Where is the Wealth of Nations? Measuring Capital for the 21st Century*, Washington, DC: World Bank, p. 31. These low-income countries exclude oil exporters.
28.   World Wildlife Fund (2010), *Living Planet Report 2010: Biodiversity, Biocapacity and Development*, Gland, Switzerland: WWF, p. 42.
29.   Ibid., p. 12.
30.   United Nations Environment Programme (2010), *Assessing the Environmental Impacts of Consumption and Production: Priority Products and Materials' (A Report of the Working Group to the International Panel for Sustainable Resource Management)*, p. 22.
31.   Simms, A. (2001), 'Ecological debt – balancing the environmental budget and compensating developing countries', *International Institute for Environmental Development Opinion*, September.
32.   Paredis, E., J. Lambrecht, G. Goeminne and W. Vanhove (2004), *VLIR-BVO Project 2003: Elaboration of the Concept of Ecological Debt, Final Report*, Ghent: Centre for Sustainable Development (CDO) Ghent University.
33.   Kitzes, J. et al. (2008), 'Shrink and share: humanity's present and future ecological footprint', *Philosophical Transactions of the Royal Society B: Biological Sciences*, **363**(1491), 467–75.
34.   One global hectare (gha) represents the productive capacity of one hectare of land at world average productivity.
35.   For details on the sources of international data and the calculation methodology, refer to the Global Footprint Network at www.footprintnetwork.org/en/index.php/GFN/.
36.   Paredis et al., *VLIR-BVO Project 2003: Elaboration of the Concept of Ecological Debt*, p. 22.
37.   See, for example, McDonald, G. and M. Patterson (2003), 'Ecological footprints of New Zealand and its regions', *Environmental Reporting Technical Paper*, Wellington, NZ: Ministry for the Environment.
38.   World Wildlife Fund, *Living Planet Report 2010*, p. 81.
39.   Ibid., p. 34.
40.   Ibid., p. 40.
41.   Ibid.
42.   Ibid.
43.   Australian Taxation Office (2015), 'Administrative treatment of retrospective leg-

islation', accessed 21 April 2016 at https://www.ato.gov.au/general/new-legislation/administrative-treatment-of-retrospective-legislation/#.
44. Sandler, D. (2009), 'Retrospective tax decisions – treading where legislation won't', *Cambridge Law Journal*, **52**(3), 399–401.
45. Vanistendael, F. (1996), 'Tax law design and drafting', in V. Thuronyi (ed.), *Legal Framework for Taxation, Volume 1*, Washington, DC: International Monetary Fund.
46. Parker et al., *The Little Climate Finance Book*, p. 21.
47. Ibid.
48. World Wildlife Fund, *Living Planet Report 2010*, p. 85.
49. Musgrave, R.A. (1967), 'In defense of an income concept', *Harvard Law Review*, **81**(1), 44–62.
50. Utz, S. (2002), 'Ability to pay', *Whittier Law Review*, **23**(3), 867; Dodge, J.M. (2005), 'Theories of tax justice: ruminations on the benefit, partnership, and ability-to-pay principles', *Tax Law Review*, **58**(4), 399–461.
51. Buehler, A.G. (1945), 'Ability to pay', *Tax Law Review*, **1**, 243.
52. Ibid., p. 252.
53. Andrews, A. (1974), 'A consumption-type or cash flow personal income tax', *Harvard Law Review*, **87**(6), 1113–88; Warren, A. (1980), 'Would a consumption tax be fairer than an income tax?', *The Yale Law Journal*, **89**(6), 1081–124.
54. Bergheim, S. (2006), 'Measures of well-being: there is more to it than GDP', *Deutsche Bank Research, Current Issues*, 8 September.
55. Stiglitz, J.E., A. Sen and J.P. Fitoussi (2009), *Report by the Commission on the Measurement of Economic Performance and Social Progress*, p. 41.
56. UNDP (2010), *Human Development Report 2010 – 20th Anniversary Edition: The Real Wealth of Nations: Pathways to Human Development*, New York: UNDP.
57. World Bank, *Where is the Wealth of Nations?*, p. 61.
58. Kaval, P. (2006), 'Valuing ecosystems services: a new paradigm shift', *Working Paper No. 6/10*, Waikato, NZ: Department of Economics, University of Waikato; Turner, R.K. et al (2003), 'Valuing nature: lessons learned and future research directions', *Ecological Economics*, **46**(3), 493–510; Wilson, M.A. and J.P. Hoehn (2006), 'Valuing environmental goods and services using benefit transfer: the state-of-the art and science', *Ecological Economics*, **60**(2), 335–42.
59. Richards, K. (1997), 'Putting a price tag on nature', *Issues in Science and Technology*, **14**(2), 88.
60. Faber, S.C., R. Costanza and M.A. Wilson (2002), 'Economic and ecological concepts for valuing ecosystem services', *Ecological Economics*, **41**(3), 375–92; Turner, 'Valuing nature: lessons learned and future research directions'.
61. Alexander, A.M., J.A. List, M. Margolis and R.C. d'Arge (1998), 'A method for valuing global ecosystem services', *Ecological Economics*, **27**(2), 161–70.
62. Voora, V.A. and H.D. Venema (2008), 'The natural capital approach: a concept paper', Winnipeg: International Institute for Sustainable Development.
63. Alexander et al., 'A method for valuing global ecosystem services', p. 162.
64. World Bank, *Where Is the Wealth of Nations?*
65. Kumar, M. and P. Kumar (2008), 'Valuation of the ecosystem services: a psycho-cultural perspective', *Ecological Economics*, **64**(4), 808–19; Kontogianni, A., G.W. Luck and M. Skourtos (2010), 'Valuing ecosystem services on the basis of service-providing units: a potential approach to address the "endpoint problem" and improve stated preferred methods', *Ecological Economics*, **69**(7), 1479–87.
66. Turner, R.K. and D. Pearce (1993), *Economics and Ecology: New Frontiers and Sustainable Development*, London: Chapman and Hall; Bingham, G. et al. (1995), 'Issues in ecosystem valuation: improving information for decision making', *Ecological Economics*, **14**(2), 73–90; Costanza, R. et al. (1997), 'The value of the world's ecosystem services and natural capital', *Nature*, **387**(6230), 253–60.
67. Kumar and Kumar, 'Valuation of the ecosystem services: a psycho-cultural perspective', p. 809.

68.   Voora and Venema, 'The natural capital approach'; Smith, R. (2007), 'Development of the SEEA 2003 and its implementation', *Ecological Economics*, **61**(4), 592–9.
69.   Barbier, E.B. and G.M. Heal (2006), 'Valuing ecosystem services', *The Economists' Voice*, **3**(3); Carpenter, S.R. et al. (2006), 'Millennium Ecosystem Assessment: research needs', *Science*, **314**(5797), 257–8.
70.   See, for example, National Research Council (2004), *Valuing Ecosystem Services: Toward Better Environmental Decision-Making*, Washington, DC: The National Academies Press; L.H. Goulder and D. Kennedy (2011), 'Interpreting and estimating the value of ecosystem services', in G. Daily, P. Kareiva, T. Ricketts, H. Tallis and S. Polasky (eds), *Natural Capital: Theory & Practice of Mapping Ecosystem Services*, Oxford: Oxford University Press.
71.   World Resources Institute (undated), 'Valuing ecosystem services', accessed 21 April 2016 at http://www.griequity.com/resources/Environment/Valuing%20Ecosystem%20 Services.htm referring to Costanza et al., 'The value of the world's ecosystem services and natural capital'.
72.   Alexander et al., 'A method for valuing global ecosystem services', pp. 162, 163.
73.   World Bank, *Where is the Wealth of Nations?*
74.   Ibid., p. 25.
75.   Voora and Venema, 'The natural capital approach', p. 52.

7. Potential environmental impacts of the Australia–South Korea Free Trade Agreement and fiscal intervention

Seck L. Tan

7.1 INTRODUCTION

> It is perfectly possible for a nation to secure sustainable development – in the sense of not depleting its own stock of capital assets – at the cost of procuring unsustainable development in another country.[1]

This quote serves to remind us that a nation's sustainable development achieved at the expense of environmental degradation in another nation is not true sustainable development.

This chapter aims to investigate the impacts of trade liberalization on Australia's ecosystem using a macroeconomic analysis of environmental utilization, and providing policy options available to protect the natural resources in Australia. Such a strategy allows natural resources to realize their full economic potential (whilst being maintained in a closed-loop arrangement) and offers recognition to the ecosystem as an essential player in sustainable trade development.

Australia is blessed with an abundance of land, clean water, rich biodiversity and fresh air. These enable the production of high-quality food and agriculture products for both domestic and export consumption. Coupled with an array of highly sought-after minerals and deposits, Australia is more than qualified as a lucky country. The source of high-quality food and agricultural products is attributed to the ecosystem; however, continual trading of food and agricultural products, energy and resource commodities utilizes the services of the ecosystem and this is not captured in national income accounting. For instance, mining fossil fuels for export degrades the environment, which may suggest that the rate of environmental capital utilization for export production is greater than the rate of utilization for domestic consumption.

Australia has signed free trade agreements (FTAs) with China, Chile, Japan, New Zealand, the United States, ASEAN (Brunei, Myanmar, Cambodia, Indonesia, Laos, Malaysia, Philippines, Singapore, Thailand and Vietnam) and the Gulf Cooperation Council. South Korea is the latest addition to the growing list of FTAs that Australia has signed. If Australia is using South Korea as a platform or springboard into the rich and deep Asian base,[2] a reduction in trade barriers will certainly enhance entry to Asia and further expand trade, output and economic development. The prospect of an FTA between Australia and South Korea was initially discussed in 2004[3] with accrued benefits and probable competitive pressure on selected industries highlighted for the Australian economy.[4] An independent feasibility study[5] estimated a boost in Australia's real gross domestic product (GDP) of US$22.7 billion to the year 2020 from an Australia and South Korea FTA, which is targeted to benefit the sectors of agriculture and food, mineral and ores, metals and manufactures. Another study[6] expects trade with South Korea to have an increase of 23 per cent by 2030, with most of the increase attributed to energy and resources.

Following five years of diplomacies (trade negotiations started in 2009), the FTA between Australia and South Korea was finally inked in December 2014. The FTA supports bilateral trade between both nations by allowing tariffs to be eliminated on Australian exports such as agricultural products, energy, manufactured goods and resources (coal, iron ore and crude petroleum) to South Korea. The key focus lies in agriculture products and allows Australia's agricultural products to compete in a protected[7] but lucrative market. In return, South Korean exports of automobiles and parts, and consumer goods will also enjoy favourable treatment in Australia. With the FTA, 84 per cent of Australia's exported goods will be exempted from tariffs; the percentage will rise to 99.8 per cent with a full implementation of the FTA.[8] Coal exports are not subjected to a tariff now and will remain so for the tenure of the FTA. The returns in employment and stabilizing money wages may be immediate but the expected contribution of US$22.7 billion to GDP would materialize possibly only in the longer term to 2020. Nevertheless, another immediate impact (which has been neglected) is the potential degradation of Australia's ecosystem where the provision of agricultural products and mineral resources[9] has utilized its stock of environmental assets.

There is high probability that Australia's FTA with South Korea may result in an increase in emissions from further trade liberalization, and at a modest expense to the environment.[10] A review of the FTA text (Chapter 18) finds minimal mention of 'environment' and no concrete policies to protect Australia's ecosystem, barring the laws of protection in Article 18.1: Levels of Protection in the FTA official document text[11] by

Australia's Department of Foreign Affairs and Trade. As more agricultural products are harvested to meet export demand, soil quality may degrade through fertilizer use. This is evident in reduced harvest and lower-quality produce. Excessive fertilizer use can also lead to algae blooms as nutrients are washed off the land into the water during rainy seasons. Although trade liberalization has the potential to deliver gains and strengthen economic relationships bilaterally, there may be other impacts beyond the expected economic and trade benefits. This chapter focuses on the potential impacts on Australia's environmental capital from free trade with South Korea.

To ensure a continual provision of ecosystem services for future trade and output expansions, care must be taken of the ecosystem. A responsible response would be one that protects the environment as opposed to a continual degradation of the environment, and one way to potentially decrease environmental degradation is to increase agricultural value.[12] The Australian agricultural industry has embraced technology to increase productivity and value in the agricultural sector via research and development (R&D), sale of patents and the management of property rights (post-R&D). Selected initiatives that engaged technological advances include: laser levelling of crops, global positioning system (GPS) image tracking, chip mounting on livestock, and helicopter herding. Such R&D forays are a sign of progress and development for the agricultural sector and a push towards sustainability for future generations.

As the basis of trade changes, there have been conflicting views of economic benefit from FTAs.[13] For instance, theories of trade state that changes in trade will affect emission levels (proxy for environmental degradation) via three main effects namely: composition, scale and technique.[14,15,16] Composition effect refers to emission changes due to relative price changes (from comparative advantage) and impacts on the production structure. Scale effect refers to changes in emissions as a result of increased level of economic activities. Technique effect refers to emissions from changes in production methods. Trade can be beneficial, or degrading, or both (beneficial and degrading) to the environment.

Trade was found to be beneficial for the environment when air quality was used to proxy environmental degradation.[17,18,19] Similarly, trade openness minimizes the growth of toxic intensity.[20] On the other hand, trade and growth can potentially worsen the measures of environmental degradation such as carbon dioxide.[21,22] Other scholars had found that free trade is both beneficial and degrading to the environment, largely dependent on the extent to which environment and trade goals are complementary and supportive,[23] along with indirect and direct impacts on the environment.[24]

Using an empirical approach, this chapter offers an explanation of the utilization of Australia's environmental capital and trade (exports and imports) trends with South Korea (FTA partner), as well as contrasting the observed relationship with South Korea. The chapter makes the case that while the expected outcomes from the FTA agreement with South Korea will benefit the Australian economy, it is highly recommended that there be initiatives in place to ensure that trade will be just as beneficial to Australia's environment. Should free trade result in environmental degradation, the anticipated outcomes will not be a true representation of the benefits from free trade. Although the study is based on historical data from 1996 to 2013, it seeks to establish a relationship for Australia's environmental utilization and trade trends with South Korea and offers a prediction during the FTA tenure.

This chapter is structured as follows with three main sections. Following this introduction, an overview of trade figures between Australia and South Korea and an empirical calculation on environmental utilization (based on a macroeconomic framework) of both nations will be presented. Section 7.3 offers proposed fiscal intervention and enhancements of trade agreements as future policy measures.

7.2   TRADE FLOWS AND ENVIRONMENTAL CAPITAL UTILIZATION FOR AUSTRALIA AND SOUTH KOREA

Trade numbers between Australia and South Korea from 1996 to 2013 are shown in Figure 7.1. South Korea is ranked third on the list of Australia's top ten countries to export to and is ranked eighth on the list of Australia's top ten importers. Australia's exports (X) to South Korea show a progressive increase from 1996 to 2008 before experiencing a slump (which could be explained by the global financial crisis (GFC)). Recovery of the exports took two years to reach a new historic high before another dip due to the strong Australian dollar and global business cycle but remains in line with a long-term rising trend. Australia's imports (M) from South Korea remain consistently lower than its exports to South Korea and display a much steadier rise relative to exports over the observed time period.

The illustration for environmental capital (KN) utilization employs a macroeconomic analysis to internalize the environment as capital. The Appendix at the end of this chapter details the steps taken to estimate KN utilization.[25] The main thrust of the argument is that the environment has been overlooked as a factor of production in the determination of national income and no appropriate measurement has been accorded to

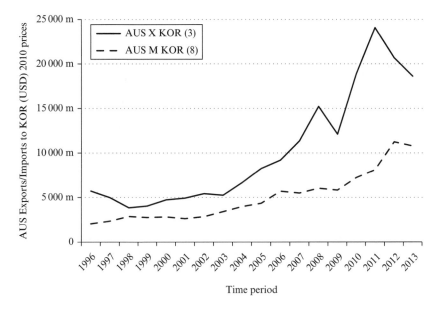

Note: m = million.

Source: Asian Development Bank 'Key indicators for Asia and the Pacific 2014'.

Figure 7.1   *Australia's exports and imports with South Korea (1996–2013)*

the environment in its utilization. This denotes that development policies were formulated with no consideration for the environment and implemented without protection of the environment. The proxy used for *KN* utilization is carbon dioxide as it is a key contributor to climate change from production and consumption of energy.

The utilization of *KN* for Australia and South Korea from 1996 to 2013 is illustrated in Figure 7.2.[26] *KN* utilization for Australia exhibits an increasing trend with peaks in 2000 and a dip the next year; utilization peaked again in 2008 followed by a plunge in the subsequent year before rising again in line with expected trends. Peaks in the utilization of *KN* fell in the immediate years that followed, that is, a dip in 2001 was due to the burst of the dot-com bubble, and a steep fall in 2009 was attributed to the GFC. In contrast, South Korea displays an overall decreasing path in its utilization of *KN*, with a steep fall during 1997–98 explained by the Asian financial crisis (AFC). The observation between both economies shows two diverging paths (barring the peaks from dot-com bubble and GFC for Australia and trough from AFC for South Korea) where Australia's utilization of

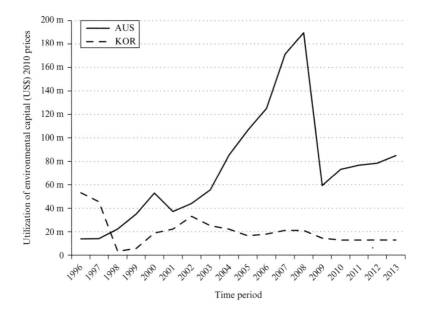

Note: m = million.

Source: *OECD Factbook 2014.*

Figure 7.2   *Environmental capital utilization for Australia and*
South Korea (1996–2013)

KN is rising at an increasing rate and South Korea's utilization of *KN* is
falling at a decreasing rate.

Although the observed *KN* utilization for both Australia and
South Korea is diverging, GDP for both economies displays a steady
rise from 1996 to 2013, with Australia showing a dominant GDP (see
Figure 7.3). In examining the trade behaviour and utilization of *KN* for
both economies, it is observed that the peak in Australia's exports to South
Korea coincides with the peak in Australia's *KN* utilization in 2008 prior
to the GFC. The evidence suggests that the potential degradation of *KN*
will rise, with more trade between Australia and South Korea. This implies
three things: first, Australia's exports to South Korea have resulted in a
high rate of its *KN* utilization; second, crises such as the AFC, dot-com
bubble and GFC offer corrections for trade flows and the utilization of
KN; and third, both observations occurred when both economies were
growing.

Even though the FTA between Australia and South Korea was inked in

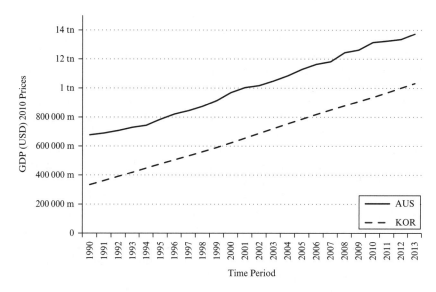

Note: m = million; tn = trillion.

Source: *OECD Factbook 2014.*

Figure 7.3 *Gross domestic income for Australia and South Korea (1996–2013)*

December 2014, it is likely that the overall rising trends for trade flows and *KN* (observed during the time period studied) will continue to rise during the FTA's tenure to 2020. The projections of *KN* utilization and trade flows beyond the observed time period suggest that Australia belongs to the category that degrades the environment with trade liberalization. The utilization patterns of *KN* for both economies tell of a contradicting outcome; that is, both economies displayed rising GDP but Australia's higher GDP was achieved at an expense of greater *KN* utilization relative to South Korea.

The next section proposes available policy options to Australia for maintaining growth whilst utilizing a lower level of *KN* via fiscal intervention and changes to trade agreements.

7.3 RECOMMENDATIONS: FISCAL INTERVENTION AND TRADE AGREEMENTS

The first recommendation is the use of environmental tax to slow the rate of *KN* utilization.[27] In general, taxes should be applied to resource throughput[28] and pricing based on carbon content to emphasize the significance of taxing environmentally harmful activities and address a nation's environment damage. The aim of such intervention is to drive the Australian economy towards a low-carbon development scenario. However, such policies and accompanying technologies may not necessarily address development constraints. As global demand for mineral resources slows in Australia, it presents an opportunity for the ecosystem to be elevated as the bedrock of the economy. A percentage of revenue collected[29] can be reinvested via a portfolio to maintain *KN* as a source and a sink. A shift of investment towards low-carbon scenarios demands that environmental goals be clearly defined with a transparent incentive structure. This enables economic development and social advancement in a responsible manner while offering appreciation to the ecosystem.

The land in Australia provides a service to the production of quality agriculture produce. With excessive farming and fertilizers, agricultural land will degrade and compromise the quality of the produce. Unfortunately, the land (or ecosystem in general) is a public good in a failed market, which explains a lack of justification to preserve the services it offers. Taxes may help to account for the cost of degradation but when regulations are not clearly laid out, the costs and risks of engaging in trade will be high and the prospects of economic expansion low. There is a range of options to address this:

- Regulate the use of environmental assets by assigning rights and provide absolute certainty on responsible ownership. This encourages owners (farmers) to practise ecosystem-friendly methods of production.
- Incentivize restoration of environmental assets (with a balance between competing land use for reforestation and agriculture). This aids in maintaining the quality of agricultural products and ensures the security of regional jobs.
- Tax revenues to finance the conservation and repair of the natural environment. An efficient response to excessive environmental degradation from trade and economic growth would require an integration of environmental taxes, or green tax reform[30] to the overall tax structure.

In an effort to reverse Australia's current trend of *KN* utilization and move Australia into the category that promotes environmental well-being with free trade, it is proposed that the strategy of fiscal policies implemented by Australia would have to focus on:

- addressing a balance in the proportion of differing goods;
- managing the level of economic activities (via some hybrid form of fiscal taxes);
- incentives for low-carbon methods of production.

There is no doubt that the FTA will offer economic expansion and secure Australian jobs into the future. However, to ensure that the eco-system continues its service towards trade and economic expansion, the agricultural land and natural resources in Australia need to be protected more and exploited less with an acknowledgement that environmental protection and economic development can happen at the same time and are not mutually exclusive.

The second recommendation is via modification of trade agreements to include protection of the environment and a sustainable use of natural resources. FTA is a basic level of economic integration between two trading partners with an agreement to eliminate tariffs on agreed goods and services. To further reduce complication (minimizing cost and delays), trade facilitation is introduced to ensure that trade procedures are simpli-fied. A step up from FTA is the Comprehensive Economic Partnership (CEP), which extends economic integration beyond trade to include invest-ment, financial aid, technological cooperation and R&D. As such, CEP seeks to broaden and deepen a mutually beneficial economic partnership agreement between partners, and consolidation towards greater economic gains.[31] As discussed earlier in the chapter, mention of the environment is restricted to laws of protection with no concrete policy actions. It is recommended that bilateral environmental agreements[32] are considered in conjunction with CEP in the future.

7.4 CONCLUSION

The FTA between Australia and South Korea is widely regarded as one of the best trading deals signed by Australia. Agricultural and mineral exports to South Korea enjoy tariff-free entry into a highly lucrative and profit-able market. The expected benefits from this trade deal are GDP growth and local employment, while the cost incurred is exploitation of land and natural resources to facilitate crop production and mining for exports. As the ecosystem services trade and development, it is conceivable that more agricultural produce and further resource extraction may intensify the rate of environmental utilization.

The empirical illustration in section 7.2 shows that while Australia's GDP is rising (due to increasing exports to South Korea), the rate of environmental utilization for Australia is also increasing during the observed time period. Path-dependent observation suggests that Australia's environmental utilization is likely to increase through the FTA's tenure. For trade development to be sustainable, it is recommended that a balance between trade and natural resource protection is sought. Trade and environment utilization are closely related and they should not be thought of in solitude. As more trade is expected, greater environmental utilization will be observed. Therefore, trade needs to encourage action that utilizes the environment less. The rate of exploitation of land and natural resources in Australia can be reduced by way of environmental taxes as well as changes to trade agreements. Of greater significance is the need for revision of the national income accounting system; that is, Australia's method of income accounting must adjust for the impact of the environment as potential environmental impacts from trade cannot be underestimated.

NOTES

1. Pearce, D.W. and J.J. Warford (1993), *World Without End: Economics, Environment, and Sustainable Development*, Oxford: Oxford University Press, p. 4.
2. UNSW Business School (2013), 'Asian partners: how Korea is overlooked in coming fourth', *BusinessThink*, 21 May, accessed 13 April 2016 at https://www.businessthink.unsw.edu.au/Pages/Asian-Partners-How-Korea-is-Overlooked-in-Coming-Fourth.aspx.
3. Harvie, C. (2004), 'Prospects for an FTA between Australia and Korea', in J. Lee, C. Kim and K. Wong (eds), *Conference on Korea and the World Economy, III*, Seoul: Akes, KDI and RCIE, pp. 643–66.
4. Robertson, J. (2006), 'Time for an Australia–South Korea Free Trade Agreement (FTA)?', *Research Note No. 31*, Department of Parliamentary Services, Parliament of Australia, 3 May.
5. ITS Global and Korean Institute for International Economic Policy (KIEP) (2008), *Australia–Republic of Korea Free Trade Agreement Feasibility Study*, 17 April.
6. Taylor, G., J. von Thien and S. Mansour (2014), 'Korea–Australia FTA: energy and resources opportunities', *Clayton Utz Insights*, 6 March, accessed 13 April 2016 at http://www.claytonutz.com/publications/edition/6_march_2014/20140306/korea-aust ralia_fta_energy_and_resources_opportunities.page.
7. Australia is likely to gain more from FTAs with nations that have higher trade barriers prior to the negotiation of FTAs. Siriwardana, M. (2006), 'Australia's involvement in free trade agreements: an economic evaluation', *Global Economic Review*, **35**(1), 3–20.
8. Le Vesconte, S. (2014), 'Focus: Korea–Australia Free Trade Agreement: strengthening cross-border investment', *Allens Linklaters*, 23 April, accessed 13 April 2016 at http://www.allens.com.au/pubs/asia/foasia23apr14.htm.
9. Under the Environmental Protection and Biodiversity Conservation (EPBC) Act, the state owns and has the rights to the minerals and resources. Based on Australia's underlying constitutional framework, the state holds the right to issue licences for the extraction of minerals and resources by third parties. Such arrangements preclude the rights of landowners. Therefore, in the absence of a shift in public resource ownership, landowners remain at the mercy of third party developers.
10. Siriwardana, M. (2015), 'Australia's new free trade agreements with Japan and

South Korea: potential economic and environmental impacts', *Journal of Economic Integration*, **30**(4), 616–43.

11.   Australian Government, Department of Foreign Affairs and Trade (undated), 'Korea-Australia Free Trade Agreement, Chapter 18: Environment', accessed 13 April 2016 at http://dfat.gov.au/trade/agreements/kafta/official-documents/Pages/chapter-18-environment.aspx.

12.   Chang, S.C. (2015), 'The effects of trade liberalization on environmental degradation', *Quality & Quantity*, **49**(1), 235–53.

13.   Harris-Rimmer, S. (2015), 'Rules-based trade as a pivotal power', in *Global Networks: Transforming How Australia Does Business*, Melbourne: Committee for Economic Development of Australia, Chapter 3.

14.   Grossman, G. and A.B. Krueger (1992), 'Environmental impacts of a North American free trade agreement', *CEPR Discussion Papers No. 644*; Copeland, B. and S. Taylor (2003), *Trade and Environment: Theory and Evidence*, Princeton, NJ: Princeton University Press.

15.   Copeland, B.R. and M.S. Taylor (2003), 'Trade, growth and the environment', *National Bureau of Economic Research Working Paper No. 9823*.

16.   Tamiotti, L., R. Teh, V. Kulacoglu, A. Olhoff, B. Simmons and H. Abaza (2009), *Trade and Climate Change, WTO–UNEP Report*, accessed 13 April 2016 at https://www.wto.org/english/res_e/booksp_e/trade_climate_change_e.pdf.

17.   Antweiler, W., B.R. Copeland and M.S. Taylor (2001), 'Is free trade good for the environment?', *American Economic Review*, **91**(4), 877–908.

18.   Frankel, J.A. and A.K. Rose (2005), 'Is trade good or bad for the environment? Sorting out the causality', *Review of Economic Statistics*, **87**(1), 85–91.

19.   Harbaugh, W.T., A. Levinson and D.M. Wilson (2002), 'Re-examining the empirical evidence for an environmental Kuznets curve', *Review of Economic Statistics*, **84**(3), 541–51.

20.   Lucas, R., D. Wheeler and H. Hettige (1992), 'Economic development, environmental regulation and the international migration of toxic international pollution: 1960–1988', in P. Low (ed.), *International Trade and the Environment Discussion Paper No. 159*, Washington, DC: World Bank.

21.   Frankel, J. (2008), 'Environmental effects of international trade', *Expert Report No. 31 to Sweden's Globalisation Council*, accessed 13 April 2016 at http://www.hks.harvard.edu/fs/jfrankel/Swenvirinlaga31proofs.pdf.

22.   Please note that studies highlighted above from notes 16–21 (inclusive) were made with no recognition of the environment in the national income accounting (NIA) system. This chapter seeks to recognize the consideration for the environment in the NIA system and identify the potential environmental impacts from trade.

23.   Korves, N., I. Martínez-Zarzoso and A.M. Voicu (2011), 'Is free trade good or bad for the environment? New empirical evidence', in J. Blanco and H. Kheradmand (eds), *Climate Change – Socioeconomic Effects*, Rijeka, Croatia: InTech, pp. 1–30.

24.   Dean, J. (2002), 'Does trade liberalization harm the environment? A new test', *Canadian Journal of Economics*, **35**(4), 819–42.

25.   Tan, S. (2016), 'Framework for valuing the utilization of the environment', *International Journal of Social Economics*, **43** (6), July 2016.

26.   The estimates of environmental capital (*KN*) utilization are specific to trade between Australia and South Korea and made with reference to the entire economy based on the income method of national income. An alternative method of *KN* estimation to capture the trade relationship is to employ the expenditure method of national income where net exports are accounted for. Please see the framework used in Tan, S. (2015), 'Sustainable development: an empirical illustration for Saudi Arabia', *The Journal of Developing Areas*, **49**(6), 517–29, based on work by Thampapillai, D.J. (2012), 'Macroeconomics versus environmental-macroeconomics', *The Australian Journal of Agricultural and Resource Economics*, **55**(3), 1–16.

27.   See, 'Australia lags its trading partners on pollution price tags: global study', accessed 13

April 2016 at http://www.climateinstitute.org.au/articles/media-releases/australia-lags-its-trading-partners-on-pollution-price-tags-global-study.html.

28.   Daly, H.E. (1996), *Beyond Growth*, Boston, MA: Beacon Press.
29.   Thampapillai, D.J., X. Wu and S. Tan (2010), 'Fiscal balance: environmental taxes and investments', *Journal of Natural Resources Policy Research*, **2**(2), 137–47.
30.   Gago, A. and X. Labandeira (2000), 'Towards a green tax reform model', *Journal of Environmental Policy & Planning*, **2**(1), 25–37.
31.   Kawai, M. and G. Wignaraja (2008), 'EAFTA or CEPEA: which way forward?', *ASEAN Economic* Bulletin, **25**(2), 113–39.
32.   A bilateral agreement was signed between the Commonwealth of Australia and Western Australia to protect the environment and promote sustainable use of natural resources in Australia on 1 January 2015.

APPENDIX

The following details the steps taken to estimate KN:

1. The OECD[1] economies selected for this study are Australia and South Korea. The variables selected from 1996 to 2013 are the following: final consumption expenditure (C); final consumption expenditure of government (G); gross capital formation (GCF); net balance of goods and services (NX); national income expenditure approach (Y); compensation of employees (CE); gross operating surplus (OS); net taxes (T); savings (S); income approach to national accounts ($IANA$); GDP deflator; and employment (labour) (L). All of the monetary estimates are in the appropriate national currency at current prices.
2. The GDP deflator was used to convert the current value estimates to constant values. Note that the base year is 2010. To smooth any cyclical variations, the Hodrick-Prescott (HP) filter was applied to the variables C, GCF, S,[2] CE, and OS. KN consists of capital stock KM (GCF), OS and CE. HP filtering applied to the three variables (which made up KN) ensures that contamination of business cycles to KN will be at a minimal.
3. The perpetual inventory method was used to estimate the capital stock (KM). GCF is the investment (I) and the logarithm of GCF is computed to express the values in a more natural way. The size of the capital at the initial time period of the time series can be determined and estimated by the coefficient w, which is defined as the ideal rate of increase for KM per annum. The initial size of the capital stock is denoted as $KM_{t=1}$ for the first year and is estimated from the GCF value. This value is defined as follows:

$$KM_{t=1} = GCF_{t=1}/(\delta + \omega) \tag{A7.1}$$

where δ is the rate at which capital stock depreciates over 30 years, which is assumed to be $(1/30) = 0.0333$. The size of the capital stock for subsequent years can now be estimated by:

$$KM_{t+1} = KM_t + GCF_{t+1} - (\delta * KM_t) \tag{A7.2}$$

4. Labour (L) is estimated to be the level of total labour force employed. This is obtained directly from the OECD database.
5. The value of θ is estimated to be (OS/Y) and λ is (CE/Y).
6. The variable ϕ is estimated to be (D_{KN}/Y) where D_{KN} is the total cost of air pollution. The value of D_{KN} is restricted to the cost of carbon

dioxide (CO_2) abatement and the measurement of gases includes the greenhouse gases such as CO_2, methane (CH_4), nitrous oxide (N_2O), and other GHG (which includes hydrofluorocarbons (HFCs), per-fluorinated compounds (PFCs) and sulphur hexafluoride (SF_6)). All of the gases are measured in tonnes of CO_2 equivalent, at a cost of US$100/tonne (2010 constant prices).[3]

7. With the introduction of ϕ (the share of income to *KN*), θ and λ must be revised to capture changes in the constituent of income.[4] If the assumption that a constant return to scale holds, then $\theta' + \lambda' + \phi = 1$. Hence, θ and λ must be revised to θ' and λ'. This revision is necessary because the original variables are overstated from the inclusion of the income share from *KN*. In this study, θ' and λ' were estimated using shadow pricing. The shadow price is the price of the factor of production when the market is perfect, for example when full employment is observed. Thus, the coefficients θ' and λ' can be defined as follows:

$$\theta' = (1 - \phi)\left(\frac{P_{KM}}{P_L + P_{KM}}\right) \qquad \text{(A7.3)}$$

$$\lambda' = (1 - \phi)\left(\frac{P_L}{P_L + P_{KM}}\right) \qquad \text{(A7.4)}$$

where P_{KM} is the shadow price of *KM*, which is estimated to be (*OS/KM*) and P_{Lt} is the shadow price of *CE*, which is estimated to be the capital equivalent price of *L*. The method adopted in Thampapillai (2012)[5] is to convert *CE* to explain the context of unemployment. This conversion is performed by dividing *CE* by the labour force to estimate a wage rate that would support full employment. The revised value of *CE*, namely CE_{St} is then the product of the employment and the shadow wage rate, which is ($L_t^* W_{St}$). Then λ' is (CE_{St}/Y). P_{Lt} is estimated to be (CE_{St}/KM_t), which is a *KM* equivalent price.

8. *KN* can be calculated by substituting all of the parameters that are described from steps 3 to 7 and derived as:

$$KN = KM^{\frac{\theta - \theta'}{\phi}} L^{\frac{\lambda - \lambda'}{\phi}} \qquad \text{(A7.5)}$$

Note that these parameters are point estimates and not estimation of long-run steady state properties.

Notes

1. The OECD database was selected because it has a full set of national income accounts with data dating from 1980.
2. Savings $(S) = GDP - C - G$.
3. The literature has proposed a cost of US$100/tonne of CO_2 emissions. Stern, N. (2007), *The Economics of Climate Change: The Stern Review*, Cambridge, UK: Cambridge University Press; Ackerman, F., E.A. Stanton, S.J. DeCanio, E. Goodstein, R.B. Howarth, R.B. Norgaard, C.S. Norman and K.A. Sheeran (2009), *The Economics of 350: The Benefits and Costs of Climate Stabilization*, Economics for Equity and the Environment Network; Hope, C.W. (2011), 'The social cost of CO_2 from the PAGE09 model', *Economics, Discussion Paper No. 2011-39, September*; Karstad, P.I. (2012), 'The price on carbon should increase', *Statoil Innovate Blog*, 24 April.
4. The model presented draws on the framework proposed by Thampapillai, D.J. (2012), 'Macroeconomics versus environmental-macroeconomics', *The Australian Journal of Agricultural and Resource Economics*, **55**(3), 1–16.
5. Ibid.

8. The impact of environmental taxes on enterprise behavior and competitiveness – China's iron and steel industry

Jian Wu, Xiao Wang and Zhe Yang

8.1 RESEARCH BACKGROUND

Environmental taxes have been studied in China for several years. In June 2007, the State Council issued the *Comprehensive Working Plan on Energy Conservation and Pollution Reduction*, in which an environmental tax was clearly proposed for the first time and its policy process formally initiated. In October 2010, the 5th Plenary Session of the 17th CPC Central Committee issued *A Proposal for Making the 12th Five-Year Plan* that contained a new tax category: the Environmental Protection Tax. In April 2014, the new environmental protection law of the People's Republic of China was promulgated, in which the name 'Environmental Protection Tax' appeared in a legal document for the first time. Eventually, in June 2015, *The Environmental Protection Tax Law of the People's Republic of China (Exposure Draft)* was issued for public comments and suggestions.

As China is facing serious environmental pollution, the main purpose of environmental taxes in China is to protect and improve the environment by adjusting the polluters' (especially enterprises') behavior. So, determining the impact of environmental taxes on enterprise behavior will be critical to ensuring the effectiveness of this newly proposed policy. This study seeks to fill this knowledge gap.

The rest of the chapter consists of four sections: section 8.2 is a review of relevant studies, section 8.3 describes the methodology and data of this study, section 8.4 is the analysis, and section 8.5 presents the conclusions and some policy implications.

8.2 LITERATURE REVIEW

Among empirical studies, there is little literature that specializes in the impact of environmental tax on enterprises' behavior, although some studies have explored the impact of various environmental management activities on enterprises' behavior, including enterprises' production and environmental strategies[1] and enterprises' innovation activities.[2] Some of the literature focuses on the relation between industrial behavior and competitiveness, but the conclusions are unclear.[3] A few studies specialize in the impact of environmental taxes on enterprises' competitiveness, but do not explain the reason for behavior change.[4] Most of them are ex post studies, while for the case of China we need an ex ante assessment.

The methods that study the impact of environmental management activities on an enterprise can be roughly divided into three types: the direct comparison method, which is good only for ex post assessment, the parametric method and the non-parametric method. The parametric method mainly uses stochastic frontier analysis (SFA) while the main representative of the non-parametric method is data envelopment analysis (DEA).

The SFA has inherent advantages when accounting for the cause of dependent variables' change due to its establishment of the frontier function. It can correctly and intuitively represent the impact on dependent variables through the independent variable coefficient and its significance. However, if the amount of data is small or the variable selection is unreasonable, the predicted results may greatly differ from the actual situation.

There are a few studies that use DEA for forecasting. Those studies can be divided into two types. One type uses DEA to replace the production function,[5] and the other type uses DEA evaluation based on multiple scenarios.[6] The main difficulty of this method is the reasonability of scenario settings.

To sum up, the applicability of the DEA method is relatively extensive. This study chooses the data envelopment analysis–range-adjusted measure (DEA-RAM) model as the main method, because existing data are limited and samples are relatively small. It is hard to carry out accurate forecasting analysis of enterprises' behaviors by establishing the production function; on this basis, this method 'has non-radial direction, non-angle, additive structure and other characteristics'.[7] It significantly minimizes the errors produced in the evaluation process by the traditional DEA method.

8.3 APPROACH, METHODOLOGY AND DATA

8.3.1 Research Approach

The research approach is as follows. First, RAM models are built to measure the relative efficiency (production efficiency, environmental efficiency and comprehensive efficiency), to represent competitiveness of different enterprises under the current policy. Then we set up the scenarios that consist of tax scenarios (different environmental tax form and tax rates) and behavior scenarios (possible behaviors that enterprises may exhibit). Thereafter, we can simulate the change of relative efficiency of enterprises under different scenarios. Eventually, under the assumption that enterprises will try to maximize their efficiency, we can predict the best behaviors that enterprises may choose under different tax scenarios.

8.3.2 DEA-RAM Model

With RAM models, we try to measure the relative efficiency of enterprises under certain input/output combinations. Considering the policy performance we will explore, we use production efficiency (only considering desired output), environmental efficiency (only considering undesired output) and comprehensive efficiency that integrates the first two efficiencies to describe the relative efficiency from different aspects.

RAM model based on desired output – production efficiency
First, in order to establish the production possibility set, we assume that each enterprise uses N types of normal factor input and M types of energy input, which are $x = (x_1, \ldots, x_N) \in R_N^+$ and $e = (e_1, \ldots, e_M) \in R_M^+$, respectively. The outputs are P types of desired outputs and I types of undesired outputs, which respectively are $y = (y_1, \ldots, y_P) \in R_P^+$ and $b = (b_1, \ldots, b_I) \in R_I^+$. Therefore the production possibility set is:

$$T = \{(x, e, y, b), x \in R_N^+, e \in R_M^+\}. \tag{8.1}$$

Suppose the slack variables of the input and desired output that are related to the production frontier projection of the jth enterprise ($j = 1, 2\ldots, J$) are $s_n^x \geq 0$, $\forall n$ and $s_P^x \geq 0$, $\forall n$. The slack variable represents the distance of input and output items of the assessed unit to what are on the efficiency frontier. In addition, the DEA-RAM model uses the proportion that the slack variable accounts for in the full range to measure the relative efficiency of the assessed unit.

Let the input range of each enterprise be $r_{nj} = [\max(x_{nj}) - \min(x_{nj})]$ and the output range be $r_{pj} = [\max(y_{pj}) - \min(y_{pj})]$. The adjustment interval of the slack variable is:

$$R_n^x = \frac{1}{(N+P)r_{nj}} \quad \text{and} \quad R_p^y = \frac{1}{(N+P)r_{pj}}. \tag{8.2}$$

Therefore, the RAM model based on desired output is as (8.3):

$$\max\left\{\left(\sum_{n=1}^{N} R_n^x s_n^x + \sum_{p=1}^{P} R_p^y s_p^y\right) \left| \begin{array}{l} \sum_{j=1}^{J} x_{nj}\lambda_j + s_n^x = x_{n0}, \forall n; \sum_{j=1}^{J} y_{pj}\lambda_j - s_p^y = y_{p0}, \forall p; \\ \sum_{j=1}^{J} \lambda_j = 1, \lambda_j \geq 0, \forall j; s_n^x \geq 0, \forall n; s_p^y \geq 0, \forall p; \end{array} \right.\right\} \tag{8.3}$$

The objective function (8.3) is the sum of relative efficiency value of each input item and output item. The value of the objective function is normalized into the interval of [0, 1]. The intuition of this objective function is that when the slack quantities of each input item and output item are 0, the objective function value will be 0, which means the assessed decision-making unit is located on the efficiency frontier; if some items' slack variables of the decision-making unit are not 0, then the objective function value at this time must be larger than 0, which means the decision-making unit is not located in the efficiency frontier.

Let λ^* be the optimal state and $\sum_{j=1}^{J} \lambda_j = 1$, $\lambda_j \geq 0$ be the weight of cross-sectional observed value of the maximum relative efficiency that each enterprise can reach when the model obtains the optimal solution. The maximized objective function value of non-efficiency extent is between 0 and 1. At the same time, the size of the non-negative slack variable will not exceed the range, then:

$$r_{nj} \geq s_n^{x*} = x_{nj} - \sum_{j=1}^{J} x_{nj}\lambda^* \geq 0, \; r_{pj} \geq s_n^{y*} = \sum_{j=1}^{J} y_{pj}\lambda^* - y_{pj} \geq 0. \tag{8.4}$$

$$1 \geq \theta_P = 1 - \left(\sum_{n=1}^{N} R_n^x s_n^x + \sum_{p=1}^{P} R_p^y s_p^y\right) \geq 0. \tag{8.5}$$

Due to the non-efficiency level of objective function, the efficiency value is written as θ_P, which equals to 1 subtracted by the objective function value. When all slack variables are 0, then $\theta_P = 1$, the enterprise is located on the optimal frontier.

RAM model based on undesired output – environmental efficiency
In the model of measuring environmental efficiency, the slack variable of pollutant emissions is written as s_i^b. In order to represent the intention of reducing the undesired output, the negative sign will be added before the slack variable. Therefore, the RAM model of undesired output is as follows (8.6):

$$\max\left\{\left(\sum_{n=1}^{N}R_n^x s_n^x + \sum_{m=1}^{M}R_m^e\left(s_m^{e+}+s_m^{e-}\right)+\sum_{i=1}^{I}R_i^b s_i^b\right) \left| \begin{array}{l} \sum_{j=1}^{J}x_{nj}\lambda_j + s_n^x = x_{n0}, \forall n; \\[2mm] \sum_{j=1}^{J}e_{mj}\lambda_j - s_m^{e+} + s_m^{e-} = e_{m0}, \forall m; \\[2mm] \sum_{j=1}^{J}b_{ij}\lambda_i + s_i^b = b_{i0}, \forall i; \\[2mm] \sum_{j=1}^{J}\lambda_j = 1, \lambda_j \geq 0, \ \forall j; \\[2mm] s_n^x \geq 0, \ \forall n; s_m^{e+} \geq 0, \ s_m^{e-} \geq 0, \ \forall m; s_i^b \geq 0, \ \forall i \end{array} \right. \right\}$$

$$(8.6)$$

What should be noted is that the increase of energy consumption of some kind of energy does not indicate the deterioration of efficiency. On the contrary, it may mean efficiency improvement. Therefore, in the energy input items, we set the slack variables in two directions to represent the possible energy shift from one energy type to other alternative energy sources.

Similar to the RAM model based on the desired output, the environmental efficiency value at this time is:

$$1 \geq \theta_E = 1 - \left(\sum_{n=1}^{N}R_n^x s_n^{x*} + \sum_{m=1}^{M}R_m^e\left(s_m^{e+*}+s_m^{e-*}\right)+\sum_{i=1}^{I}R_i^b s_i^{b*}\right) \geq 0. \quad (8.7)$$

When all slack variables are $\theta_E = 1$, the enterprise is located on the optimal frontier.

RAM model based on dual output – comprehensive efficiency
The RAM model based on dual output is the sum of the RAM model based on desired output and the RAM model based on undesired output:

$$\max \left\{ \begin{pmatrix} \displaystyle\sum_{n=1}^{N} R_n^x s_n^x + \sum_{m=1}^{M} R_m^e \left(s_m^{e+} + s_m^{e-} \right) \\ + \displaystyle\sum_{p=1}^{P} R_p^y s_p^y + \sum_{i=1}^{I} R_i^b s_i^b \end{pmatrix} \middle| \begin{array}{l} \displaystyle\sum_{j=1}^{J} x_{nj}\lambda_j + s_n^x = x_{n0}, \forall n; \\[2ex] \displaystyle\sum_{j=1}^{J} e_{mj}\lambda_j - s_m^{e+} + s_m^{e-} = e_{m0}, \forall m; \\[2ex] \displaystyle\sum_{j=1}^{J} b_{ij}\lambda_j + s_i^b = b_{i0}, \forall i; \\[2ex] \displaystyle\sum_{j=1}^{J} y_{pj}\lambda_j - s_p^y = y_{p0}, \forall p; \\[2ex] \displaystyle\sum_{j=1}^{J} \lambda_j = 1, \lambda_j \geq 0, \quad \forall j; \\[1ex] s_n^x \geq 0, \quad \forall n; s_m^{e+} \geq 0, \quad s_m^{e-} \geq 0, \quad \forall m; \\[1ex] s_p^y \geq 0, \quad \forall p; \ s_i^b \geq 0, \quad \forall i \end{array} \right\}$$

$$(8.8)$$

The comprehensive efficiency at this time is:

$$1 \geq \theta_C = 1 - \left(\sum_{n=1}^{N} R_n^x s_n^{x*} + \sum_{m=1}^{M} R_m^e (s_m^{e+*} + s_m^{e-*}) + \sum_{p=1}^{P} R_p^y s_p^{y*} + \sum_{i=1}^{I} R_i^b s_i^{b*} \right) \geq 0.$$

$$(8.9)$$

8.3.3 Samples and Data

This study takes as samples all the enterprises in operation in the iron and steel industry in Shijiazhuang City in 2011. The information data sources include the pollutant charges data and pollution census data provided by the Shijiazhuang Municipal Environmental Protection Bureau, and the firm-level financial dataset provided by the State Administration of Taxation Electronic Information Center. After data cleansing and integration, this study takes seven iron and steel companies as the final samples.

Table 8.1   Input and output items for efficiency measurement

	Output	Input
Production efficiency	Total industrial output value – current year's prices (10 000 RMB)	Registered capital (10 000 RMB) the number of employees
Environment efficiency	Environmental expenditure (10 000 RMB)	Registered capital (10 000 RMB), the number of employees, coal consumption (tons), coke consumption (tons), natural gas consumption (10 000 m³), other fuel consumption (tons of coal equivalent) electricity consumption (10 000 kW)
Comprehensive efficiency	Total industrial output value – current year's prices (10 000 RMB), environmental expenditure (10 000 RMB)	

8.3.4   Scenario Settings

Selection of variables
The major input and output items we identified to measure the relative efficiency include capital input, labor input, energy input, desired output and undesirable output.

Due to data availability and quality, this study adopts the registered capital as the capital input, the number of employees as labor input and takes the output value of enterprises as the desired output items, to measure the production efficiency of enterprises.

After introducing the environmental efficiency evaluation, we add the energy consumption into the input items, and use the environmental expenditure of the enterprise to represent the undesired output (Table 8.1).

Policy scenarios: environmental taxes package
This study specifically creates two environmental tax packages: one is emissions tax only; the other is a combined tax of emissions tax plus carbon tax. The emissions tax will tax conventional pollutants as under the current pollution charge policy and the carbon tax will tax carbon emissions.

For the tax rate scenarios, this study sets three levels of tax rate that are high, medium and low rates of emissions tax and carbon tax. The low rate of air pollutants (SO_2, NO_x, industrial dust) and water pollutants (COD (chemical oxygen demand), NH_3-N) is 1.2 yuan and 1.4 yuan per pollutant equivalent; the medium rate of air and water pollutants is 2.4 yuan and

Table 8.2 Summary of scenario settings

	Environmental Tax Package		Emissions Behavior	
			Unchanged	−50%
Baseline	No environmental tax			
Scenario	Emissions tax w/o carbon tax	High		
		Medium		
		Low		
	Emissions tax with carbon tax	High		
		Medium		
		Low		

2.8 yuan per pollutant equivalent; the high rate is 4.8 yuan and 5.6 yuan per pollutant equivalent, respectively. For carbon tax, the low, medium and high rates are 10, 50, 100 yuan/ton CO_2.[8]

The measure of emission taxes and carbon taxes in this study follows the current measurement formula of pollutant charges, which is the emissions tax amount = pollutant equivalent * tax rate. The equivalent of carbon dioxide = consumption of each energy * emissions factors of carbon dioxide.

Scenario settings of enterprises' behaviors
When facing environmental tax policy, the enterprise can demonstrate three types of behavior change as its response: production behavior, emissions control behavior and technological innovation. As emissions reduction is the objective of the current environmental tax reform, in this chapter we mainly discuss enterprises' emissions behaviors in scenario settings. This study will use the price-taker assumption, therefore price will be kept stable.

Enterprises will have two options regarding emissions: emissions unchanged (emissions control expenditure remains the same) and emission reduction (by increasing emissions control expenditure). This study sets the emissions reduction scenario to be air pollutants reduced by 50 percent.

We assume the desired output under each scenario remains unchanged, but the emissions reduction will need to absorb some production resource because of the emissions control cost. Based on the average pollution abatement operating cost of all sample enterprises in 2011, the emissions reduction cost of SO_2, NO_X and industrial dust are 9.95, 9.95 and 5.05 yuan/kg.

Table 8.3   Efficiency and emissions behavior change (by enterprises of different scales)

Scale of Enterprise	Baseline (Comprehensive Efficiency)		
Large-scale	0.786652		
Medium-scale	1.000000		
Small-scale	1.000000		

	Emissions tax (low)	Emissions tax (medium)	Emissions tax (high)
Large-scale	0.774463	0.771361	1.000000
Medium-scale	1.000000	0.983652	1.000000
Small-scale	1.000000	1.000000	1.000000

	Emissions tax (low): −50% emissions	Emissions tax (medium): −50% emissions	Emissions tax (high): −50% emissions
Large-scale	0.774814	0.774203	0.773069
Medium-scale	0.970996	0.970059	0.968239
Small-scale	1.000000	0.991005	0.991030

	Combined tax (low)	Combined tax (medium)	Combined tax (high)
Large-scale	0.781259	0.779945	0.779107
Medium-scale	1.000000	0.975000	0.973389
Small-scale	1.000000	0.988862	0.988531

	Combined tax (low): −50% emissions	Combined tax (medium): −50% emissions	Combined tax (high): −50% emissions
Large-scale	0.775866	0.777462	0.778019
Medium-scale	0.971044	0.970736	0.970431
Small-scale	0.990246	0.989137	0.988664

Scenario summary

A summary of the environmental tax scenario and the enterprise behavior scenario is shown in Table 8.2. With the 12 'environmental tax-emissions behavior' scenarios, we can understand the impact of environmental tax on relative efficiency and so whether emissions control behavior is favorable for an enterprise.

8.4 ANALYSIS OF RESULTS

The efficiency values simulated in the model represent the efficiency of the assessed decision-making units. The closer that efficiency values approach to 1, the higher is the efficiency. When the efficiency value is 1, the decision-making units are located on the efficiency frontier.

8.4.1 Efficiency and Behavior Change for Enterprises of Different Scales

Although there are only seven sample enterprises from Shijiazhuang City's iron and steel industry, the enterprise scales are relatively complete, including two large-scale enterprises, two medium-scale enterprises and three small-scale enterprises. The efficiency changes of all different scale enterprises are shown in Table 8.3.

According to Table 8.3, large enterprises' competitiveness is relatively lower than that of medium/small enterprises. After emissions tax is levied, with the tax rate increased from low to medium level, the comprehensive efficiency of large and medium enterprises slightly declines. The small enterprises are always located on the efficiency frontier under the different tax rates. Only under the high tax rate level can large enterprises reach the efficiency frontier. That indicates that the increase in tax rate will have an obvious impact only on the large enterprises.

With the inclusion of carbon tax, under the medium and low tax rates, the large enterprises can reduce the distance from the efficiency frontier. But under the high rate of combined emissions taxes, both medium and small enterprises deviate from the efficiency frontier. With an increase in the tax rate, the comprehensive efficiency of all large, medium and small enterprises declines in different degrees.

Regarding the potential of emissions behavior change, under the high rate of emissions taxes, increasing emissions control effort will have an adverse impact on the competitiveness of scales of enterprises, especially the large enterprises, whose efficiency value declines from the efficiency frontier to 0.773069. But under the medium and low tax rate levels, the large enterprises can enhance competitiveness through emissions reduction. However, under the scenario of combined taxes, the emissions reduction behaviors of large enterprise and medium enterprises will have an adverse impact on their enterprise competitiveness under each tax rate level. Only the small enterprises can see opportunities to gain the higher comprehensive efficiency through emissions control.

Table 8.4 Efficiency and emissions behavior change (by enterprises of different ownership)

Enterprise Ownership	Baseline (Comprehensive Efficiency)		
State-owned	1.000000		
Privately owned	0.928884		

Scenarios (Comprehensive Efficiency)

	Emissions tax (low)	Emissions tax (medium)	Emissions tax (high)
State-owned	1.000000	1.000000	1.000000
Privately owned	0.924821	0.918338	1.000000
	Emissions tax (low): −50% emissions	Emissions tax (medium): −50% emissions	Emissions tax (high): −50% emissions
State-owned	1.000000	1.000000	1.000000
Privately owned	0.915270	0.910256	0.909284
	Combined tax (low)	Combined tax (medium)	Combined tax (high)
State-owned	1.000000	1.000000	1.000000
Privately owned	0.927086	0.912746	0.911764
	Combined tax (low): −50% emissions	Combined tax (medium): −50% emissions	Combined tax (high): −50% emissions
State-owned	1.000000	1.000000	1.000000
Privately owned	0.910759	0.910634	0.910482

8.4.2 Efficiency and Behavior Change for Enterprises with Different Ownership

Among our seven sample enterprises, there is one state-owned enterprise, and the other six are all privately owned. The efficiency changes for enterprises with different ownership are shown in Table 8.4.

In the samples, the comprehensive efficiency values of state-owned enterprise under all scenarios are 1, which means it is always located on the efficiency frontier. Therefore, the state-owned enterprise in the sample enterprises will have more space for adjusting its behavior under the different environmental tax forms and different tax rate levels.

For private enterprises, when the current pollution charge policy changed to an environment tax, their efficiency declines from 0.928884 to 0.924821. This indicates that, compared with the state-owned enterprises, the private enterprises have enjoyed the environmental bonuses due to the poor enforcement of pollution levy policy. This fits with the reality that China's enforcement of environmental regulations always focuses on state-owned enterprises and is less strict for the private sector.

An increase of emissions tax rate has different impacts on the efficiency value of private enterprises: when the tax rate is increased to the medium level, the overall combined efficiency of private enterprises is further reduced to 0.918338. This means that at this time, private enterprises will bear more environmental tax pressures with an elevation of the tax rate. But when the tax rate is further elevated to the high level, the combined efficiency of private enterprises is elevated to 1. This shows that the higher environmental cost will not necessarily enlarge the gap of competitiveness between different enterprises.

With the inclusion of carbon taxes, under the low tax rate, private enterprises will not lose competitiveness compared with the state-owned enterprise. However, with an elevation of the environmental tax rate, the combined efficiency of private enterprises shows a gradual decline trend. Compared with the emissions taxes scenario, the impact on enterprises is more relevant to an increase in the tax rate under the combined taxes scenario.

Regarding the potential of emissions behavior change, under all different tax packages and different tax rate levels, there will be adverse impacts on the enterprises' comprehensive efficiency if private enterprises increase their efforts for emissions reduction. This means that under each scenario, the private enterprises will have no self-incentive to increase their emissions control efforts. But what should be noted is that, under the scenario of combined taxes, an elevation of the tax rate will reduce the negative impact on efficiency, so that under the combined taxes scenario, it could be easier to push enterprises to make emissions reduction efforts.

8.5 CONCLUSION

This study focuses on the impact of environmental taxes at different tax rates on the enterprises' competitiveness and behavior patterns. By simulating the influence of different behaviors on the relative efficiency of enterprises with different scales when facing different tax rates, the best behaviors that enterprises may choose under different tax design and rates were analyzed. Some conclusions have been reached as follows:

- Under the scenario of an emissions tax, a low or medium tax rate will have only a slight impact on enterprises' relative efficiency. Only a high tax rate can drive large enterprises to reach the efficiency frontier. Generally, an increase tax rate will have more impact on large enterprises and private ones. State-owned enterprise under all scenarios is always located at the efficiency frontier. Therefore, large enterprises and private enterprises are more sensitive to changes in the tax rate.
- With the inclusion of carbon tax and an increase in the tax rate, the comprehensive efficiency of all large, medium and small enterprises declines in different degrees. Compared with the emissions taxes scenario, the impact on enterprises under the combined taxes scenario is more relevant to the increase of tax rate.
- Regarding the potential of emissions behavior change, increasing emissions control efforts will have an adverse impact on the competitiveness of scales of enterprises, especially large enterprises. However, under the scenario of combined taxes, small enterprises can see opportunities to gain higher comprehensive efficiency through emissions control, so that small enterprises have greater flexibility in choosing emissions behaviors.
- Under all scenarios, private enterprises will have no incentive to increase their emissions control efforts, but under the combined taxes scenario, the increase tax rate will reduce the negative impact on efficiency, so it could be easier to push enterprises to make emissions reductions.

The above findings remind us that, if only an emissions tax is levied, a low tax rate will not have any impact on enterprises' competitiveness, therefore, no behavior change can be expected. In order to achieve emissions reduction through the implementation of environmental tax, a high tax rate should be applied. A carbon tax can obviously have more impact on all enterprises. Since large and private enterprises will be more sensitive to a change in the tax rate, supplementary measures should be designed to help buffer negative impacts on these enterprises, to ensure environmental tax reform can achieve its goal at minimum social cost.

NOTES

1. Henriques, I. and P. Sadorsky (1996), 'The determinants of an environmentally responsive firm: an empirical approach', *Journal of Environmental Economics and Management*, **30**(3), 381–95; Hartl, R.F. and P.M. Kort (1997), 'Optimal input substitution of a firm facing an environmental constraint', *European Journal of Operational Research*, **99**(2), 336–52; Rugman, A.M. and A. Verbeke (2000), 'Six cases of corporate strategic responses to environmental regulation', *European Management Journal*, **18**(4), 377–85.
2. Lanjouw, J.O. and A. Mody (1996), 'Innovation and the international diffusion of environmentally responsive technology', *Research Policy*, **25**(4), 549–71; Li, P. and X.R. Mu (2013), 'The hysteresis of Porter hypothesis and the optimal intensity of regulation – inspection based on system GMM and the threshold effect', *Industrial Economics Research*, **4**, 21–9.
3. Hamilton, J.T. (1995), 'Pollution as news: media and stock market reactions to the Toxics Release Inventory data', *Journal of Environmental Economics and Management*, **28**(1), 98–113; Russo, M.V. and P.A. Fouts (1997), 'A resource-based perspective on corporate environmental performance and profitability', *Academy of Management Journal*, **40**(3), 534–59.
4. National Environmental Research Institute (2007), *Competitiveness Effects of Environmental Tax Reforms*, final report to the European Commission, DG Research and DG TAXUD, Aarhus, Denmark: NERI.
5. Wang, S.H., M.L. Song and J. Wu (2011), 'Extension of DEA model and its application in economic forecasting', *Journal of Central University of Finance & Economics*, **6**, 56–60.
6. Chen, S.Y. (2009), 'Energy consumption, CO_2 emission and sustainable development in Chinese industry', *Economic Research Journal*, **4**, 41–55.
7. Li, T. (2013), 'Measuring the win-win performance of China's carbon reduction and economic growth with energy constraints: a range-adjusted measure of non-radial DEA', *China Economic Quarterly*, **12**(2), 667–92.
8. Guo, X.J. (2014), *Impact of Environmental Tax on Enterprises Pollution Control Behavior – Empirical Study Based on Key Industries and Enterprises in Shijiazhuang*, Beijing: Renmin University of China.

PART III

National experiences with fuel and energy
pricing

9. Distributional effects of motor-fuel taxation in the Czech Republic*

Jan Brůha, Hana Brůhová-Foltýnová and Vítězslav Píša

9.1 ENVIRONMENTAL AND DISTRIBUTIONAL EFFECTS OF FUEL TAXATION

Transport emissions rose by 20 percent between 1990 and 2010 and accounted for more than 20 percent of all GHG emissions in the EU; this indicates that the transport sector is the second biggest greenhouse gas-emitting sector after energy and the only major sector where greenhouse gas emissions (GHGs) are still rising or stagnating.[1] Pricing policies in the transport sector are thought to be an important tool to reduce these global emissions and other pollutants from transport, either alone or as a part of a policy mix. Fuel excises in particular have a direct impact on the fuel efficiency of vehicles (which generally comes at a cost) and, indirectly, reduce mileage – and in this way reduce GHG emissions.[2]

The effect of fuel excise duties depends on price elasticity. The price elasticity of demand for fuels differs among time frames, countries and applied methods of estimation. The estimated values for the long run are usually elastic, which suggests substantial regulatory effects. A meta-analysis of motor-fuel demand made by Dahl (2012)[3] showed that the price elasticity for gasoline is −0.2 on average in the short run and −0.7 in the long run. In the Czech Republic, the long-term price elasticity even reached −0.99 for gasoline and −0.80 for diesel.[4]

One of the prime arguments against raising fuel taxes is the perception that they are regressive, that is, they are more costly to the poor than to the rich.[5] This perception makes it politically harder to implement or increase such taxes. Contrary to this general perception, a more detailed analysis reveals that this rule is not generally valid and that there are different distributional effects depending on the tax base and socioeconomic characteristics of households. The OECD has recently published a very detailed analysis of 21 countries that demonstrates that taxes on transport fuels are not regressive on average, as households in lower expenditure deciles spend a lower proportion of their expenditure on taxes on transport fuels.[6] There are differences regarding the size of the households: larger households spend a higher share of their expenditure on taxes on transport fuels than smaller ones. Similarly, households living in rural areas spend, on average, more of their expenditure on fuel taxes than households in urban areas, and if the household head is over 60 years of age, households tend to spend a smaller share of their expenditure on taxes on transport fuels.

The aim of this chapter is to analyze distributional effects of motor-fuel taxation on different kinds of households in the Czech Republic. Our detailed statistical analysis of microdata on households' expenditure goes farther beyond the present knowledge because our focus is on different groups of households differentiated not only according to their incomes but also according to availability of vehicles, location of households and their size and other socioeconomic and demographic characteristics.

The rest of the chapter is organized as follows. The next section describes the transport sector in the Czech Republic from the environmental point of view and discusses the impact of taxation on this sector. In section 9.3, the motor-fuel consumption of various household groups is analyzed. Section 9.4 then applies a formal measure of motor-fuel tax progressivity to Czech data. The last section concludes.

9.2   MOTOR-FUEL CONSUMPTION IN THE CZECH REPUBLIC

The Czech Republic, as a part of the European Union, should contribute to the European Commission's ambitious goal to reduce GHG emissions from the transport sector by 60 percent by 2050 compared with the 1990 levels, as is stated in the 2011 White Paper *Roadmap to a Single European Transport Area*.[7]

Contrary to this European goal, emissions of CO_2 from the transport sector and, above all, from passenger cars, were increasing especially during the 1990s and 2000s; there has been a small slowdown as a result of the financial crisis only during the last few years in the Czech Republic. In 1995, the transport sector produced 10 660 000 tons of CO_2, to which cars contributed 5 080 000 tons, while in 2014 it was 18 208 000 tons in total, and 10 109 000 tons emitted only by cars. This represents an increase of about 80 percent (32 percent between 2000 and 2014).

This growth was caused by both an increase in the number of cars on the streets and in the number of kilometers driven. The number of registered cars in the Czech Republic reached 3 043 316 in 1995 and 4 833 386 in 2014, which comprises an increase of nearly 60 percent (the population of the Czech Republic was oscillating around 10.4 million for the whole period). Gasoline cars dominated the car fleet (in 2014, about 3 189 890 gasoline cars and 1 631 014 diesel cars were registered). More than half of all the registered cars (2 845 833) were older than ten years in 2014 and the average age of the car fleet was 14.5 years in the same year.[8]

Excise duty on fuels and VAT are the dominant regulatory tools applied to cars in the Czech Republic measured by revenues. Road tolls in the Czech Republic are only collected on motorways. Furthermore, businesses have to pay a vehicle tax. Because the age of the car fleet in the Czech Republic is a serious problem, an ecological tax on old vehicles has been implemented. It is charged upon the registration of a used car and is differentiated according to the EURO standards. Cars compatible with EURO 3 and higher are exempt from this tax.

Despite the fact that taxes influence the consumer motor-fuel prices significantly, literature on distributional effects of fuel taxes in the Czech Republic – contrary to the case of other advanced countries – has been scarce. The only exception is a relatively old study by Brůha and Ščasný (2008)[9] and one by Ščasný (2011).[10] They discovered that motor-fuel taxation is slightly progressive in the Czech Republic. However, this progressivity is counterbalanced by value-added tax on energy, which is regressive; the overall distributional impact of environmentally related taxation is thus almost neutral. In this chapter, we use improved methodology and newer data, and focus in detail on fuel-related expenditure and the distributional effects of fuel taxation.

9.2.1 Taxation of Motor Fuels in the Czech Republic and in Central Europe

In the Czech Republic, the indirect tax rates have to fulfill EU minimum rates stipulated by EU Tax Directives (2006/112/EC sets the framework for VAT, 2003/96/EC for excise duties on energy products). The VAT rate on gasoline and diesel has to be the same, but for the excise taxes the rate on diesel is generally lower. The lower diesel rate is historically given despite the higher energy and CO_2 emission content of diesel for the same volume.

In the Czech Republic, the VAT rate on motor fuels has been changed three times since 2000. The rate of 22 percent (effective from 1995) was decreased to 19 percent in 2004. Consequently, the rate was increased twice to 20 percent in 2010 and to 21 percent in 2013. The current VAT rate is the 18th highest among the EU countries.

Excise duty rates on traditional motor fuels have been changed twice since 1999. The petrol rate increased from CZK 10 840/1000 L (€401/1000 L)[11] to CZK11 840/1000 L (€438/1000 L) in 2004 and to CZK12 840/1000 L (€475/1000 L) in 2010. The diesel rate increased from CZK8150/1000 L (€302/1000 L) to CZK9950 1000 L (€368/1000 L) in 2004 and to CZK10 950/1000 L (€405/1000 L) in 2010.

Currently, the Czech Republic has the 19th highest gasoline and the 15th highest diesel excise tax among the EU countries. Compared to its neighboring countries (Slovakia, Poland, Austria and Germany), the Czech Republic has the second lowest excise tax on gasoline and the second highest excise tax on diesel. Revenues from the excise tax on motor fuels are approximately CZK80 billion (€3 billion). The share of diesel and its substitutes in motor-fuel tax revenues has been growing since 2009 and reached 68 percent in 2014. This is mainly the result of permanently decreasing demand for gasoline.

The vehicle tax rate on passenger cars differs according to engine capacity from CZK1200 (€44) for engines with less than 800cm^3 capacity to CZK4200 (€155) for engines with capacity above 3000cm^3, while the tax rate on other vehicles is set according to maximum permissible laden weight and number of axles. These tax rates range from CZK1800 (€67) to CZK50 400 (€1864). The annual revenue from the vehicle tax is CZK5.5 billion (€3 million), which is approximately 6.8 percent of the revenues from the motor-fuel excise duty.

Cars with a total weight not exceeding 3.5 tons using motorways need to display a sticker. The price of the sticker differs according to the period of permitted use of the motorway. The price of the annual sticker is CZK1500 (€55) and the associated revenue reached CZK4.1 billion (€152 million) in 2014. The revenue is approximately 5.1 percent of revenues from the excise tax on motor fuels.

An ecological tax on old vehicles applies to vehicles of the types EURO 0 to EURO 2. The revenues from the tax were CZK272 million (€10.1 million) in 2014, which is 0.3 percent of the revenues from the motor-fuel taxes.

9.3   MOTOR-FUEL CONSUMPTION ACROSS HOUSEHOLD GROUPS

In this section, we focus on the patterns of household motor-fuel consumption and hence the burden of related taxes across household groups.

We analyze socioeconomic data for a repeated cross-section sample of Czech households called the Household Budget Survey (HBS). The HBS is an annual survey conducted by the Czech Statistical Office on income and expenditure of households. Each year, about 3000 households based on quota sampling are surveyed. The dataset contains information on characteristics of a household's economic status, occupation, ownership of industrial goods, living conditions, income and expenditure on various items, including expenditure on motor fuels. Given the information on motor-fuel expenditure and average motor-fuel prices, we can calculate (although somewhat imprecisely) the motor-fuel consumption in liters.

Traditionally in studies on distributional effects of taxes, income is used to measure tax burden and to distinguish between rich and poor households. Recently, Flues and Thomas (2015)[12] have proposed using expenditure rather than income to measure the magnitude of the consumption-tax burden. In this chapter, we follow their expenditure-based approach as the default, but we also comment the results of the income-based approach.

We are interested in how households differ in their motor-fuel consumption and expenditure. We divide households into several groups according to where the households are located, their socioeconomic characteristics and their wealth.

A non-negligible number of Czech households do not report positive expenditure on motor fuels. Not surprisingly, this set of households almost perfectly corresponds with the set of households without a car. What are the characteristics of such households? Figure 9.1 displays the reported car ownership across household types and expenditure deciles.

Apparently, reported car ownership is positively related to wealth: there is a higher probability that richer households will own a car than poorer households. In fact, almost all households in the 9th and 10th expenditure deciles report owning at least one car, while only about 20 percent of households in the 1st expenditure decile own at least one car.

Second, there are differences in the reported car ownership across households' locations. Households located in villages (i.e., in a municipality with fewer than 2000 inhabitants) have a significantly higher probability of owning a car than households located in larger towns (i.e., in municipalities with more than 50000 inhabitants). On the other hand, the composition of the household does not matter for the reported car ownership. Given the expenditure decile, the reported car ownership is almost the same for households of economically active persons with or without children and for households of pensioners. These results continue to hold qualitatively even when the households are sorted using income deciles rather than expenditure deciles.

Furthermore, we analyze the typical consumption of motor fuels and taxes paid across household groups. Figure 9.2 displays the share of motor-fuel taxes in the total pre-tax expenditure across household deciles and types.

Apparently, the share differs across household groups. Poorer households have a lower share of the motor-fuel taxes in their expenditure on

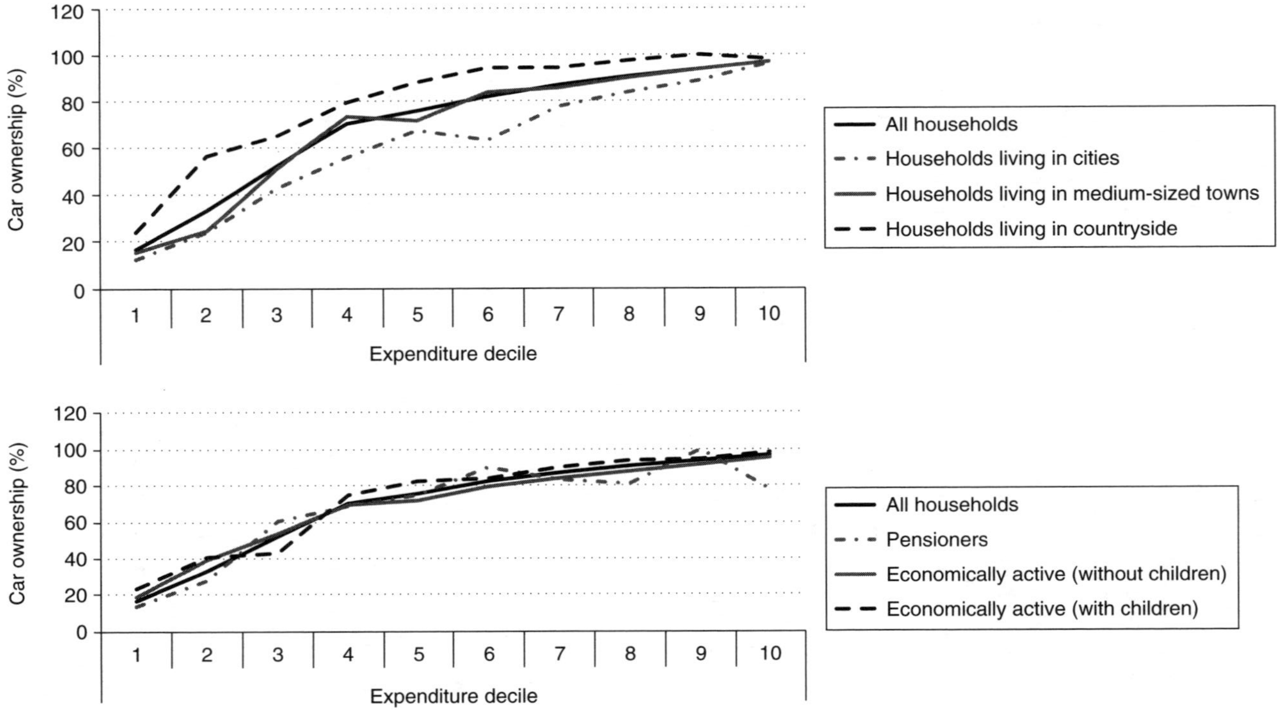

120
100
80
60
40
20
0
Car ownership (%)
1
2
3
4
5
6
7
8
9
10
Expenditure decile
All households
Households living in cities
Households living in medium-sized towns
Households living in countryside
120
100
80
60
40
20
0
Car ownership (%)
1
2
3
4
5
6
7
8
9
10
Expenditure decile
All households
Pensioners
Economically active (without children)
Economically active (with children)

Figure 9.1 Car ownership across household types

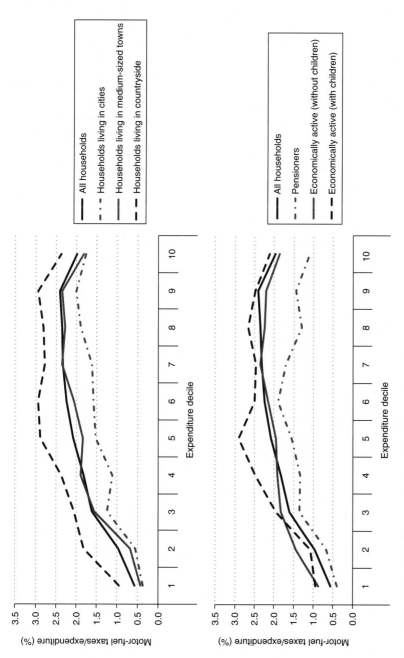

Figure 9.2   Motor-fuel taxes as share in pre-tax expenditures

147

average. The only exception is the 10th decile: these richest households tend to pay a lower share than the households in the 9th decile, and this feature is consistent with international evidence from other countries.[13] The usual explanation is that the richest households tend to use other means of transport, such as taxis. The Czech data do not support this explanation. The expenditure shares of all transport types fall in the richest decile, while the absolute value of motor-fuel expenditure increases across all the deciles. While the absolute expenditure on motor fuels increases by about 20 percent from the 9th to the 10th decile, the total expenditure increases almost twofold between the two deciles, which explains the fall in the expenditure share in motor fuels for the richest decile. This pattern in general also holds for various subgroups of households.

Another factor that influences the distributional effect is – similarly to the case of car ownership – the size of the municipality in which the household is located. Households located in small villages pay a significantly higher share of motor-fuel taxes in their expenditure than households located in medium-sized towns. But, unlike the case of car ownership, the composition of households also matters: households of economically active individuals with children tend to pay a larger share of motor-fuel taxes than economically active households without children or households of pensioners.

Since it is a generally expected fact that the poorer pay more, we should ask why the poorer households pay a lower share of motor-fuel taxes in their expenditure in the Czech Republic. It turns out that this is because of lower car ownership among these households. Figure 9.3 replicates the analysis but only for households that report owning at least one car.

For the subset of households that own at least one car, the expenditure share of motor fuels decreases with the wealth of households: poorer households pay a higher share of motor-fuel taxes in their expenditure. On the other hand, it still holds that – conditional on car ownership and the expenditure decile – households located in villages pay a larger share of these taxes than households located in cities. It also continues to hold that economically active households with children pay a larger share than households of pensioners.

Qualitatively, all the results mentioned above survive if the expenditure deciles are replaced by the net income deciles and if the income share is used instead of the expenditure share.

9.4   THE SUITS INDEX

In this part of the chapter, we employ a formal measure to inquire about the progressivity or regressivity of motor-fuel taxation in the Czech Republic.

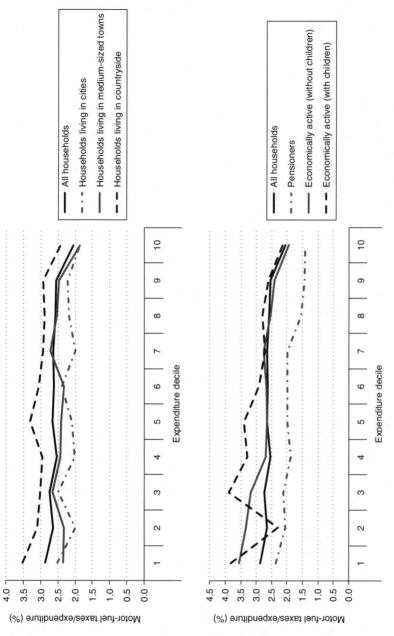

Figure 9.3   Motor-fuel taxes as share in pre-tax expenditures (for households owning a car)

149

A popular measure of tax progressivity is the so-called Suits index, which was introduced by Suits (1977).[14] It is based on a comparison of cumulative income or expenditure with cumulative tax burden (y-axis). The index is formally defined as:

$$S = 1 - L/K,$$

where $L = \int_0^{100} T(x)\, dx$, $K = 5000$, and the function T characterizes the tax payments by a household with expenditure x, that is, it is an accumulated percentage of the total tax burden (households are sorted according to their expenditure).

The Suits index always varies between -1 and 1, and the negative value of the Suits index indicates a regressive tax (poorer households pay more tax relative to their income than the rich households), while the positive value signals tax progressivity. A proportional tax (i.e., a tax where each household pays an equal fraction of its income) has a Suits index of zero. A theoretical tax where the richest person pays all the tax has a Suits index of 1, and a tax where the poorest person pays everything has a Suits index of -1.

The Suits index can be easily estimated for a random sample of n data on households' income/expenditure and tax payments. Then the integral L above can be approximated by the trapezoid rule as follows:

$$L \equiv \int_0^{100} T(x)\, dx \cong \sum_{i=1}^{n} \frac{1}{2}[T(x_i) + T(x_{i-1})]\,(x_i - x_{i-1}),$$

where x_i is the cumulative percentage of total expenditure of households, and $T(x_i)$ is the estimated tax payment for each person. This approach can be easily generalized for stratified samples and samples with weights.

We use our sample of Czech households and estimate the index for the four years that were used in the preceding section. We also consider a modification to the Suits index (henceforth called the modified Suits index), where the variable x_i does not represent the cumulative expenditures, but instead the cumulative percentage of households (households are again sorted by their total pre-tax expenditures). The results for the year 2013 are demonstrated in Figure 9.4 and Table 9.1.

The advantage of the Suits index (as well as its modification) is that it can be nicely represented graphically. The conventional Suits index is given in the upper left-hand chart in Figure 9.4. The x-axis displays the normalized cumulative expenditures (of households sorted by their net income), while the y-axis displays the cumulative tax payments on motor

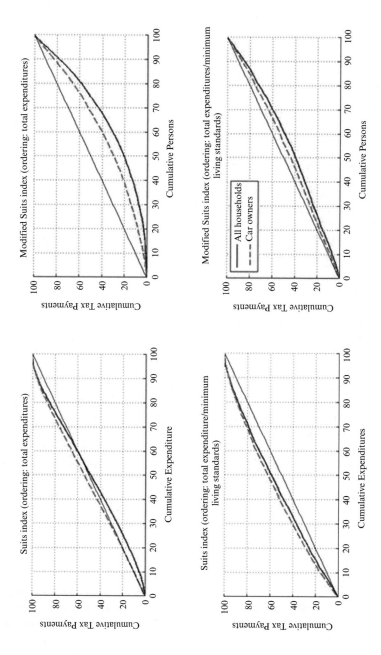

Figure 9.4   Suits index for excise duty for Czech households

Table 9.1   Suits indexes calculated for motor-fuel excise taxes in the Czech Republic

	Sorting	2004	2007	2010	2013
Suits index	Total expenditure	0.084	0.071	0.087	0.153
Modified Suits index		0.360	0.361	0.379	0.398
Suits index	Expenditure/min.	−0.057	−0.110	−0.080	−0.014
Modified Suits index	living standards	0.170	0.142	0.164	0.184

fuels by households sorted in the same way. The excise tax on motor fuels seems to be progressive: for example, the set of households with, together, 30 percent of the total expenditure pays only about 20 percent of the total excise duty. For richer households, the excise tax becomes flat. We report the index for all the households in the sample as well as for the subsample of car owners. As the poorer households are more likely not to own a car, it is not surprising that the Suits curve for the subsample of car owners exhibits lower tax progressivity.

The upper right-hand chart in Figure 9.4 graphically displays the modified Suits index. The graphical representation is revealing for this case as well. The modified Suits index shows that 50 percent of the poorest households pay only about 20 percent of the total tax revenues.

The lower charts display both the indexes for an alternative ordering of households that is based on the ratio of the total expenditure to the minimum living standards. If this perspective is taken, then the excise tax is almost a flat tax.

Finally, we inquire whether the Suits indexes have changed over time. We have computed these indexes for the four years and the results are given in Table 9.1.

The numerical values of the Suits indexes seem to exhibit an increasing trend and attain the highest value for the last year in our sample: 2013. Therefore, we test the hypothesis that the Suits indexes in 2013 are statistically significantly higher than in the previous years, that is, whether the variation in the indexes in time represents a genuine feature rather than sampling variability.

One way of testing the significance of the difference is the bootstrap, which is a statistical method based on a resampling of the original sample; see, for example, Mills and Zandvakili (1997).[15] However, as shown by Davidson and Flachaire (2007),[16] the usual bootstrap should be modified if applied to inequality measures. We therefore applied the method advocated by Davidson and Flachaire (2007) to see whether the year 2013 is really different from the previous years. We failed to reject the hypothesis that the year 2013 would be statistically different from the previous years and the relatively higher value for that year is attributed to sampling issues rather than a change in the excise tax progressivity.

9.5   CONCLUDING REMARKS AND POLICY IMPLICATIONS

Because of its relatively high elasticity, particularly in the long run, excise duty on fuels can be an effective tool for environmental regulation of transport in the Czech Republic. Indeed, nowadays it represents the dominant regulative measure affecting transport-related GHG emissions in the Czech Republic. However, the existing level of taxation slightly above the minimum EU excise duty rate has not slowed down the increase in these global emissions; they have been continuously rising.

In this chapter, we made two main contributions. On one front, we updated the previous analyses of distributional effects of motor-fuel taxation for the Czech Republic. On the methodological front, we applied a new set of methods to this task. Our findings suggest that if excise duty on fuels were increased substantially, the distributional effects would not be large; however, different groups of households would be affected differently. The most affected groups of households would be households located in rural areas and households of economically active citizens with children. To decrease the tax burden on these societal groups, they should be compensated directly or indirectly by different mitigating measures. The distributional argument against environmental taxation of motor fuels might be eliminated.

A specific group from the equity point of view includes those who do not own a car: households of pensioners and those located in larger urban areas and belonging in most cases to the lowest income groups of the analyzed households. The aforesaid might be households that may have an income constraint on buying a car. It is a political goal to provide enough options for mobility for this specific socioeconomic group.

NOTES

*   The research for this chapter has been supported by Czech Science Foundation Grant No. 14-22932S. The support is gratefully acknowledged.
1.   Bosetti, S., H. Brůhová-Foltýnová, C. Di Bartolo, R. Jordová, P. Kurfürst and

P. Malgieri et al. (2014), *Policy Recommendations for EU Sustainable Mobility Concepts Based on CIVITAS Experience*, Brno, Czech Republic: ICLEI, p. 68.

2. EC (1995), *Green Paper: Towards Fair and Efficient Pricing in Transport. Policy Options for Internalizing the External Costs of Transport in the European Union*, COM(95)691.
3. Dahl, C.A. (2012), 'Measuring global gasoline and diesel price and income elasticities', *Energy Policy*, **41**(C), 2–13.
4. Brůha, J., H. Brůhová-Foltýnová and V. Píša (2015), 'Motor fuel taxation in Central Europe and international tax competition: simulation of motor fuel tax harmonization', in L. Kreiser, M.S. Andersen, B.E. Olsen, S. Speck, J.E. Milne and H. Ashiabor (eds), *Carbon Pricing. Design, Experiences and Issues. Critical Issues in Environmental Taxation, Volume XV*, Cheltenham, UK and Northampton, MA, USA: Edward Elgar Publishing, pp. 159–76.
5. Flues, F. and A. Thomas (2015), 'The distributional effects of energy taxes', *OECD Taxation Working Paper No. 23*, Paris: OECD.
6. Ibid.
7. EC (2011), *White Paper: Roadmap to a Single European Transport Area: Towards a Competitive and Resource Efficient Transport System*, COM(2011) 144 final.
8. Ministry of Transport of the Czech Republic (2014), *Transport Yearbook 2014*, accessed 14 April 2016 at https://www.czso.cz/csu/czso/ministry-of-transport.
9. Brůha, J. and M. Ščasný (2008), 'Tax progressivity measurement: empirical applications for the Czech Republic', in M. Ščasný and M. Braun Kohlová et al. (eds), *Modelling of Consumer Behaviour and Wealth Distribution*, Prague: Matfyzpress, pp. 157–79.
10. Ščasný, M. (2011), 'Who pays taxes on fuels and public transport services in the Czech Republic? Ex post and ex ante measurement', in T. Sterner (ed.), *Fuel Taxes and the Poor: The Distributional Effects of Gasoline Taxation and their Implications for Climate Change*, Washington, DC: Resources for the Future, pp. 269–98.
11. The rates are converted to euros via the exchange rate applicable on 20 November 2015.
12. Flues and Thomas, 'The distributional effects of energy taxes'.
13. Ibid.
14. Suits, D. (1977), 'Measurement of tax progressivity', *American Economic Review*, **67**(4), 747–52.
15. Mills, J.A. and S. Zandvakili (1997), 'Statistical inference via bootstrapping for measures of inequality', *Journal of Applied Econometrics*, **12**(2), 133–50.
16. Davidson, R. and E. Flachaire (2007), 'Asymptotic and bootstrap inference for inequality and poverty measures', *Journal of Econometrics*, **141**(1), 141–66.

10. Renewable electricity support in the EU – what lessons can be learned?

Claudia Kettner and Daniela Kletzan-Slamanig

10.1 INTRODUCTION

Renewable energy technologies play a decisive role for climate change mitigation and environmental protection but also in the context of energy security and cost competitiveness. So far, renewable energy technologies are generally not cost competitive compared to fossil energy technologies.[1] Therefore, the European Union and its member states have introduced policy targets and renewable support schemes with the aim of offsetting the higher costs of electricity from renewable energy sources (RES), thereby achieving a certain share of renewables in total electricity generation.

Since 2001, common guidelines for renewable electricity support in the EU have been provided for in Directive 2001/77/EC.[2] In addition, this directive contained indicative national targets for the EU member states in order to achieve an overall increase of the share of renewables in the electricity mix to 21 per cent by 2010. In the context of the EU's *2020 Climate & Energy Package*, the overall comprehensive policy framework for the production and promotion of energy from renewables, including electricity, was established in Directive 2009/28/EC.[3] This directive also stipulated a target of 20 per cent renewables in gross final energy consumption for the EU in the year 2020, along with individual targets for the member states ranging between 11 per cent (Luxembourg) and 49 per cent (Sweden).[4] In order to achieve the respective targets member states can either make use of national instruments or 'cooperation mechanisms' (statistical transfers, joint RES projects, joint RES support schemes). Most member states have opted for national regulation and renewable electricity support schemes will play an important role in this context. However, the instruments chosen by the member states differ considerably.

In this chapter we give an overview of available support instruments and summarize the evolution of renewable electricity support and generation in the EU. We first discuss the economics of different instruments that can be used for renewable electricity support in terms of aspects like risk minimization, investment security or dynamic incentives for technological innovation (section 10.2).

In section 10.3 the instruments applied in the EU member states are described, as well as the changes in RES support that have taken place since 2009. In addition the regulative aspects are complemented by an appraisal of the development of renewable electricity generation in the EU. Finally, section 10.4 offers conclusions on the effectiveness of support instruments for incentivizing the deployment of renewable electricity technologies.

10.2   INSTRUMENTS FOR RENEWABLE ELECTRICITY SUPPORT

The aim of renewable electricity support is to offset the higher costs of producing electricity from renewable energy sources, thereby promoting deployment of respective technologies and achieving a certain level of renewable electricity supply.

The policy measures should reduce the project risk, either in the investment phase through investment incentives or in the operating phase through a guaranteed remuneration for electricity from renewable sources.[5] The design of the support scheme and the guarantee of stable conditions for a certain period can influence the investors' risk perception, thus increasing investment incentives.[6]

Renewable support schemes should be designed to maximize environmental effectiveness and economic efficiency. Environmental effectiveness here refers to the contribution of the instrument to the achievement of a predefined level of renewable energy sources; economic efficiency refers to a minimization of total costs for achieving a certain renewables target and might be seen from a static perspective – that is, minimization of current costs – and from a dynamic perspective – minimization of long-term costs due to the provision of innovation incentives.

For the promotion of electricity from renewable energy sources, generally the following instruments are applied:[7]

- feed-in tariffs;
- feed-in premia;
- quota systems with tradable green certificates;
- tendering schemes; and
- fiscal measures and other forms of support (investment subsidies, tax reductions or exemptions, low interest loans, and so on).

The support instruments are either price based (such as feed-in tariffs or premia, or investment subsidies), quantity based (in the case of a quota system) or hybrid, that is, a mixture between price- and quantity-based instruments, in the case of tendering schemes focusing on electricity generation.[8] In the following the different support instruments are described in detail.

10.2.1 Feed-in Systems

The underlying principle of feed-in systems is that a specific 'fee' for each unit of electricity generated from renewable energy sources is paid. This fee is either a lump sum compensation per unit of electricity produced (feed-in tariff) or is paid in addition to the current market price (feed-in premium). The level of compensation is related to the specific electricity generation costs (possibly including a risk premium) and is guaranteed for a certain period. The duration of support and the level of compensation thus determine the funding intensity.

The guaranteed compensation provides high investment security and favourable financing conditions for the supported projects.[9] The revenues for investors become more predictable. In a feed-in tariff system the only uncertainty is related to the development of operating and maintenance costs and the amounts of electricity generated. In the feed-in bonus system the predictability is slightly lower as the revenues also depend on the future market price of electricity. In case of feed-in tariffs an increase in electricity prices does not affect the amount of electricity generated from renewable sources, but reduces the difference between the market price and the feed-in tariff. In a feed-in premium system, in contrast, with increasing market prices the specific remuneration for renewable electricity increases as well as the exploitation of renewable energy.

With respect to price-based instruments the challenge lies in determining the 'right' level of compensation, or, in other words, in avoiding excessive as well as insufficient support. In theory, feed-in tariffs should be based on the marginal electricity generation costs.[10] In fact, however, producer surpluses – that is, the amount by which the compensation level exceeds production costs – can occur, when the production costs are comparably low, for example due to favourable locations (for instance, locations with high wind speeds in the case of wind power). Producer surpluses can be reduced by technology-specific and differentiated tariffs (by region or time of day), which increase the static efficiency of the system.[11] However, producer surpluses also offer potentials for research and development as well as for investments in less mature technologies, which in turn contribute to technological diversification. Since the objective of renewable energy promotion is not only achieving current renewable targets at the lowest possible cost but also exploiting future potentials, in terms of technological diversification technologies should also be supported that currently still exhibit high specific electricity generation costs.

Degressive tariffs, that is, compensation that declines over time, ensure dynamic efficiency, that is, the realization of learning effects and cost reductions due to an increased implementation of the technologies. When the marginal costs of electricity generation decrease, a further expansion of renewable electricity generation as well as rising producer surpluses (if not tackled by tariff degression) will occur. A predetermined path for the degression of the tariffs can increase the transparency and predictability for investors.[12]

Periodic reviews and adjustments of the tariffs accounting for changes in production costs can be integrated in the design of a support scheme in order to maintain the effectiveness and efficiency of the system.

10.2.2 Quota Systems with Tradable Green Certificates

In quota systems, a minimum share of electricity from renewable sources is set as the target. Evidence of the achievement of the renewable targets has to be provided by the parties (electricity generators or traders) via tradable green electricity certificates.[13] The quantity target should be set ex ante in quota systems; it should rise continuously – in accordance with a defined path – and be valid over a longer period of time. The compensation is based on the market price of electricity and the market price of the green certificates,[14] and is thus formed on two separate markets. Future revenues are hence subject to considerable uncertainty as both remuneration components are variable.[15]

In a quota system, penalties have to be defined in case a party fails to fulfil its target. The penalties should be set at a level well above the average certificate price in order to establish a functioning market, or in other words to provide an incentive for buying and selling certificates, and to guarantee the environmental effectiveness of the system.[16] Ultimately, the fines also constitute a price ceiling for the tradable green certificates, as in the case where the market price exceeds the level of the penalty firms will pay the fine instead of acquiring additional certificates on the market.

In theory, quota systems with tradable green certificates lead to competition among electricity generators and thereby to the development of cost-effective technology options, which should lead to lower overall system costs compared to feed-in tariffs. In practice, the financing conditions are unfavourable for plant operators in quota systems as, due to the uncertain revenues, risk premiums are added to the capital costs in order to hedge against the price risk. These higher costs of capital may lead to larger producer surpluses and lower technological diversity since investments will be limited primarily to lower-risk, mature technologies. In order to reduce the risk for plant operators, minimum prices for the certificates can be defined.[17]

Quota systems originally aimed at the general promotion of electricity from renewable energy sources, that is, no technological differentiation was provided for. However, a distinction between different technologies is feasible. On the one hand, the issued green certificates could be weighted according to the technology type. On the other hand, a technology-specific differentiation of the certificate market would be possible; this would, however, lead to smaller market segments and lower liquidity associated with higher compliance costs. In both cases, a technology-specific differentiation would reduce the risk of windfall profits for mature technologies.[18]

10.2.3 Tendering Schemes

In most cases, tendering schemes represent a combination of a quantity-based and a price-based instrument, in which projects are selected in a competitive process by specifying a desired capacity, production volume or technologies.[19] Projects that are selected in this process usually receive long-term purchase contracts; the price paid for the electricity is determined in the competitive process.[20] Changes in electricity prices have no impact on the quantity produced in a tendering system, since the quantity produced is determined ex ante.

In the case of tendering schemes, the risk for plant operators is on the one hand related to the uncertainty of the competition process and on the other to the fact that the actual costs might exceed the expected costs. Great Britain and Ireland, for instance, have abandoned tendering schemes due to a lack of success, as even projects that succeeded in the competitive process had not been realized due to insufficient profitability.[21] Also, the planning effort for the tenders can be significant for the administrative entities as well as for the losing bidders.[22]

10.2.4 Fiscal Instruments

Fiscal measures – such as tax incentives, investment subsidies, loans, and similar – are often used as complementary support measures. These instruments reduce the capital costs of renewable electricity projects (investment promotion, flexible depreciation models, loans) or the operating costs (tax reductions, exemptions). One drawback of fiscal instruments is their dependence on the public budget, thus the level of available funds can vary from year to year. In the case of budget constraints, funding might also be suspended entirely. In order to provide a stable investment signal, these fiscal incentives should hence also be guaranteed ex ante for a few years in order to create predictability and reduce the risk for the electricity generator.

10.2.5   Summary of the Main Instruments for Renewable Electricity Support

The components of the remuneration for electricity from renewable energy sources as well as the market risk for electricity generators in quota systems and feed-in schemes are summarized schematically in Figure 10.1. In a tradable green certificate scheme, renewable electricity generators receive a two-part compensation: the market price of electricity and the price of the certificates. As both components are variable, green certificate schemes are connected with a comparably high risk for the plant operators. With a feed-in premium, the remuneration also consists of two components: the (variable) market price of electricity and the fixed bonus for renewable electricity. Compared to tradable green certificate schemes, the market risks are partly reduced by the fixed remuneration component. Feed-in tariffs, in contrast, consist of a single, fixed compensation component. Feed-in tariffs hence largely remove the market risk related to renewable electricity projects.[23]

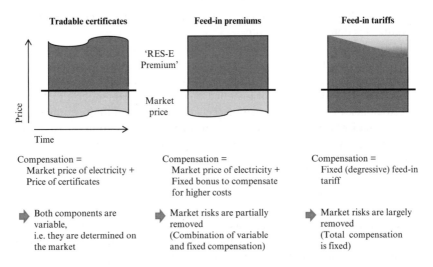

Source: Based on De Jager and Rathmann and Bode and Groscurth.[24]

Figure 10.1   Remuneration of electricity from renewable energy sources in different support systems

Effective renewable electricity support schemes should in general comply with the following guidelines:[25]

- Ambitious long-term goals for the development of renewable electricity should be defined in order to provide a sufficiently stable and predictable investment environment. If realized electricity generation from renewables comes near to attaining the target, targets should be revised.
- Stability of regulation is another prerequisite for investment security; support systems hence should not be subject to abrupt changes. Changes in support schemes should only apply to new installations and should be communicated well in advance in order to provide a stable investment environment.
- Support should be technology specific in order to reflect differences in the maturity of the technologies. This does not only apply to price-based mechanisms but also to quota systems where the number of certificates received for a given amount of electricity produced should reflect underlying generation costs. With respect to feed-in tariffs, an alignment to plant size and location could improve the economic efficiency of funding.
- For a successful expansion of renewable energy sources it is essential to also remove non-economic barriers. On the one hand, these include administrative and legal barriers, such as inefficient administrative procedures involving a large number of, or poorly coordinated authorities or long lead times, and grid-related barriers, such as difficulties in obtaining grid access on the other hand.[26]

10.3 RENEWABLE ELECTRICITY SUPPORT IN THE EU

Renewable electricity support schemes differ between the European countries (see Table 10.1). Feed-in tariffs and feed-in premia are the most frequently applied instruments in the European Union; often they are complemented by other instruments such as investment grants, tax exemptions or fiscal incentives. In 2013 feed-in tariffs for renewable electricity generation have been deployed in Austria, Bulgaria, Croatia, France, Greece, Hungary, Ireland, Latvia, Lithuania, Luxembourg, Malta, Portugal, Slovakia and the United Kingdom. In Denmark, Estonia, Finland and the Netherlands, a feed-in premium system has been used to support renewable electricity generation. The Czech Republic,

Table 10.1 Overview of renewable electricity support schemes in the EU-28

	Austria	Belgium	Bulgaria	Cyprus	Croatia	Czech Republic	Denmark	Estonia	Finland	France	Germany	Greece	Hungary	Ireland	Italy	Latvia*	Lithuania	Luxembourg	Malta	Netherlands	Poland	Portugal	Romania	Slovakia	Slovenia	Spain*	Sweden	UK
Feed-in tariff	x	–	x	–	x	x		–		x	x	x	x	x	x	x	x	x	x			x		x	x	x		x
Feed-in premium	x	x		x	x	x	x	x	x		x				x					x	x		x		x	x		
Quota obligation		x																			x		x				x	x
Tendering schemes										x					x													
Investment grants	x		x	x	x	x	x	x	x	x		x	x	x	–	x	x	x	x	–	x	–	x	x			x	x
Tax exemptions	x				x	x	x			x	x	x		x	x		x	x	–	x	x		x	x			x	x
Fiscal incentives	–	–	x		x	x	x		–			–	–		–		x		–	x	x				x			

Notes:
* Currently suspended.

x No changes between 2009 and 2014;   x instrument added since 2009   ☐ instrument removed since 2009.

Source: Kettner et al. and RES LEGAL.[28]

162

Germany, Italy, Slovenia and Spain have applied a combination of feed-in tariffs and feed-in premiums. Quota obligations have been implemented in five EU member states: Belgium, Poland, Romania, Sweden and the United Kingdom. Frequently, this instrument has also been combined with feed-in tariffs for specific technologies and/or plant sizes. For instance, the United Kingdom offered feed-in tariffs for small-scale projects below 5MW. In addition to the instruments chosen, the support level for renewable energy also differs significantly between EU member states, only partly reflecting regional differences in generation costs.[27]

Furthermore the support schemes have been frequently adapted by member states not only with respect to the support level but also with respect to the predominant policy instrument. Between 2009 and 2013, for instance, the promotion of renewable energy sources was switched from feed-in tariffs to feed-in premia in two member states (Belgium and Estonia) while three other countries (Finland, Germany and Italy) installed feed-in premia as a complement to existing support measures (Table 10.1). Italy ceased the previously applied quota scheme and Denmark switched from tendering to feed-in premia. Even more fluctuation can be observed with respect to the complementing instruments like grants, tax exemptions and so on.

However, even without major changes in instrument choice, various adaptations in the support conditions can be and were frequently made in recent years (e.g., changes in the level of tariffs or duration of support, introducing a ceiling to electricity volumes eligible for support ,etc.). Such variations – if made frequently and randomly – can have a disrupting effect as they reduce investment security and confidence.

Changes in the support instrument applied can be necessary in order to ensure effectiveness and efficiency when the previous scheme did not deliver the intended results. If the adaptation is well planned and announced well in advance, the effects are likely to be less detrimental than those of frequent changes within a scheme that significantly affect investment conditions.

Renewable electricity generation has been characterized by significant increases over the past decades. In the EU-28, electricity generation from renewable energy sources has risen from 1139 petajoules (PJ) to 2890 PJ between 1990 and 2013, which corresponds to an annual growth rate of more than 4 per cent. Thus, the share of renewables in electricity generation grew from 12 to 25 per cent in the EU-28 in the period 1990 to 2013 (see Figure 10.2).

In all member states, except for Latvia, renewable electricity generation increased between 1990 and 2013.[29] As might be expected, countries in which renewable energy sources played only a minor role in electricity generation in 1990, such as Denmark, the Netherlands or Belgium, showed the strongest growth rates. In 2013 the share of renewable energy electricity supply in the 28 member states ranged between 2 per cent (Malta) and 74 per cent (Austria);[30] in 1990, in comparison, the contribution of renewable energy sources amounted only up to 65 per cent (Austria), while in three countries (Cyprus, Estonia and Malta) there was no electricity generation from renewable energy sources at all.

Evidence from the EU member states shows that the most pronounced growth rates of renewable electricity generation were observed in countries using price-based instruments (such as Denmark, Germany or Greece) – these countries also exhibited the highest increases with regard to the respective renewable electricity generation potentials (as indicated by Figure 10.2).[31] The effectiveness of quota systems (as used, for instance, in Belgium, Sweden and the United Kingdom) is comparatively low.[32] Evaluations of the economic efficiency of renewable support schemes also point at larger producer surpluses in member states with quota systems.[33]

10.4   CONCLUSIONS

In the context of renewable electricity support schemes, the challenge is to account for volatile market prices and for the cost degression of renewable electricity technologies – especially of new technologies like photovoltaics – with increasing deployment and learning effects. At the same time, investors have to be compensated for the risk associated with renewable electricity investments.

The risk perception of investors determines the success of renewable electricity support schemes; the effectiveness of the instruments crucially depends on their credibility. A stable regulatory environment increases planning and investment security and leads to lower economic costs. Administrative barriers (grid integration, licensing procedures) can reduce the effectiveness of the instruments significantly.

Evidence from EU member states shows that feed-in tariffs tend to have a high level of effectiveness and are economically efficient. However, so far there is little experience with quota systems; these are nevertheless generally more complex in design.

While feed-in tariffs have proven to be effective in increasing the generation of renewable electricity and also the deployment of new technologies with higher risk associated with them, it has to be taken into account that they result in higher costs for electricity users as they have to pay the support as an add-on to the electricity price.

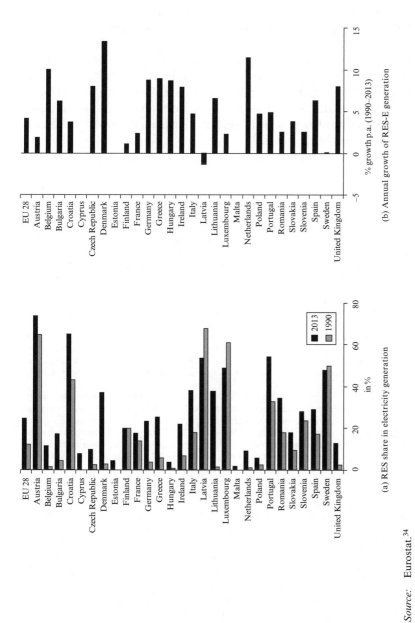

(a) RES share in electricity generation

(b) Annual growth of RES-E generation

Source: Eurostat.[34]

Figure 10.2 *Development of renewable electricity (RES-E) generation by member state*

165

Therefore, countries like Germany have introduced evaluations of the support scheme at regular intervals and subsequent adaptations if required due to technological progress and learning/scale effects. However, in implementing major system changes, the potential disruptive effects on the development of technology providers and plant operators have to be considered.

Design elements like tariff degressivity and regional or temporal tariff variations as well as the increased use of feed-in bonuses instead of fixed tariffs are further safeguards for minimizing the risk of over-subsidization.

In addition, a reduction of the administrative burden related to the planning and licensing of renewable projects can significantly lower the cost of compliance for all instruments.[35]

NOTES

1. In the case of high market prices more mature technologies like small hydropower and onshore wind can be competitive. In 2008, for instance, several installations opted out of the Austrian support schemes as market prices were higher than feed-in tariffs.
2. Directive 2001/77/EC of the European Parliament and of the Council of 27 September 2001 on the promotion of electricity produced from renewable energy sources in the internal electricity market.
3. Directive 2009/28/EC of the European Parliament and of the Council of 23 April 2009 on the promotion of the use of energy from renewable sources and amending and subsequently repealing Directives 2001/77/EC and 2003/30/EC.
4. The target values reflect a lump sum increase of 5.5 percentage points for each member state compared to the share of renewables in gross final energy consumption in 2005 on the one hand, and on the other taking into account the countries' GDP per capita as well as their respective potentials of renewable energy sources. The maximum share is limited to 50 per cent.
5. Wohlgemuth, N. and R. Madlener (2001), 'Financial support of renewable energy systems: investment vs operating cost subsidies', in *Proceedings of the Norwegian Association for Energy Economics (NAEE) Conference 'Towards an Integrated European Energy Market'*, Bergen, 31 August–2 September 2000; Haas, R., C. Panzer, G. Resch, M. Ragwitz, G. Reece and A. Held (2011), 'A historical review of promotion strategies for electricity from renewable energy sources in EU countries', *Renewable and Sustainable Energy Reviews*, **15**(2), 1003–34.
6. Dinica, V. (2006), 'Support systems for the diffusion of renewable energy technologies – an investor perspective', *Energy Policy*, **34**(4), 461–80; Held, A., M. Ragwitz and R. Haas (2006), 'On the success of policy strategies for the promotion of electricity from renewable energy sources in the EU', *Energy and Environment*, **17**(6), 849–68; Klessmann, C., C. Nabe and K. Burges (2008), 'Pros and cons of exposing renewables to electricity market risks – a comparison of the market integration approaches in Germany, Spain, and the UK', *Energy Policy*, **36**(10), 3646–61; De Jager, D. and M. Rathmann (2008), *Policy Instrument Design to Reduce Financing Costs in Renewable Energy Technology Projects*, Utrecht: ECOFYS, IEA Renewable Energy Technology Deployment; Bürer, M.J. and R. Wüstenhagen (2009), 'Which renewable energy policy is a venture capitalist's best friend? Empirical evidence from a survey on international cleantech investors', *Energy Policy*, **37**(12), 4997–5006.

7. Ackermann, T., G. Andersson and L. Söder (2001), 'Overview of government and market driven programs for the promotion of renewable power generation', *Renewable Energy*, **22**(1–3), 197–204; Held et al., 'On the success of policy strategies'; De Jager and Rathmann, *Policy Instrument Design*; Haas et al., 'A historical review'; Haas, R., G. Resch, C. Panzer, S. Busch, M. Ragwitz and A. Held (2011), 'Efficiency and effectiveness of promotion systems for electricity generation from renewable energy sources – lessons from EU countries', *Energy*, **36**(4), 2186–93; Green, R. and A. Yatchew (2012), 'Support schemes for renewable energy: an economic analysis', *Economics of Energy & Environmental Policy*, **1**(2), 83–98.

8. Haas et al., 'A historical review'; Hass et al., 'Efficiency and effectiveness of promotion systems'; Held et al., 'On the success of policy strategies'; Fouquet, D. (2013), 'Policy instruments for renewable energy – from a European perspective', *Renewable Energy*, **49**(C), 15–18.

9. Dinica, 'Support systems'; Bürer and Wüstenhagen, 'Which renewable energy policy is a venture capitalist's best friend?'

10. The marginal electricity generation costs are the costs of producing an additional unit of electricity.

11. Klessman et al., 'Pros and cons of exposing renewables'.

12. Klein, A., E. Merkel, B. Pfluger, A. Held, M. Ragwitz and G. Resch et al. (2010), *Evaluation of Different Feed-in Tariff Design Options – Best Practice Paper for the International Feed-In Cooperation*, 3rd edition, Karlsruhe: Fraunhofer ISI.

13. In the case that traders have to fulfil the obligation, all certificates have to be bought on the market; in the case that electricity producers are obligated, they could either increase their production of renewable electricity or acquire certificates on the market.

14. The value of allowances is determined by the quantity target and respectively resulting supply and demand on the certificate market.

15. Menanteau, P., D. Finon and M.-L. Lamy (2003), 'Prices versus quantities: choosing policies for promoting the development of renewable energy', *Energy Policy*, **31**(8), 799–812; De Jager and Rathmann, *Policy Instrument Design*.

16. De Jager and Rathmann, *Policy Instrument Design*.

17. Minimum prices for tradable green certificates exist, for example, in Belgium. De Jager and Rathmann, *Policy Instrument Design*.

18. If the diversity of renewable electricity generation technologies (and especially cost differences) are not taken into account in the design of a quota system, investors in mature renewable technologies might gain considerable windfall profits when the tradable green certificate scheme operates at 'at the edge of the marginal RES-E [renewable electricity] technology'. See Verbruggen, A. (2004), 'Tradable green certificates in Flanders (Belgium)', *Energy Policy*, **32**(2), 165–76.

19. In principle, however, tendering procedures could also relate to investment grants. In this case the tendering scheme would represent a pure quantity-based instrument.

20. De Jager and Rathmann, *Policy Instrument Design*.

21. Haas et al. 'A historical review'.

22. De Jager and Rathmann, *Policy Instrument Design*.

23. Dinica, 'Support systems'; De Jager and Rathmann, *Policy Instrument Design*; Bürer and Wüstenhagen 'Which renewable energy policy is a venture capitalist's best friend?'; Menanteau et al. 'Prices versus quantities'.

24. See De Jager and Rathmann, *Policy Instrument Design*; Bode, S. and H.-M. Groscurth (2008), 'Anreize für Investitionen in Anlagen zur Stromerzeugung aus erneuerbaren Energien unter verschiedenen Förderinstrumenten' (Incentives for investment in renewable electricity under different funding instruments), *Discussion Paper No. 1*, Hamburg: arrhenius Institut für Energie- und Klimapolitik.

25. De Jager and Rathmann, *Policy Instrument Design*; Klessmann, C., A. Held, M. Rathmann and M. Ragwitz (2011), 'Status and perspectives of renewable energy policy and deployment in the European Union – what is needed to reach the 2020 targets?', *Energy Policy*, **39**(12), 7637–57.

26. Swider, D.J., L. Beurskens, S. Davidson, J. Twidell, J. Pyrko and W. Prüggler et al. (2008), 'Conditions and costs for renewable electricity grid connection: examples in Europe', *Renewable Energy*, **33**(8), 1832–42; ECORYS, eclareon, EREC and Golder Associates (2010), *Assessment of Non-Cost Barriers to Renewable Energy Growth in EU Member States – AEON, DG TREN No. TREN/D1/48 – 2008*, Rotterdam: ECORYS.
27. Ragwitz, M., A. Held, B. Breitschopf, M. Rathmann, C. Klessmann and G. Resch et al. (2011), *Review Report on Support Schemes for Renewable Electricity and Heating in Europe*, a report compiled within the European research project RE-Shaping, Karlsruhe: Fraunhofer ISI; Bode and Groscurth, 'Anreize für Investitionen in Anlagen'. However, a comparison of the support levels is not appropriate as the tariffs should reflect the potential of a given technology in a country as well as the economic capacity of a country or regulatory decisions to particularly favour a certain technology.
28. Kettner, C., D. Kletzan-Slamanig and S. Schleicher (2010), *Instrumente für die Umsetzung von Maßnahmen zur Erreichung der Ziele für erneuerbare Energien* [Instruments for the Implementation of Measures to Achieve Renewable Energy Goals], Vienna: Oesterreichs Energie; RES LEGAL (2015), 'Legal sources on renewable energy', accessed 19 December 2014 at http://www.res-legal.eu/search-by-country/.
29. In Latvia most renewable electricity generation is based on hydropower; the decline in the share of renewables in Latvia reflects a reduction in hydropower after a record high in 1990.
30. Hydropower has a long tradition in Austria, but in the period 1990–2013 significant growth rates were achieved in wind power, which accounted for 4.5 per cent of total Austrian electricity generation in 2013.
31. Held et al., 'On the success of policy strategies'; Bode and Groscurth, 'Anreize für Investitionen in Anlagen'; Swider et al., 'Conditions and costs for renewable electricity grid connection'.
32. This might be partly due to inadequate instrument design and strategic behaviour.
33. Held et al., 'On the success of policy strategies'; Swider et al., 'Conditions and costs for renewable electricity grid connection'.
34. Eurostat (2015), *Eurostat Database*, accessed 17 November 2015 at http://ec.europa.eu/eurostat/data/database.
35. Klessmann et al. 'Status and perspectives of renewable energy policy'; Bode and Groscurth, 'Anreize für Investitionen in Anlagen'.

11. Protecting Australian gas resource and the need to reserve and promote the use of natural gas for Australian industries

Prafula Pearce

11.1 INTRODUCTION

Australia's natural gas endowment has been estimated to be 132 trillion cubic feet (tcf) as of 2012[1] and Australia is the world's third largest exporter of liquefied natural gas (LNG).[2] Natural gas has an advantage over other fossil fuels in that it produces lower emissions. In addition, natural gas products can be close substitutes for oil and diesel and therefore overcome some of the problems associated with oil and diesel, including higher emissions, price fluctuations and lack of availability. Due to these qualities of natural gas products, there has been a recent increase in worldwide demand and this has created pressure to exploit Australia's natural gas resource. The Council of Australian Governments (COAG), through the COAG Energy Council, recognizes that a significant transformation is occurring in the gas market and that there is a need for the Australian government to guide gas market development and provide certainty for all stakeholders.[3] The future aim for Australia's significant gas resource can be gleaned from the *Energy White Paper 2015*, which is to increase the supply of gas in order to meet domestic and international gas demand.[4] This chapter questions whether the Australian government's adoption of the market-based policy and its intention to 'not to pursue national reservation policies or national interest tests'[5] for natural gas is the best approach to benefit the current and future generations of Australians. In addition, Australian government policy should take into consideration the long-term environmental impact of extracting unconventional gas.

This chapter also addresses Australia's energy security and emissions with regard to transportation fuels as it is currently dependent on imported oil and diesel. In this respect, the Australian government's *Strategic*

Framework for Alternative Transport Fuels states that from now until 2030, Australia has an opportunity to lay the foundations for a market-based diversification of its transport fuel mix.[6] Compressed natural gas (CNG) and LNG could be alternative fuels for transportation. Both CNG and LNG are products derived from natural gas and are cheap, abundant and widely available in Australia. Despite recognizing this opportunity, current Australian government policies, including taxation policies, do not encourage a shift from the use of oil and diesel to the use of natural gas products for Australia's domestic transportation. The fiscal reforms required to promote gas as a transportation fuel in Australia can be directed to assist in acquiring, converting or fuelling vehicles, and can include accelerated depreciation, special tax deduction and the adjustment of excise rates.

11.2   THE STATUS OF THE AUSTRALIAN GAS RESOURCE AND THE REGULATORY REGIME

Natural gas in Australia is derived from conventional sources or unconventional sources, the difference being the type of reservoirs from which it is produced. Conventional gas is stored in porous sandstone formations capped by hard rock and has a high flow rate when it is extracted through production wells without the use of a pump. Unconventional gas is not stored in porous sandstone reservoirs, but in structures containing coal or clay-rich sedimentary rock and is therefore called coal seam gas (CSG), shale gas or tight gas. The extraction of unconventional gas often requires a large quantity of water to induce fracturing, or other advanced technology.[7]

Another form of gas is liquefied petroleum gas (LPG), which is a by-product of natural gas processing and petroleum refining. The properties of LPG are different from LNG and CNG. LPG is heavier than air and can therefore be hazardous, whereas natural gas is lighter than air.

Australia's Economic Demonstrated Resources (EDR) of conventional natural gas as of January 2011 have been reported to be 113 400 petajoules (PJ) or 103 tcf.[8] The resource life at the end of 2010 was estimated to be 54 years at current levels of production, and this reserve-to-production ratio was set to decline with the commissioning of five new LNG projects.[9] The outlook to 2035 projections forecasts an increase in use of gas in the Australian economy as well as increased LNG exports for Australia's resource market; however, it is also anticipated that new discoveries of conventional gas can assist in dissipating this increased demand.[10]

Australia also has abundant unconventional gas resources, which are CSG, tight gas and shale gas. As of January 2012, the EDR of CSG was reported to be 35 905 PJ or 33 tcf, amounting to a 150-year reserve-to-production ratio.[11] This ratio can also change as more projects involving the extraction of unconventional gas come on board.

The Australian government is in the process of setting up and reviewing the regulatory regime for the energy market (including gas) in Australia. In April 2007 a review of the governance arrangements for the Australian energy market was initiated by COAG, which created three bodies: the Australian Energy Regulator (AER); the Australian Energy Market Commission (AEMC); and the Australian Energy Market Operator (AEMO). The role of the AER is to regulate the retail energy market and enforce the rules made by the AEMC.[12] The role of the AEMC is to make the National Gas Rules under the National Gas Law in order to deliver reliable and efficient gas supplies.[13] The role of the AEMO is to operate the retail and wholesale gas markets across eastern and south-eastern Australia where most of the unconventional gas resources are located, and has no influence on the north-west Australian gas market[14] where most of the conventional gas is located.[15] These three bodies are to be overseen by the ministerial council known as the Energy Council. A further review of the institutional structure of the three regulatory bodies has been conducted through the release of an Issues Paper in April 2015.[16] The final report of the outcome of the review was released in October 2015 and concludes that although the governance arrangements are fundamentally sound, the COAG Energy Council is not providing policy leadership to the energy sector.[17]

The focus of the Australian government through the COAG Energy Council is only market driven and not motivated by the preservation or the reservation of the gas resource for Australian industries. This is evident in the Energy Council's vision, which states:

> The Council's vision is for the establishment of a liquid wholesale gas market that provides market signals for investment and supply, where responses to those signals are facilitated by a supportive investment and regulatory environment, where trade is focused at a point that best serves the needs of participants, where an efficient reference price is established, and producers, consumers and trading markets are connected to infrastructure that enables participants the opportunity to readily trade between locations and arbitrage trading opportunities.[18]

The COAG Energy Council's *Meeting Communiqué* of 11 December 2014 specifically rejected the need for national interventions and to 'not pursue national reservation policies or national interest tests'.[19] The Australian government's *Energy White Paper* also stated that 'the Australian Government does not support calls for a national gas reservation policy or other forms of subsidy to effectively maintain separation between domestic and international gas markets or to quarantine gas for domestic supply'.[20]

The question as to whether the Australian government should preserve natural gas for Australia's long-term prosperity is discussed in the next section.

11.3   THE AUSTRALIAN GOVERNMENT'S ROLE TO PRESERVE THE NATURAL RESOURCE OF GAS

Although the Commonwealth government does not have gas reservation policies, the states of Western Australia and Queensland have safeguards to secure domestic gas supplies. Western Australia has adopted the Domestic Gas Reservation (DGR) policy as from October 2006, requiring proponents to reserve 15 per cent of production from each prospective LNG project in order to 'secure affordable domestic gas supply to meet Western Australia's long term energy needs and to sustain economic growth, development and value adding investment'.[21] However, the final report to the Inquiry into Microeconomic Reform in Western Australia produced by the Economic Regulation Authority (ERA) has called for its abolition.[22] Queensland has not adopted the 15 per cent reservation policy, but instead adopted the Prospective Gas Production Land Reserve policy as from May 2011, under which the Queensland government has the option to release land and preserve it for the domestic market and also the option to impose conditions on exploration licences and direct future production for the domestic market.[23]

There are opposing views amongst stakeholders as to whether the DGR policy should be implemented in Australia. Energy user groups such as Manufacturing Australia, DomGas Alliance and the Australian Industry Group (AIG) support government intervention, including a DGR or some form of national interest test, whereas exploration groups such as the Australian Petroleum Production and Exploration Association (APPEA) do not support any government intervention.[24]

The Australian government has not carried out an independent study on the costs, benefits and consequences of not pursuing a DGR policy or a national interest test. However, private institutional studies have reported contradictory outcomes. A study commissioned by AIG and the Plastics and Chemicals Industries Association undertaken by the National Institute of Economic and Industry Research has revealed that the likely consequences of the current policy to export natural gas are serious due to the following facts: gas exports from eastern Australia will rise from 2 million tonnes in 2015 to 20 million tonnes in 2018; export commitment is putting pressure on domestic gas supply contracts; significant economic loss is likely to be felt in the near future due to domestic users' inability to secure an affordable supply of natural gas; and by shifting natural gas away from Australia's industrial use towards export either due to tight supply or uneconomic pricing results in giving up AU$255 million in lost industrial output for a AU$12 million gain in export output.[25] This study estimated the net GDP cost of unrestricted LNG exports to be AU$22 billion (2009 dollars) in 2040.[26] Another study that used a different methodology was commissioned by APPEA and conducted by Deloitte Access Economics. This study estimated the net GDP cost of a national reservation policy to be AU$6 billion (2011–12 dollars) in 2025.[27] A briefing paper prepared in December 2013 for the NSW Parliamentary Research Service correctly sums up that a DGR in the short term would benefit gas consumers and produce losses for gas producers, but the long-term impacts are uncertain.[28]

It cannot be said with certainty that the Australian people are benefiting sufficiently through a large increase in employment prospects or from the revenues that the Australian government raises from the exploitation of the gas resource. As regards government revenues from gas extraction, the states impose royalties on onshore gas production of generally 10 per cent of the wellhead value. After allowing for expenses, the royalty percentage is only approximately 5 to 7 per cent.[29] The Commonwealth government imposes petroleum resource rent tax (PRRT) on petroleum products, including gas for both onshore and offshore petroleum projects at the rate of 40 per cent. In dollar terms, the revenue collections are insignificant compared with the total value of gas extracted. The LNG exports alone were valued at nearly AU$17 billion for 2014–15.[30] However, the 2015–16 forecasted revenue from the total Commonwealth PRRT is only AU$1.77 billion.[31] The states' total budgeted income for 2015–16 from all royalties and land rent is also small, for example, Queensland at AU$2444 million[32] and AU$3670 million for Western Australia.[33]

The revenues collected by the Australian government from gas extraction are not significant and should therefore be weighed against what the country is giving up from exploiting the country's gas resource. It may be argued that the extraction and export of natural gas may improve Australia's current GDP. However, the question that should be addressed is whether the improvement in the current GDP is the right measure with which to make policy decisions pertaining to a non-renewable resource of gas that has taken millions of years to form. An improvement in the current GDP should be weighed against the need to preserve the gas resource for future generations. A study carried out by the National Institute of Economic and Industry Research states that the Australian government should set aside sufficient reserves of natural gas for domestic use for the next 30 to 40 years in order to counter the unintended consequences of large-scale export of natural gas.[34] However, the question is whether 30 to 40 years' outlook is long enough considering the non-renewable nature of natural gas. The policy decision pertaining to a non-renewable resource should be based on a well-defined national interest test.

The Treasury explored the meaning of the national interest test in the examination of Australia's foreign investment policy. The factors that should be taken into consideration in assessing national interest were stated to include national security, competition, impact on the economy and the community.[35] However, these factors should be observed in relation to the long-term impact including environmental impacts and not just short-term revenue raising. By only focusing on the short-term benefit of extra income from gas exports, the Australian government is also not keeping up its commitment to the global community that it has committed to by being signatory to United Nations declarations and resolutions.[36]

Precautionary and sustainability principles require that the need of the current generation should be satisfied without compromising the ability of future generations to meet their own needs.[37] If the needs of future generations are measured against the same amount of time it took for the non-renewable resource of natural gas to be created (millions of years), then arguably it cannot be said with scientific certainty that the needs of the future generations will not be compromised when the current resource of natural gas has been substantially diminished in a few hundred years.[38]

The precautionary principle requires that a substance or activity that poses a threat to the environment should be curbed and the public should be protected where scientific investigation discovers a plausible risk.[39] The environmental implications of developing the unconventional gas resource and extracting LNG from coal seam gas are uncertain. A report prepared by ABC News states that, based on the impact statement of the AU$35 billion Origin Energy/Conoco Phillip project in Queensland, all CSG and LNG projects under construction in the Gladstone areas could produce more than 34.7 million tonnes of greenhouse gases and this would amount to 80 per cent of the emissions produced by passenger cars in Australia.[40]

Problems associated with the excessive use of water to extract CSG as well as water contamination have also been forecasted in Queensland. It has been predicted that over 40 000 wells may be drilled in Queensland in the next decade and the amount of water that will be used is contentious, with various estimates ranging from 61 gigalitres per year by energy companies, 300 gigalitres a year by the National Water Commission and 1500 gigalitres per year by the Federal Government Water Group. The dewatering processes used in CSG extraction cause contamination with heavy minerals, radionuclides and salt. It is estimated that 21 to 31 million tonnes of salt will be produced over the next 30 years.[41] The Australian government should therefore act with caution as the adverse environmental effects can include long-term damage to land and reduced agricultural productivity. The Law Society of New South Wales Young Lawyers Environment and Planning Committee in its *Submission on the Green Energy Paper* strongly urged 'the Federal Government to commit to the principles of ecologically sustainable development as it governs the gas sector in Australia'.[42]

Considering that there may be long-term environmental impacts from extracting natural gas makes the case for preserving and reserving the Australian resource of gas for its domestic market even stronger, especially when the harmful environmental impacts may far outweigh the benefits from extracting and exporting gas. Many countries in the world have gas preservation policies in order to first satisfy their domestic needs. A review of the policies of the countries producing most of the world's supply of gas indicates that the United States and Canada require government export approval to export gas; the Netherlands, Norway and the United Kingdom operate in a liberalized and integrated European gas market; and many non-OECD countries have government interventions in restricting supply or stimulating demand that affect the wholesale price of gas.[43] The Australian government should consider preserving the gas for its domestic market and use the fiscal system to favour particular causes, users or industries in order to promote policies such as energy security, reduced emissions, energy affordability, economic development and the long-term benefit of the nation.

11.4 THE NEED TO USE FISCAL POLICY TO PROMOTE THE USE OF NATURAL GAS FOR PARTICULAR USERS AND INDUSTRIES IN AUSTRALIA

Fiscal policy should be used to promote the use of natural gas in the transportation sector in order to advance Australia's energy security and reduce emissions. Australia has limited resources of crude oil, that is, seven to ten years of estimated crude oil resources to production.[44] Australia imports about 80 per cent of the crude oil and the oil products it requires[45] and the transport sector accounts for about 70 per cent of the total use of oil.[46] The transport sector consumes 73 per cent of all liquid fuel supplies,[47] and 95 per cent of this consumption in the year 2011–12 was crude oil–derived liquid fuels and 2.7 per cent was LPG.[48] The National Roads and Motorists' Association (NRMA) commissioned report released on 28 February 2013 stated the position of the transport sector as being crippled within weeks if there was a disruption in the overseas supply chain.[49] This data and reasoning have recently been confirmed in a report released in June 2015 by the Senate Rural and Regional Affairs and Transport References Committee on their inquiry into Australia's transport energy resilience and sustainability.[50]

The Senate report confirmed the threats to Australia's liquid fuel security[51] and pointed to the *Energy White Paper: Green Paper 2014*, which encouraged the use of alternative transport fuels to strengthen Australia's liquid fuel security.[52] Since Australia has an abundant natural gas resource, the government should develop policies to encourage the shift from crude oil products to natural gas products for Australia's passenger and freight transportation requirements. It is costing Australians more than double in terms of energy content to import crude oil products compared with the price of LNG exports. In 2012, the average price of LNG exported was AU\$10.57 per gigajoule (GJ) compared with an average price of AU\$20.30 per GJ for crude oil imports and AU\$26.80 per GJ for refined fuel imports.[53]

Using natural gas products for Australia's transportation needs will also assist in reducing CO_2 emissions from road transport as the transport sector accounts for 92.5 megatonnes or 17.1 per cent of Australia's annual greenhouse gas emissions.[54] The Australian government projected that emissions from road transport would increase by 24 per cent over the period from 2000 to 2020.[55] The *Australia's Emissions Projections 2012* report states that the transport sector is the third largest emitting sector in Australia.[56] Within the transport sector, road transport contributed 84 per cent of all transport emissions in 2012,[57] caused by continued growth in passenger vehicle numbers, and greater consumption of diesel fuel by heavy vehicle users.[58] Gas Energy Australia, in its 2030 vision for natural gas fuels, states that natural gas fuels are the only feasible alternative for heavy transport and has proven technology and products available for cars, heavy-duty trucks, buses, forklifts, trains, marine vessels and stationary energy.[59] Other advantages of promoting natural gas for Australia's transportation needs have been identified and include: a saving of AU\$870 million in import costs for every 10 per cent substitution of imported diesel; natural gas–powered heavy trucks emit 23 per cent less greenhouse gas than diesel-powered trucks; converting one diesel truck to a natural gas–powered truck can reduce 35 tonnes of CO_2 per annum, which compares with removing 12 cars from the road; and compared with diesel, natural gas emits 30 per cent less CO_2, 75 per cent less NO_2, 90 per cent less particulate matter and 99 per cent less SO_2.[60] Natural gas fuel has been recognized as having the lowest cost of production of any fuels in Australia up until 2050.[61]

In addition to preserving and targeting the use of natural gas for the transport industry, gas-powered electricity generators can assist in reducing emissions. The recent Intergovernmental Panel on Climate Change (IPCC) *Synthesis Report* has stated that renewable energy sources such as solar and wind power are intermittent and cannot provide continuous power generation, and decarbonization of electricity generation is encouraged by substituting coal and oil for power generation with lower carbon-emitting natural gas.[62] A study on the national interest effects of the structure of the Australian gas industry state that the current government policy will result in high domestic prices for gas and this would jeopardize the viability of substituting coal-powered electricity generators with new gas-fired electricity generators.[63]

There are many other major industries that are dependent on natural gas availability, namely: basic chemicals, paints, pharmaceuticals, soap and detergents, cosmetics, rubber products and plastic products,[64] and these are likely to benefit from a reliably priced supply of natural gas.

11.5 FISCAL POLICY TO PROMOTE USE OF NATURAL GAS FOR PARTICULAR USERS AND INDUSTRIES IN AUSTRALIA

The Australian government should use fiscal and other measures to direct the use of natural gas in specific industries. It is not possible to explore all of the measures in detail without further research. However, the conceptual reasoning for some of the measures that the Australian government can adopt to target and benefit specific industries is outlined below.

There is a need to improve transport energy security as discussed above. Australia is vast in area and it is common for diesel-powered trucks to transport goods across the country. In the year 2012, approximately 191 billion tonne-km of freight was moved, of which 75 per cent was transported by 87000 trucks that consumed 4.3 billion tonnes of diesel.[65] Thus fiscal policy could be directed towards assisting the acquisition, conversion and fuelling of natural gas vehicles used for the transportation of goods in Australia.

Without a fiscal policy direction from the government, the uptake of natural gas trucks for transportation purposes is likely to be only 5 per cent or less over a five-year period.[66] The acquisition of natural gas–fuelled vehicles can be assisted through accelerated depreciation rates, which are currently far below those in other countries. The average age of a heavy-duty vehicle for depreciation purposes is 13.7 years in Australia, compared with 7.8 years in the UK, 4.9 years in Spain and 6.7 years in the USA.[67] In addition, there are no Australian government rebates or assistance programmes to encourage the purchase of or conversion to an LNG- or CNG-powered truck. Even an outright tax deduction for the cost of conversion would encourage the use of gas for transportation. The Australian government could grant a special tax deduction of up to 50 per cent on the acquisition and modification of new and existing depreciable gas-fuelled vehicles, similar to the 2008 to 2009 business tax break that was granted by the Australian government. In 2008–09, the Australian government granted a 50 per cent deduction to small businesses and a 30 per cent deduction to other businesses for eligible investments made between 13 December 2008 and 31 December 2009.[68] It is common for governments to use tax expenditures as an environmental incentive to invest in specific assets to reduce pollution or protect the environment. The Australian government should design a special deduction as an environmental incentive to encourage investment in gas-fuelled vehicles.

Another discouragement to the uptake of natural gas trucks is the excise rates. The current excise rate for diesel is 38.143 cents per litre, but a fuel tax credit of 12.003 cents applies when used in a vehicle with a gross vehicle mass greater than 4.5 tonnes. In comparison, the excise rate for natural gas (CNG and LNG) is 26.13 cents per kilogram with no fuel tax credit. When compared in energy terms, the duty for diesel is significantly less, that is, 59 per cent when compared with LNG and 64.5 per cent when compared with CNG.[69] An adjustment should be made to the excise rates so that diesel does not have an advantage over natural gas when it is used in vehicles for the transportation of goods. Otherwise, the Australian government will appear to be contradicting itself since it has recently released a methodology for reducing emissions from land and sea transport under the Emission Reduction Fund (ERF).[70]

In addition to the transport industry, other industries should be encouraged to use natural gas, for example for electricity generation. A proposed fiscal mechanism for the Australian government could be similar to the 'provider-gets-principle'[71] that it has used in the ERF[72] to reserve gas and to ensure the availability of gas to specific industries for a specific period at known prices that are not based on world market fluctuations. The same provider-gets-principle can be applied by giving entities that engage in specified projects and satisfy criteria set out in a defined national benefit test the privilege and the right to purchase gas at set prices for a set period. The reduction of emissions may be only one of the defined criteria. Other criteria could include national security, competition and impact on the economy and the community.

A percentage of the gas extracted by gas developers could be set aside in a 'Gas Reserve Bank' controlled by a government body such as the AEMO. This government body could then auction the rights to purchase gas at set domestic prices to domestic industries based on approved limits.

If the government is willing to provide money under the ERF for industries to reduce emissions, then the question is why this principle can't be extended to preserve the non-renewable natural gas resource that would bring about benefits such as national energy security to the economy and the nation as a whole, including benefits to current and future generations.

11.6   CONCLUSION

The benefit of exploiting the non-renewable natural resource of gas for an immediate return from export sales should be measured against other policies such as energy security, energy affordability, economic development and the long-term benefit of the nation. On the one hand, the Australian government is encouraging the reduction of emissions in the transport sector through the ERF[73] and seeking to strengthen Australia's liquid fuel security.[74] However, the Australian government's free market policy on natural gas could jeopardize the promotion of these policies. Therefore, there is an urgent need for an independent government study to determine the best policy approach for Australia's gas endowment.

Gas Energy Australia has correctly questioned the Australian government's vision for natural gas as follows:

> Australia has a decision to make – do we take more control of our own future, by enabling the growth of a cheaper, cleaner, secure Australian energy source that supports jobs, boosts our economy and leads to a cleaner and healthier environment for our children?
> OR
> Do we bumble along with our current energy mix, watching our dependency on foreign imports continue to escalate, our cost of transportation, electricity and goods rise, and Australian jobs sent overseas – with Australia losing power over its own destiny?[75]

Natural gas is a fossil fuel that took millions of years for our planet to produce and being non-renewable, it is irrecoverable. If we continue to deplete our natural resource of conventional and unconventional gas, it is worth questioning the type of country we will be leaving for our children and grandchildren, especially if we damage the valuable land and our water resources in the process.

NOTES

1. US Energy Information Administration (2014), *Australia: International Energy Data and Analysis*, accessed 5 June 2015 at www.eia.gov/beta/international/analysis.cfm?iso=AUS, p. 7.
2. Ibid., p. 1.

3. COAG Energy Council (2014), 'Australian gas market vision', accessed 23 August 2015 at https://scer.govspace.gov.au/files/2014/12/COAG-Energy-Council-Australian-Gas-Market-Vision-Dec-2014-FINAL1.pdf.
4. Australian Government, Department of Industry and Science (2015), *Energy White Paper 2015*, Canberra: Commonwealth of Australia, p. 17.
5. See COAG Energy Council (2014), 'Meeting communiqué (11 December 2014)' and 'Gas market development plan (summary as at July 2015)', accessed 14 April 2016 at https://scer.govspace.gov.au/files/2014/05/COAG-Energy-Council-Communique-11-Dec-2014-FINAL2.pdf and http://www.scer.gov.au/sites/prod.energycouncil/files/publications/documents/Australian%20Gas%20Market%20Development%20Plan%20%28July%202015%29.pdf respectively.
6. Australian Government, Department of Resources, Energy and Tourism (2011), *Strategic Framework for Alternative Transport Fuels*, Canberra: Commonwealth of Australia, p. 5.
7. Gas Industry Social & Environmental Research Alliance (2011), 'General coal seam gas frequently asked questions', accessed 15 April 2016 at http://www.gisera.org.au/publications/faq/faq-csg-general.pdf.
8. Australian Government Department of Resources, Energy and Tourism, Geoscience Australia and Bureau of Resources and Energy Economics (2012), *Australian Energy Resource Assessment*, Canberra: Commonwealth of Australia, p. 13.
9. Ibid, p. 16.
10. Ibid., p. 24.
11. Ibid., p. 17.
12. See Australian Government, Australian Energy Regulator website, accessed 1 August 2015 at http://www.aer.gov.au/about-us.
13. See Australian Energy Market Commission website, accessed 1 August 2015 at http://www.aemc.gov.au/.
14. See Australian Energy Market Operator website, accessed 1 August 2015 at http://www.aemo.com.au/Gas.
15. Australian Government, Department of Industry, Geoscience Australia and Bureau of Resources and Energy Economics (2014), *Australian Energy Resource Assessment*, Canberra: Commonwealth of Australia, p. 81.
16. Vertigan, M., G. Yarrow and E. Morton (2015), 'Review of governance arrangements for Australian energy markets', issues paper, Canberra: Commonwealth of Australia.
17. Vertigan, M., G. Yarrow and E. Morton (2015), *Review of Governance Arrangements for Australian Energy Markets: Final Report*, Canberra: Commonwealth of Australia, p. 7.
18. COAG Energy Council, 'Australian gas market vision', p. 1.
19. COAG Energy Council, 'Meeting communiqué'.
20. Australian Government, Department of Resources, Energy and Tourism (2012), *Energy White Paper 2012*, Canberra: Commonwealth of Australia, p. 134.
21. Department of Premier and Cabinet (2006), *Western Australian Government Policy on Securing Domestic Gas Supplies*, extracted from Economic Regulation Authority (2014), *Inquiry into Microeconomic Reform in Western Australia Final Report*, Perth, Western Australia: Economics Regulation Authority, p. 355.
22. Economic Regulation Authority (2014), *Inquiry into Microeconomic Reform in Western Australia: Final Report*, Perth, Western Australia: Economics Regulation Authority, p. 355.
23. Haylen, A. and D. Montoya (2013), 'Gas: resources, industry structure and domestic reservation policies', *Briefing Paper No. 12/2013*, New South Wales: NSW Parliamentary Research Service, p. 64.
24. Ibid., pp. 66–9.
25. National Institute of Economics and Industry Research (2012), *Large Scale Export of East Coast Australia Natural Gas: Unintended Consequences: A Study of the National Interest Effects of the Structure of the Australian Gas Industry*, report to the Australian

Industry Group and the Plastics and Chemical Industries Association, Victoria: National Institute of Economics and Industry Research, p. ii.

26. Haylen and Montoya, 'Gas: resources, industry structure and domestic reservation policies', p. 78.
27. Ibid.
28. Ibid., p. 105.
29. Clark, R. and M. Thomson (eds) (2014), *Transport Fuels from Australia's Gas Resources*, Sydney: University of New South Wales Press Ltd, pp. 270–72.
30. Department of Industry, Innovation and Science (2016), *Energy in Australia 2015*, Canberra: Commonwealth of Australia, p. 87.
31. Financial Review Data (2015), 'Budget explorer 2015–16: revenue and expenditure', accessed 23 August 2015 at http://www.afr.com/data/budget.aspx?budgetId=2015-16&type=parties&dimensions=wide, p. 1.
32. Queensland Government (2015–16), 'Budget strategy and outlook 2015–16: Budget paper no. 2: Revenue', Queensland: Queensland Treasury, p. 45.
33. Government of Western Australia (2015), 'Where the money comes from and where it goes', *2015–16 Budget Fact Sheet*, Western Australia: Department of Treasury, p. 2.
34. National Institute of Economics and Industry Research, *Large Scale Export of East Coast Australia Natural Gas*, p. 49.
35. Senate Rural and Regional Affairs and Transport Reference Committee, Parliament of Australia (2013), *Foreign Investment and National Interest*, accessed 15 April 2016 at http://www.aph.gov.au/Parliamentary_Business/Committees/Senate/Rural_and_Regional_Affairs_and_Transport/Completed_inquiries/2012-13/firb2011/report/index.
36. See United Nations (1992), *Report of the United Nations Conference on Environment and Development*, Rio Declaration (3–14 June 1992), Principle 15. Also see United Nations (1987), *Report of the World Commission on Environment and Development, Our Common Future*. Also see *United Nations Framework Convention on Climate Change*, opened for signature 4 June 1992, 1771 UNTS 107 (entered into force 21 March 1994); *Kyoto Protocol to the Framework Convention on Climate Change*, opened for signature 16 March 1998, 2303 UNTS 148 (entered into force 16 February 2005).
37. See *Telstra Corporation Ltd* v. *Hornsby Shire Council* [2006] 67 NSWLR 256.
38. For a discussion of the precautionary principle applied to the sustainability of oil, see Pearce, P. (2014), 'The role of the precautionary principle in designing energy taxes in Australia', in L. Kreiser, S. Lee, K. Ueta, J.E. Milne and H. Ashiabor (eds), *Environmental Taxation and Green Fiscal Reform: Theory and Impact, Critical Issues in Environmental Taxation, Volume XIV*, Cheltenham, UK and Northampton, MA, USA: Edward Elgar Publishing, pp. 39–52.
39. Stein, P.L. (1999), 'Are decision-makers too cautious with the precautionary principle?', paper presented at the Land and Environment Court of New South Wales Annual Conference, Blue Mountains, 14–15 October.
40. Australian Broadcasting Corporation News (2012), 'Coal seam gas by the numbers', accessed 23 August 2015 at http://www.abc.net.au/news/specials/coal-seam-gas-by-the-numbers/.
41. Ibid.
42. The Law Society of New South Wales Young Lawyers Environment and Planning Law Committee (2014), *Submission on the Energy Green Paper*, Canberra: Energy White Paper Taskforce, p. 10.
43. Energy Quest (2013), *Domestic Gas Market Interventions: International Experience*, Adelaide, South Australia, pp. 4–8.
44. Bureau of Resources and Energy Economics (2014), *Energy in Australia 2014*, Canberra: Commonwealth of Australia, p. 16.
45. Ibid., pp. 108 and 110.
46. Australian Government, Department of Industry, Geoscience Australia and Australian

Bureau of Agriculture and Regional Economics (2010), *Australian Energy Resource Assessment*, Canberra: Commonwealth of Australia, p. 63.

47. Department of Resources, Energy Economics and Bureau of Resources and Energy Economics (2012), *Energy in Australia 2012*, Canberra: Commonwealth of Australia, p. 99.
48. Bureau of Resources and Energy Economics, *Energy in Australia 2014*, p. 121.
49. Blackburn, J. (2013), *Australia's Liquid Fuel Security. A Report for NRMA Motoring and Services*, accessed 15 March 2015 at http://www.mynrma.com.au/media/Fuel_Security_Report.pdf, pp. 7, 10. Also see Stewart, C. (2013), 'Doomsday warning on fuel stock', *The Australian*, 28 February 2013. Also see Pearce, P. and D. Pinto (2013), 'The role of motor vehicle taxes in shaping Australia's oil policy', *The Tax Specialist*, **17**(1), 75–88.
50. The Senate Rural and Regional Affairs and Transport Reference Committee (2015), *Australia's Transport Energy Resilience and Sustainability*, Canberra: Commonwealth of Australia.
51. Ibid., p. 40.
52. Ibid., pp. 54–5.
53. Gas Energy Australia (2015), *Cleaner, Cheaper Australian Fuels: A 2030 Vision for Natural Gas Fuels – CNG and LNG*, New South Wales: Gas Energy Australia, p. 4.
54. Commonwealth of Australia, Department of the Environment (2015), *Australian National Greenhouse Accounts: National Inventory Report 2013 Volume 1* (Table 2.1). GHG emissions are measured as being equivalent to the most common gas, carbon dioxide ('CO_2-e').
55. Department of Environment (2013), *Australia's Abatement Task and 2013 Emissions Projections*, Canberra: Commonwealth of Australia, p. 5.
56. Department of Climate Change and Energy Efficiency (2012), *Australia's Emissions Projections 2012*, Canberra: Commonwealth of Australia, p. 25.
57. Department of Environment, *Australia's Abatement Task and 2013 Emissions Projections*, p. 11.
58. Australian Government, Department of Infrastructure, Transport and Regional Development (2012), 'State and Capital City vehicle kilometres travelled 1990–2012' (Information Sheet No. 44), Canberra: Commonwealth of Australia.
59. Gas Energy Australia, *Cleaner, Cheaper Australian Fuels*, p. 1.
60. Ibid., pp. 4–6.
61. Australian Government, Office of the Chief Economist (2014), *Australian Liquid Fuels Technology Assessment 2014*, Canberra: Commonwealth of Australia, p. 14.
62. Intergovernmental Panel on Climate Change (2014), *Climate Change 2014 Synthesis Report: Summary for Policymakers*, accessed 16 August 2015 at http://www.ipcc.ch/report/ar5/syr/, p. 28.
63. National Institute of Economics and Industry Research, *Large Scale Export of East Coast Australia Natural Gas*, p. ii.
64. Ibid., p. 17.
65. Clark and Thomson, *Transport Fuels from Australia's Gas Resources*, p. 24.
66. Ibid., p. 6.
67. Gas Energy Australia, *Cleaner, Cheaper Australian Fuels*, p. 8.
68. Tax Laws Amendment (Small Business and General Business Tax Break) Bill 2009 (Cth).
69. Gas Energy Australia, *Cleaner, Cheaper Australian Fuels*, p. 28.
70. Minister for the Environment (Cth) (2015), *Carbon Credits (Carbon Farming Initiative – Land and Sea Transport) Methodology Determination 2015*, 13 February, accessed 17 August 2015 at https://www.comlaw.gov.au/Details/F2015L00163.
71. See European Commission (2015), 'Integrating environmental concerns into CAP', accessed 15 August 2015 at http://ec.europa.eu/agriculture/envir/cap/index_en.htm.
72. The ERF is a direct financial assistance mechanism that has been implemented by the Australian government to deliver AU$2.55 billion to support entities that implement eligible greenhouse gas (GHG) emissions reduction projects between 1 July 2014 and 30

June 2017. See Australian Government (2014), *Emissions Reduction Fund: White Paper*, Canberra: Commonwealth of Australia, p. 8.
73. Minister for the Environment (Cth), *Carbon Credits*.
74. The Senate Rural and Regional Affairs and Transport Reference Committee, *Australia's Transport Energy Resilience and Sustainability*.
75. Gas Energy Australia, *Cleaner, Cheaper Australian Fuels.*

PART IV

Evaluating green economic instruments

12. The Australian Renewable Energy Target scheme: a case study of the impact of uncertainty on a market-based mechanism

David Leary*

12.1 INTRODUCTION

A wide range of policy options, including a range of market-based mechanisms, are available to governments to support the development of renewable energy. These options include provision of investment incentives such as grant programmes, tax measures such as investment and production tax credits, government procurement policies, and guaranteed price systems such as feed-in tariffs. More common mechanisms include various market-based schemes built around obligations to purchase renewable energy, including portfolio standard or quota systems, and a binding renewable energy target. All of these options are present in some form or other in various government responses to climate change and in efforts to promote the development of renewable energy across Australia.

By far the most important of these mechanisms has been the Mandatory Renewable Energy Target (MRET) scheme established under the Renewable Energy (Electricity) Act 2000 (Cth) (the MRET Act). This scheme was originally established to spur investment in renewable energy generation in Australia. This chapter argues that this core policy objective has been undermined by a constant stream of government-sponsored inquiries, reviews and legislative amendments that have created uncertainty and undermined investor confidence in the renewable energy industry. This chapter argues that the Australian experience demonstrates a fundamental lesson that the best way to destroy, or at a minimum undermine, the effectiveness of a market-based mechanism is to create a continual climate of uncertainty through inquiries and reviews and numerous amendments to the scheme. The following discussion traces the history of reviews and amendments to the MRET scheme to demonstrate this fundamental lesson.

12.2   INITIAL EFFORTS RELATING TO CLIMATE CHANGE AND TO PROMOTE RENEWABLE ENERGY IN AUSTRALIA

The MRET scheme originated from policy initiatives of the conservative government of Prime Minister John Howard in the mid-1990s. In 1997, federal government support for renewable energy was first announced by the Howard government with the release of its policy statement *Safeguarding the Future: Australia's Response to Climate Change*.[1] This policy statement outlined a number of initiatives, including direct financial assistance, to help with development of the renewable energy industry.[2] Significantly it gave a commitment to set mandatory legally binding targets for the inclusion of renewable energy in electricity generation by 2010.[3] It also outlined proposals for electricity retailers and other large electricity buyers to be legally required to source an additional 2 per cent of their electricity from renewable or specified waste-product energy sources by 2010.[4] This was aimed at assisting the accelerated uptake of renewable energy in grid-based power applications, and thereby providing an ongoing base for commercially competitive renewable energy.[5] A secondary stated goal was that the scheme would contribute to the development of internationally competitive industries that could participate effectively in the burgeoning Asian energy market.[6]

Subsequent policy documents issued by the Howard government included the *Renewable Energy Action Agenda* issued by the then Department of Industry, Science and Resources and a *Renewable Energy Technology Roadmap*.[7] But like many policy documents since then these initiatives were long in rhetoric and short on any real substance. Substantial financial support to realize significant growth in renewable energy projects in Australia was not forthcoming. Significantly, a period of four years elapsed before the MRET scheme was finally enacted in 2001.

12.3   THE MRET SCHEME

The MRET Act established the legislative framework for the MRET scheme. The original MRET Act was in turn supported by the Renewable Energy (Electricity) (Charge) Act 2000 (Cth) and the Renewable Energy (Electricity) Regulations 2001 (Cth).

The aim of the original legislation was to encourage the additional generation of electricity from renewable sources, the reduction of emissions of greenhouse gases, and to ensure that renewable energy sources are ecologically sustainable.[8] Subsequent amendments have clarified that the scope of the second of these objectives is limited to reducing emissions of greenhouse gas emissions in the electricity sector.[9]

The original MRET Act sought to achieve its objects by providing for the issue of renewable energy certificates (RECs) for the generation of qualifying electricity, requiring certain liable entities to surrender a specified number of RECs for the electricity that they acquired during a year. Where a liable entity did not have enough certificates to surrender they could either purchase them on the REC market or the liable entity was obliged to pay a renewable energy shortfall charge (discussed below).[10]

The legislation enacted in 2001 also covered registration of electricity generators under the scheme; accreditation of power stations; creation of RECs; acquisition of electricity; the renewable energy shortfall charge; statements and assessments; objections; reviews and appeals relating to decisions made under the Acts; collection, recovery and refunds of the renewable energy shortfall charge; auditing of liable entities under the scheme; confidentiality of information collected under the scheme; various registers kept under the scheme; and criminal offences for breaches of provisions of the original MRET Act. The legislation also provided for the creation of a Renewable Energy Regulator and Office of the Renewable Energy Regulator to administer the MRET scheme. Much of this basic structure remains in force today, but since 2012 has been administered by the Clean Energy Regulator.

The MRET scheme established a target of 9500 GWh or 2 per cent of electricity to be sourced from renewable energy sources by 2010. The scheme also provided for gradual annual increases in the amount of electricity sourced from renewable energy for the period 2001 to 2010 and later years.

12.4   THE UNCERTAINTY OF INITIAL REVIEWS

While it is true that the MRET scheme was an initiative of the Howard government, subsequent actions taken by that government were to undermine the effective implementation of the MRET scheme. A constant stream of government-sponsored inquiries into the MRET scheme did much to undermine certainty and investor confidence in the emerging renewable energy industry.

The MRET scheme had barely come into operation when the Independent Review of Energy Market Directions (the 'Parer Review') delivered its report in December 2002.[11] The Chair of the Review was Senator Warwick Parer, a former Minister for Resources and Energy and leading coal industry advocate.[12] Recommendations from the Parer Review, including a recommendation that the MRET scheme be abolished, raised significant concern amongst investors in renewable energy in Australia, even though those recommendations were ultimately not adopted by the government.[13] During the course of the Tambling Review (discussed below) key industry players in their submissions highlighted the chilling effect the Parer Review recommendations had on investment in the sector. For example, the Wind Energy Association commented:

> [M]arket uncertainty introduced as a result of some of the Parer Energy Market Review recommendations has made it increasingly difficult for many wind developers to achieve financial closure on projects. AusWEA is therefore concerned that these factors are acting as a barrier to the widespread adoption of new wind generation as an energy source.[14]

The Parer Review was followed shortly after by the Tambling Review, which delivered its report in September 2003. Section 162 of the MRET Act had mandated a review of the operation of the Act after only two years of operation. Section 162 required the review to consider the extent to which the Act had contributed to reducing greenhouse gas emissions and encouraged additional generation of electricity from renewable energy sources. A range of other issues had to be considered by the review.

Unlike the Parer Review, the Tambling Review was broadly supportive of the MRET scheme. Noting the MRET scheme's impact on growth of the renewable energy industry the Tambling Review observed:

> By August 2003, MRET had contributed significantly to additional renewable energy generation with 190 power stations accredited. Of these, 84 have been commissioned since MRET came into operation. MRET's interim targets for electricity generation during its first two years of operation have been exceeded with no evidence of significant shortfalls by liable parties.[15]

The Tambling Review recommended that the MRET measures continue to operate in addition to another 29 recommendations, including several recommendations for specific amendments to the MRET Act. Key recommendations by the Tambling Review included a recommendation that MRET targets continue to increase beyond 2010 at a rate equal to the rate before 2010, up to 20 000 GWh by 2020.[16]

However, the Howard government rejected the Tambling Review recommendations to increase and extend the MRET. The government increasingly adopted an approach that was sceptical of the potential of renewable energy. Government policy increasingly came to resemble the recommendations of the Parer Review. The *Energy White Paper* released by the federal government in 2004, for example, adopted one of the key recommendations of the Parer Review that the MRET scheme be abandoned and replaced with an emissions trading scheme as the principle policy tool to drive renewable energy development.[17] Similarly, while the *Energy White Paper* allocated an impressive AU$700 million to the Low Emissions Technology Demonstration Fund, the bulk of those funds (some AU$500 million) were to be allocated to developing carbon capture and storage (CCS) projects rather than renewable energy.[18] In such a policy environment further significant changes to the MRET scheme had to wait for a change of government.

12.5 THE MRET SCHEME AND THE FAILED CARBON POLLUTION REDUCTION SCHEME

The 2007 election was fought and won by Kevin Rudd and Labor on several key issues. While not the only issue, climate change was one of the leading issues in that election campaign. Three key policy measures lay at the heart of the climate change policies that Labor took to the 2007 election: (1) a promise to ratify the Kyoto Protocol[19] to the 1992 United Nations Framework Convention on Climate Change (UNFCCC);[20] (2) a promise to introduce a national emissions trading scheme; and (3) a commitment to expand the target for the MRET scheme to 20 per cent by the year 2020.

On winning the 2007 election, the first act of the Rudd government when it was sworn in on 3 December 2007 was to sign the instrument of ratification of the Kyoto Protocol. This entered into force for Australia on 11 March 2008. Legislating for an expanded Renewable Energy Target and a national emissions trading scheme was to be more problematic.

The Rudd government released its *White Paper on the Carbon Pollution Reduction Scheme*[21] in December 2008 setting out the government's policy in relation to the medium-term target range for national emissions and the final design for the national emissions trading scheme, known as the Carbon Pollution Reduction Scheme (CPRS).[22] The White Paper also set out a range of complementary and supporting measures, including assistance for emissions-intensive trade-exposed industries (EITE industries), as well as support for low- and middle-income households who would be affected by the scheme's introduction.

The CPRS was designed as a market-based mechanism – a cap-and-trade scheme – to limit greenhouse gas emissions. Bills to establish the CPRS were introduced to Parliament on 14 May 2009 but were subsequently rejected by the Senate in August 2009. Both the Liberal and National Opposition Parties and the Greens were opposed to key elements of the proposed CPRS, although for different reasons. The Liberal and National Parties were concerned in particular that the level of assistance to EITE industries was insufficient, while the Greens opposed the legislation on the basis that the assistance was too great and that the 5 per cent emissions reduction target was set too low.

Following this first failed attempt to legislate for the CPRS the Rudd government once again introduced bills to Parliament to create the CPRS on 2 February 2010. The government subsequently entered into negotiations with the opposition in an effort to seek passage of the bills. Despite reaching an agreement with the opposition on amendments to the bills, they were never passed because of the replacement of then opposition leader Malcolm Turnbull by Tony Abbott on 1 December 2009. Labor itself ultimately abandoned the CPRS in April 2010, leading to a dramatic slump in opinion polls and ultimately to Julia Gillard replacing Kevin Rudd as prime minister.

12.6   THE ENHANCED RENEWABLE ENERGY TARGET

Despite being unable to achieve passage of legislation to create the CPRS, the Rudd government did secure agreement from the opposition (then led by now Prime Minister Malcolm Turnbull) to de-link the enhanced Renewable Energy Target (e-RET) from the troubled CPRS. This led ultimately to passage of legislation to expand the Renewable Energy Target in line with the promise that Labor took to the 2007 election.

Amendments to the scheme introduced by the 2009 amendments included increasing the Renewable Energy Target from 9500 GWh to 45 000 GWh by 2020 and extending the scheme's operation out to the end of 2030.[23]

In addition, the e-RET scheme consolidated the various state-based Renewable Energy Target schemes into one national scheme. In Victoria, for example, the Victorian Renewable Energy Act 2006 (Vic) established the Victorian Renewable Energy Target (VRET) scheme, which mandated that Victoria's consumption of electricity generated from renewable sources be increased to 10 per cent by 2016.[24] This scheme operated in a very similar way to the MRET. Other jurisdictions such as New South Wales (NSW) and the Australian Capital Territory (ACT) adopted a slightly different approach, setting mandatory benchmarks for electricity retailers and other parties who sell or buy electricity, as well as mandatory state-wide emission reduction targets.[25] Increased generation and supply of renewable energy was one way retailers could meet the mandatory reduction targets.

As part of the compromise necessary to achieve passage of the enhanced Renewable Energy Target, existing projects generating electricity from waste coal-mine gas were also included in the scheme for a transitional period, subject to them meeting certain additional eligibility requirements. Waste coal-mine gas includes methane, which is a fossil fuel and significant greenhouse gas. It is not a source of renewable energy, but its temporary inclusion in the scheme was a necessary compromise to ensure passage of the expanded scheme.

Perhaps more controversially the amendments introduced in 2009 also introduced the so-called Solar Credits REC Multiplier. These amendments created an REC multiplier scheme that initially awarded five RECs per MWh to each small residential solar photovoltaic, wind or hydro system instead of the usual one.[26] The Solar Credits REC Multiplier effectively created 'phantom' RECs by counting all five RECs as contributing towards the Renewable Energy Target, even though four of them did not give rise to any additional renewable energy generation, effectively undermining the achievement of the Renewable Energy Target.[27] The inclusion of these 'phantom' RECs was in turn a significant factor in the massive collapse in the market price of RECs in late 2009 and early 2010. REC prices collapsed from around AU$50 in April 2009 to just AU$28 by late 2009.[28]

In a belated response to the collapse of the REC market further amendments to the scheme were introduced by the Renewable Energy (Electricity) Amendment Act 2010 that broke the e-RET scheme into two separate schemes, the Large-scale Renewable Energy Target (LRET) and the Small-scale Renewable Energy Scheme (SRES).

12.7 LARGE-SCALE RENEWABLE ENERGY TARGET

From 1 January 2011 the LRET created a financial incentive for large-scale renewable power stations by providing for the creation of large-scale generation certificates (LGCs) by power stations according to the amount of renewable energy they produce.[29] Generally, one LGC is created for each whole MWh of electricity created by the power station during a year that is in excess of the power station's 1997 eligible renewable power baseline.[30]

The amount of electricity generated by an accredited power station is worked out in accordance with the regulations.[31] Initially the regulations only dealt with electricity generated by hydroelectric systems, solar (PV) systems, and wind turbines.[32] Further amendments may be needed when other sources of renewable energy become more widespread.

LGCs are effectively an electronic form of currency created on the REC registry.[33] They may be created at any time after the generation of the final part of the electricity to which they relate, up until the end of the year after the year of generation (or a later date if approved by the Clean Energy Regulator).[34]

It is important to note that an LGC is not valid until after it has been registered by the Clean Energy Regulator.[35] Effectively this requires both the creation of the certificate in the electronic registry by the registered person and the validation by the Clean Energy Regulator. This process also involves the Clean Energy Regulator making a decision as to whether the LGC is eligible for registration.[36]

Liable entities (usually electricity retailers) who make a relevant acquisition of electricity are obliged to purchase an annual amount of LGCs from power stations to meet an annual target set out in the amended Act.

12.8   THE SMALL-SCALE RENEWABLE ENERGY SCHEME

Operating separately from the large-scale scheme, the SRES created a financial incentive for property owners to install small-scale installations. These include solar water heaters, air-sourced heat pumps and small generation units including small-scale solar panel, wind and hydro systems.[37] This was achieved by legislating demand for small-scale technology certificates (STCs).[38] Solar water heaters or heat pump installations are only eligible if they are new and installed after 1 April 2001.[39] They must also be listed in the Register of Solar Water Heaters, which is maintained by the Clean Energy Regulator.[40]

The owner of a solar water heater or small generation unit was entitled to create a certificate based on how much renewable electricity the systems produce or displace.[41] The number of STCs that can be produced depends on the technology involved and calculated in accordance with the provisions of the regulations.[42] The regulations permitted varying amounts of STCs to be created depending on a range of factors including the geographic location, what kind of system was installed and the operation of the Solar Credits mechanism (see below). As a general rule the number of STCs a system can create is based on the amount of electricity in MWh generated or displaced over a set time frame. In the case of small-scale solar panel, wind or hydro systems the number of STCs is based on the amount of electricity in MWh generated by such systems over the course of their lifetime up to 15 years.[43] For solar water heaters or heat pumps the number of STCs that can be generated is determined having regard to the amount of electricity displaced by the system over the course of its lifetime of up to ten years.[44]

Solar Credits are a mechanism for increasing the number of STCs that can be created for eligible installations of small-scale solar panel, wind or hydro systems by means of a multiplier set out in the regulations.[45] Due to higher than expected growth in solar panel installations and the flow-on cost to electricity prices the Solar Credits multiplier was reduced significantly from 1 July 2011 onwards. Solar Credits then applied to the first 1.5 kW of on-grid capacity installed in an eligible location or to the first 20 kW of capacity for systems not connected to the electricity grid.[46]

Unlike the LRET, the SRES did not have a target or cap on the number of certificates that can be created each year. However, the SRES made liable entities (i.e., electricity retailers) obliged to purchase a specified amount of STCs each year.[47] The amount of STCs liable entities are obliged to purchase in any one year is determined by the small-scale technology percentage (STP) set by the regulations each year.[48] Liable entities making wholesale purchases of electricity are required to purchase STCs and surrender those to the Clean Energy Regulator on a quarterly basis.

Typically registered agents assist in coordinating the purchase and installation of the small-scale systems for property owners. They generally provide a financial benefit to the owner (such as a discount on the purchase price and cost of installation of the system) in exchange for the right to create and sell the STCs.[49] Registered agents may then in turn sell the STCs either to the STC market or through the STC Clearing House. If sold directly to a buyer the market price is determined by supply and demand. The STC Clearing House on the other hand facilitates the exchange of STCs between buyers and sellers at a fixed price.

12.9   PARTIAL EXEMPTION FOR EITE ACTIVITIES

Under the original scheme certain entities that carry on EITE activities can apply for partial exemption from the LRET and the SRES. To obtain exemption, prescribed persons must apply for a partial exemption certificate (PEC).[50] A detailed examination of this aspect of the scheme is outside the scope of this chapter, but it is worth noting that a wide range of EITE activities qualified for a PEC, which effectively means large sectors of heavily polluting industry are exempt. This list of exemptions was further expanded in 2012.[51]

The provisions dealing with EITE activities were included in recognition that the RET scheme would increase costs to firms that carry on EITE activities. These industries are trade exposed and are constrained due to international competition in their ability to pass on increases in electricity costs and costs of emissions. The combined emissions intensity and trade exposure of these activities makes them susceptible to 'carbon leakage' if transitional assistance was not provided.[52] These provisions were originally included consistent with the policy intent that these partial exemptions be provided for all activities that qualify for the EITE assistance under the originally proposed CPRS. While these have been refined over time, they still largely reflect the policy reflected in early versions of the CPRS. Thus, even though the enhanced Renewable Energy Target scheme (and now the LRET and the SRES) were decoupled from the CPRS (which was never legislated by Parliament), aspects of the CPRS live on. They were in fact ultimately incorporated in the carbon price mechanism legislated in 2011.

12.10   CERTIFICATE SURRENDER AND SHORTFALL CHARGES

The heart of both schemes is the requirement that a liable entity surrender the required number of LGCs or STCs. If a liable entity does not surrender the required number of LGCs or STCs then it will be liable to pay a shortfall charge for each LGC or STC it has failed to surrender. The MRET Act recognizes two types of charge that are calculated separately. These are the small-scale technology shortfall charge (STSC) and the large-scale generation shortfall charge (LSGSC). While typically the STSC and LSGSC will be calculated in the manner outlined below, both schemes do provide default mechanisms for assessment of such charges by the Clean Energy Regulator.[53] It is also worth noting that both LGCs and STCs may also be surrendered voluntarily.[54]

The STSC is calculated by reference to a liable entity's relevant acquisitions of electricity, its partial exemptions (calculated with regard to its EITE activities), the number of STCs it surrenders and the small-scale technology percentage.[55] To avoid payment of the STSC, liable entities may choose to purchase STCs directly from the STC market or from the STC Clearing House at a set cost per STC prior to the surrender deadlines.[56]

If a liable entity has not surrendered sufficient STCs then the amount of the STSC payable by a liable entity is worked out by multiplying its small-scale technology shortfall by the rate of charge.[57] The rate of charge is as set out in the Renewable Energy (Electricity) Small-scale Technology Shortfall Charge Act 2010 (Cth), Section 6.

The LSGSC is calculated by reference to a liable entity's relevant acquisitions of electricity, its partial exemptions (calculated with regard to its EITE activities), the number of LGCs it surrenders and the renewable energy power percentage.[58] The amount of large-scale generation shortfall charge payable by a liable entity is worked out by multiplying its large-scale generation shortfall by the rate of charge specified in the Renewable Energy (Electricity) (Large-scale Generation Shortfall Charge) Act 2000 (Cth).

12.11   FINISHING THE UNFINISHED BUSINESS – A PRICE ON CARBON THAT FINISHED A GOVERNMENT

On the road to transitioning to a low carbon future, the great unfinished business of Australia's climate change law and policy was the creation of a mechanism for putting a price on carbon. The outcome of the 2010 election proved a major impetus to moving this issue forward. In order to gain the support of key independents and the Greens for the Labor Party to form a minority government in 2010, it was agreed that a Multi-Party Climate Change Committee would be formed to work on developing a carbon price mechanism.

After extensive negotiations on 24 February 2011, the Multi-Party Climate Change Committee agreed on the broad architecture for the carbon pricing mechanism. Bills to create the mechanism were introduced into Parliament in September 2011 and ultimately became the Clean Energy Act 2011 (Cth) that came into force on 1 July 2012.

Despite containing generous transitional measures to compensate low-income earners and extensive exemptions and assistance for EITE industries, the carbon pricing mechanism became the centrepiece of a toxic political campaign by the conservative opposition parties who committed to repeal the carbon price mechanism if elected. While the carbon price mechanism was essentially an emissions trading scheme with a fixed price for the first three years of its operation, in terms of political rhetoric it became known as a 'carbon tax', although any informed examination of the legislation shows it was clearly not a tax. After a highly successful campaign to repeal the 'carbon tax' the opposition was elected and ultimately was successful in repealing the Clean Energy Act.

In late 2013 measures to repeal the Clean Energy Act were also accompanied by legislation to destroy other elements of the previous government's response to climate change including bills to abolish the independent Climate Change Authority,[59] the Clean Energy Finance Corporation[60] and the Australian Renewable Energy Agency.[61]

12.12   PUTTING THE FOX IN CHARGE OF THE HEN HOUSE – THE WARBURTON REVIEW

Following on directly from the repeal of the carbon pricing mechanism the federal government then launched a direct assault on the entire renewable energy scheme. Despite the fact a full review of the RET scheme by the Climate Change Authority (mandated by Section 162) had only taken place in 2012, just two years later two major reviews of the MRET scheme were carried out in 2014. This was despite the fact that the Climate Change Authority review in 2012 explicitly recognized the negative impact constant reviews were having on investor confidence in the renewable energy sector. As the review noted:

> Confidence, including in the sustainability of important policy frameworks, is critical in persuading investors (and their financiers) to continue with their plans for long-term investments in renewable generation. Shocks to confidence from whatever source, tend to be followed by curtailments and deferrals of investment plans . . . Given the importance it attaches to supporting investor confidence the Authority's recommendation is that the frequency of scheduled reviews should be amended from every two years to every four years.[62]

Despite this clear recommendation only two years earlier, in February 2014 the federal government announced the appointment of a so-called Expert Panel chaired by Mr Dick Warburton to examine the MRET scheme. The establishment of yet another review into the MRET concerned industry, not the least because the review was to be chaired by Dick Warburton, a self-confessed climate change sceptic known for his outspoken views critical of climate science.[63]

In August 2014 the Warburton Review released its report, making 12 key recommendations. Most significantly the report recommended two options for the future of the LRET: either the LRET should be closed to new entrants or it should be amended to slow down the growth of renewable energy generators' share of the electricity market.[64] Similarly, the Warburton Review also recommended that the SRES either be abolished or that its phase-out be brought forward from 2030 to 2020.[65]

If these recommendations had been adopted they would have had a devastating impact on future renewable energy projects in Australia. While these recommendations were ultimately not adopted by the government, the uncertainty created by the Warburton Review had an unprecedented impact on investor confidence in the renewables sector. In 2014, investment in large-scale renewable energy projects in Australia dropped by 88 per cent. In contrast, overseas investment in renewable energy projects increased by 16 per cent in the same period.[66]

For many companies active in the renewables sector the uncertainty was enough for them to take the unusual step of explicitly acknowledging the impact of this uncertainty on their profitability and future trading prospects. For example, leading energy company AGL Energy Limited commented in its *Annual Report* in 2015:

> [C]urrent energy market and policy settings are inhibiting investment in new large-scale renewable electricity generation projects ... projects are unlikely to receive sufficient revenue over their lives to be economically sustainable ... Despite recent developments, uncertainty persists in relation to new investment to meet the Renewable Energy Target, which has been the subject of numerous reviews in recent years.[67]

Other companies such as Meridian were more forthright in their *Annual Report*. As Meridian observed:

> Australia is currently an uncertain market for renewable energy operators. The recently issued Warburton Report on Australia's Renewable Energy Target (RET) recommended two options to the Government for consideration. Materially downgrading the RET would result in little, if any, investment in renewable projects in Australia for some considerable time ... Along with all the other participants in the renewable energy industry, we are concerned with the possible effects of a repeal of or material alteration to the terms of the current RET, which might make renewable projects uneconomical ... The Australian Government's final decision may materially affect our view on further generation opportunities in Australia.[68]

For other companies the impact of the uncertainty spilled over into the share market, with share prices falling in response to the uncertainty. Carnegie Wave Energy Ltd is one such ASX-listed company that acknowledged publicly the impact of uncertainty surrounding the MRET on its share price.[69] For other companies the uncertainty over the future of the MRET was the key reason for cancellation of renewable energy projects at advanced stages of development. One such example is Enviromission Limited's cancellation of its planned 100MW Mildura Power Station Solar Tower Project.[70]

In contrast to the Warburton Review, in December 2014 the Climate Change Authority (which had not yet been abolished) released its biannual review of the MRET scheme. Independent of the government, and pursuant to its statutory mandate, its report acknowledged the massive harm to the renewable energy sector that had been caused by the uncertainty surrounding the MRET and by the Warburton Review in particular. Picking up on its early comments on investor confidence in its 2012 report the 2014 report observed the following:

> In its 2012 review, the Authority considered the feasibility of achieving the 2020 LRET target. It concluded that the task was challenging but could be met, provided there was ongoing confidence on the part of renewables investors . . . since then, confidence in the industry has waned and now investment has tapered off, on the back of the erosion of bipartisan support . . . confidence within the industry that bipartisan support for the LRET can be restored quickly in a convincing manner is essential to have a strong chance of achieving the 2020 goal of 41,000 GWh. At this time this is looking rather problematic.[71]

This later review therefore rejected the major findings of the Warburton Review and instead proposed the preservation of the existing LRET target, but with some minimal changes including extending the time for achieving the target by three years.[72]

Uncertainty surrounding the future of the MRET continued for several more months into the new year. However, by June 2015 after intense political debate and lobbying by the renewable energy industry a political compromise was reached that guaranteed the future of the renewable energy industry, albeit with further significant changes to the MRET scheme.

The enactment of the Renewable Energy (Electricity) Amendment Act 2015 (Cth) reduced the 2020 Renewable Energy Target from 41 000 GWh to 33 000 GWh.[73] It also amended the scheme by amending the Renewable Energy (Electricity) Regulations 2001 by controversially allowing biomass from native forests to be recognized as a source of renewable energy.[74] This had previously been excluded because of concerns about the environmental impact of logging in native forests.

On the positive side, however, the Renewable Energy (Electricity) Amendment Act 2015 (Cth) removed the requirement for periodic reviews of the renewable energy legislation by repealing Section 162 from the Renewable Energy (Electricity) Act 2000.[75] Curiously this had been a recommendation of the Warburton Review.

12.13 CONCLUSION

As we enter 2016, the future of the Australian renewable energy sector looks somewhat more secure than it did at the beginning of 2015. For the time being bipartisan support for the Renewable Energy Target scheme, albeit in a further amended form, appears to have been restored. Nonetheless, over the past two decades the MRET scheme has been the subject of numerous enquiries and reviews and several major amendments. Most of these have been driven by political agendas hostile to real action on climate change and the growth of a stable and effective renewable energy market. The Australian experience over the last two decades demonstrates an obvious but fundamental lesson: the best way to destroy a market-based mechanism is to constantly make changes to the mechanism, and create a continual climate of uncertainty about its future. What the industry needs now more than anything else is a long period of stability so that investor confidence can be restored.

NOTES

*   The author acknowledges the assistance of his research assistant Eric Law with background research for this chapter.
1. Jones, S. (2009), 'The future of renewable energy in Australia: a test for cooperative federalism', *Australian Journal of Public Administration*, **68**(1), 3, 4.
2. Ibid.
3. Howard, J. (2003), *Safeguarding the Future: Australia's Response to Climate Change*, cited in *Australian Greenhouse Office, Renewable Opportunities. A Review of the Operation of the Renewable Energy (Electricity) Act 2000*, p. 2.
4. Ibid.
5. Ibid.
6. Ibid.
7. Jones, 'The future of renewable energy in Australia', p. 4.
8. See Renewable Energy (Electricity Act) 2000 (Cth), s. 3 as originally enacted.
9. Renewable Energy (Electricity Act) 2000 (Cth), s. 3 (b) as at 7 March 2011.
10. See the description of the scheme by Deputy President Forgie in *Hydro Power Pty Ltd and the Renewable Energy Regulator* [2008] AATA 385, 13 May 2008, paragraphs 14–38 from which this short overview is drawn. Accessed 24 April 2016 at http://www.austlii.edu.au/cgi-bin/sinodisp/au/cases/cth/AATA/2008/385.html?stem=0&synonyms=0&query=Re%20Hydro%20Power%20Pty%20Ltd%20and%20the%20Renewable%20Energy%20Regulator.
11. See Council of Australian Governments (2002), *Towards a Truly National and Efficient Energy Market*, accessed 15 April 2016 at http://www.efa.com.au/Library/ParerFinRpt.pdf.
12. Jones, 'The future of renewable energy in Australia', p. 8.
13. Kelly, G. (2007), 'Renewable energy strategies in England, Australia and New Zealand', *Geoforum*, **38**(2), 326, 331.
14. Australian Wind Energy Association (2003), Submission 198, p. 29, quoted in Australian Greenhouse Office, *Renewable Opportunities. A Review of the Operation of the Renewable Energy (Electricity) Act 2000* (Tambling Review), accessed 15 April 2016 at http://pandora.nla.gov.au/pan/121641/20101007-1302/www.mretreview.gov.au/report/index.html.
15. Australian Greenhouse Office, *Renewable Opportunities. A Review of the Operation of the Renewable Energy (Electricity) Act 2000* (Tambling Review), accessed 15 April 2016 at http://pandora.nla.gov.au/pan/121641/20101007-1302/www.mretreview.gov.au/report/index.html.
16. Ibid., p. xxvii.
17. Jones, 'The future of renewable energy in Australia', p. 10.
18. Ibid.
19. Kyoto Protocol to the United Nations Framework Convention on Climate Change, opened for signature 11 December 1997, 37 ILM 22 (entered into force 16 February 2005).
20. United Nations Framework Convention on Climate Change, opened for signature 9 May 1992, 31 ILM 849 (entered into force on 21 March 1994).

21. Australian Government, Department of Climate Change (2008), *White Paper on the Carbon Pollution Reduction Scheme: Australia's Low Pollution Future*.
22. Ibid., p. 1.
23. Office of the Renewable Energy Regulator (2009), 'Amendments to the legislation from the expansion of the Renewable Energy Target', accessed 24 April 2016 at http://pandora.nla.gov.au/pan/42809/20091020-0005/www.orer.gov.au/legislation/index.html.
24. Victoria Essential Services Commission (2009), 'Victorian Renewable Energy Target (VRET) scheme', accessed 24 April 2016 at http://pandora.nla.gov.au/pan/99491/20091029-1058/www.esc.vic.gov.au/public/VRET/index.html.
25. See 'Greenhouse Gas Reduction Scheme' (undated), accessed 24 April 2016 at http://pandora.nla.gov.au/pan/93701/20130130-0000/www.greenhousegas.nsw.gov.au/index.html.
26. Buckman, G. and M. Diesendorf (2010), 'Design limitations in Australian renewable energy policies', *Energy Policy*, **38**(7), 3365, 3373.
27. Ibid.
28. Nelson, T., J. Nelson, J. Ariyaratham and S. Camroux (2013), 'An analysis of Australia's large scale Renewable Energy Target: restoring market confidence', *Energy Policy*, **62**(C), 386–400.
29. Office of the Renewable Energy Regulator, 'LRET/SRES – the basics', accessed 24 April 2016 at http://pandora.nla.gov.au/pan/42809/20111020-0000/www.orer.gov.au/publications/lret-sres-basics.html.
30. Renewable Energy (Electricity Act) 2000 (Cth), s. 18 (1).
31. Ibid., s. 18 (3).
32. Renewable Energy (Electricity) Regulations 2001, Division 2.3, reg. 20.
33. Office of the Renewable Energy Regulator, 'LRET/SRES – the basics'.
34. Renewable Energy (Electricity Act) 2000 (Cth), s. 19.
35. Ibid., s. 26 (1).
36. Ibid., s. 26 (2) and s. 26 (3).
37. Office of the Renewable Energy Regulator, 'LRET/SRES – the basics'.
38. Office of the Renewable Energy Regulator (2010), *Increasing Australia's Renewable Electricity Generation*, accessed 24 April 2016 at http://pandora.nla.gov.au/pan/42809/20111020-0000/www.orer.gov.au/publications/pubs/ORER_booklet.pdf.
39. Renewable Energy (Electricity Act) 2000 (Cth), s. 21 (1).
40. Ibid., s. 21 (1A) and s. 23AA. See also Renewable Energy (Electricity) Regulations 2001, reg. 19C.
41. Ibid.
42. See Renewable Energy (Electricity Act) 2000 (Cth), s. 22 and s. 23B and Renewable Energy (Electricity) Regulations 2001, regs 19–20A.
43. Office of the Renewable Energy Regulator (2010), *Increasing Australia's Renewable Electricity Generation*.
44. Ibid.
45. Ibid. See Renewable Energy (Electricity Act) 2000 (Cth), s. 23B (2).
46. Office of the Renewable Energy Regulator (2010), *Increasing Australia's Renewable Electricity Generation*.
47. Ibid.
48. Renewable Energy (Electricity Act) 2000 (Cth), s. 40A.
49. Office of the Renewable Energy Regulator (2010), *Increasing Australia's Renewable Electricity Generation*.
50. Renewable Energy (Electricity Act) 2000 (Cth), s. 38B.
51. EITE activities are defined in Section 5 of the Renewable Energy (Electricity Act) 2000 (Cth) as those activities prescribed by the regulations. The Renewable Energy (Electricity) Regulations 2001, reg. 22D in turn defines EITE activities as those specified in Schedule 6 to the regulations.
52. Minister for Climate Change, Energy Efficiency and Water (2010), *Renewable Energy (Electricity) Amendment Regulations 2010 (No. 1) (SLI No. 46 of 2010), Explanatory*

Statement, accessed 17 April 2016 at http://www.austlii.edu.au/au/legis/cth/num_reg_es/rear20101n46o2010582.html.
53. See Renewable Energy (Electricity Act) 2000 (Cth), s. 48 and s. 48B.
54. Ibid., s. 28A.
55. Ibid., s. 34A.
56. Office of the Renewable Energy Regulator (2011), 'Liable entities guide: obligations and reporting under the LRET and SRES', accessed 24 April 2016 at http://pandora.nla.gov.au/pan/42809/20111020-0000/www.orer.gov.au/liable-entities/index.html.
57. Renewable Energy (Electricity Act) 2000 (Cth), s. 38AC.
58. Renewable Energy (Electricity Act) 2000 (Cth), s. 34A.
59. Climate Change Authority (Abolition) Bill 2013 (Cth).
60. Clean Energy Finance Corporation (Abolition) Bill 2013 (Cth).
61. Australian Renewable Energy Agency (Repeal) Bill 2014 (Cth).
62. Climate Change Authority (2012), *2012 Renewable Energy Target Review*, p. vi, accessed 17 April 2016 at http://climatechangeauthority.gov.au/files/20121210%20Renewable%20Energy%20Target%20Review_MASTER.pdf.
63. See, for example, comments attributed to Mr Warburton in media reports of his appointment such as Arup, T. (2014), 'Climate change sceptic Dick Warburton to head Tony Abbot review into renewable energy target', *Sydney Morning Herald*, 17 February, accessed 17 April 2016 at http://www.smh.com.au/federal-politics/political-news/climate-sceptic-dick-warburton-to-head-tony-abbott-review-into-renewable-energy-target-20140217-32vve.html; see also White, A. (2014), 'Australia needs the renewable energy target (and should increase it)', *The Guardian*, 18 August, accessed 17 April 2016 at http://www.theguardian.com/environment/southern-crossroads/2014/aug/18/renewable-energy-target-abolish-abbott-hunt-warburton.
64. See Commonwealth of Australia (2014), *Renewable Energy Target Scheme. Report of the Expert Panel*, Recommendation 2, p. vii, accessed 17 April 2016 at http://apo.org.au/files/Resource/ret_review_report_2014.pdf.
65. Ibid., Recommendation 3, pp. vii–viii.
66. Clean Energy Council (2014), *Clean Energy Australia Report 2014*, accessed 17 April 2016 at https://www.cleanenergycouncil.org.au/policy-advocacy/reports/clean-energy-australia-report.html, p. 4.
67. AGL Energy Limited, *Annual Report 2015*, p. 16, accessed 17 April 2016 at https://www.agl.com.au/about-agl/investor-centre/reports-and-presentations/annual-reports.
68. Meridian Energy Limited (2014), *Annual Report 2014*, p. 7, accessed 17 April 2016 at https://www.meridianenergy.co.nz/assets/Investors/Reports-and-presentations/Annual-results-and-reports/2014/Annual-Report-2014.PDF.
69. See Carnegie Wave Energy Limited (2015), *Annual Report 2015*, p. 33, accessed 17 April 2016 at http://carnegiewave.com/wp-content/uploads/2015/09/150925_Report-to-Shareholders.pdf.
70. See Enviromission Limited and Controlled Entities (2014), *Financial Report for the Year ended 30 June 2014*, p. 1, accessed 17 April 2016 at http://www.enviromission.com.au/EVM/PDF/1464/AnnualReporttoshareholders.
71. Climate Change Authority (2014), *Renewable Energy Target Review Report*, pp. 1–2, accessed 17 April 2016 at http://www.climatechangeauthority.gov.au/reviews/2014-renewable-energy-target-review.
72. Ibid.
73. Renewable Energy (Electricity) Amendment Act 2015 (Cth), Schedule 1 Part 1 (2).
74. Ibid., Schedule 1, Part 4.
75. Ibid., Schedule 1, Part 3.

13. Economic instruments in pollution law in New South Wales, Australia: a case for greater use and refinement

Sarah Wright

13.1 INTRODUCTION

The first generation of New South Wales ('NSW') pollution laws in the 1960s–70s were based on 'command-and-control' regulation. For example, a licence was required for water pollution discharges with consequent criminal offences for failure to comply.[1] Low maximum penalties offered little incentive to implement environmentally beneficial technology and practices. In the 1990s NSW pollution law underwent reform. A new regulator, the NSW Environment Protection Authority ('EPA'), was provided with more innovative and flexible measures to address pollution in addition to command-and-control. As the EPA recognized, 'the traditional approach to pollution regulation [could] no longer guarantee the best outcomes for the environment',[2] even with substantially increased maximum penalties. First-generation laws that had dealt separately with air, water, noise, as well as some aspects of waste, were replaced by an integrated approach in the Protection of the Environment Operations Act 1997 (NSW) ('POEO Act')[3] that forms the centrepiece of NSW pollution laws.

The POEO Act and regulations give the EPA a range of economic measures to tackle pollution. These have been utilized to differing degrees and with varied success. Economic instruments have been used in conjunction with, not instead of, the command-and-control framework. This chapter considers the use of economic measures under the POEO Act. Given (1) the integrated approach adopted in the POEO Act to pollution regulation, and (2) the limited use of economic instruments in NSW pollution law, this chapter does not focus on the use of economic instruments in relation to a specific pollutant medium such as air or water. Rather it considers the use of economic instruments regarding licensing and also monetary benefit orders ('MBOs') within the sentencing process. One of the case studies in relation to MBOs is also drawn from the licensing arena, relating to a breach of licence conditions. The aim is to consider how effectively those instruments have been utilized in NSW pollution law and whether either their limitations or infrequent use might impede environmental protection. The chapter first considers load-based licensing ('LBL') and risk-based licensing ('RBL') fees as an economic incentive to drive improved environmental performance. Second, it examines the limited use of emissions trading schemes ('ETSs') by the EPA. Third, the failure to use MBOs within the sentencing process is discussed. The chapter concludes that while the EPA has a number of economic tools to aid environmental protection and there are examples of their successful use, some have been underutilized, while others have significant design flaws. This may impact on the EPA's ability to combat pollution. Further consideration should be given to the use and improvement of economic instruments in NSW pollution law.

13.2   LICENSING FEES

In NSW a licence must be obtained from the EPA for 'scheduled activities'. These are activities listed in Schedule 1 of the POEO Act and are generally higher polluting industries.[4] Licences are also required for non-scheduled activities that pollute waters.[5] A licence regulates all pollution generated at a site.[6] Annual licence fees contain two different components, which now both incorporate an economic incentive to improve environmental performance. First, an administrative licence fee applies that varies in amount depending on the activity and the licensee's environmental management performance.[7] Second, an LBL fee may apply.[8]

13.2.1   Load-based Licensing (LBL)

A fundamental premise underlying LBL is the polluter-pays-principle.[9] LBL aims to force industry to reduce pollutants and improve existing technology by providing a financial incentive: the more pollutants discharged, the higher the fee.[10] The fee is based on annual pollutant amounts, not discharge concentrations.[11] The fee only applies to specified activities and listed pollutants, such as NO_x, SO_x, volatile organic compounds (VOCs), lead, mercury, particulate matter, phosphorus and nitrogen.[12] The fee also depends on the pollutant's environmental harmfulness and how sensitive the receiving environment is.[13] After a specified threshold amount of pollutants have been discharged, the LBL fee doubles.[14] This threshold represents the point where emissions fall below current industry technological standards.[15] Licensees must also comply with licence emission limits.[16]

LBL seeks to encourage licensees to achieve discharges that are beneath those limits.[17]

There have been few assessments of LBL effectiveness. The EPA is currently reviewing the scheme. The available material evidences mixed outcomes. LBL can work effectively as an economic incentive to reduce pollution where the pollutant can be diverted to another beneficial use rather than being discharged to the environment. For example, sewage treatment plants that would discharge high amounts of nutrients such as phosphorus and nitrogen to waters can reduce LBL fees by diverting effluent to other uses, for instance as farm fertilizer.[18] LBL has encouraged such licensees to find a relatively easy way of reducing discharges (and fees) and also potential environmental harm.

LBL effectiveness has perhaps been the subject of greater uncertainty where cleaner technology needs to be implemented to abate pollution. The Environmental Defender's Office of NSW ('EDO') argues that LBL fees are too low and do not address enough pollutants, resulting in insufficient incentives to reduce pollutants.[19] Graham and Wright (2012) argued that given numerous catchments suffer from degraded water quality LBL fails to 'provide a real incentive for cleaner production'.[20] However, licensed discharges are generally only one source of pollutants within a catchment. Many sources, particularly diffuse pollution, are unregulated. This makes it difficult to determine the impact of LBL on environmental quality. Some indication of its success may be provided by the reduction in pollutants discharged by licensees. However, other issues also affect emission levels. As Ancev et al. (2012) recognized, this includes altered production output caused by factors such as the global financial crisis, or the use of other regulatory instruments to address pollution. For example, cleaner production technologies may be required by pollution reduction programmes ('PRPs') imposed on licences.[21] This may make it difficult to determine if abatement has occurred in response to the financial incentive provided by LBL or external factors.[22]

Ancev et al. studied ten years of data between 2000 and 2009 for NO_x emissions under NSW LBL. They sought to determine whether the scheme acted effectively as an economic incentive to reduce emissions. This was the first economic assessment of NSW LBL.[23] For LBL fees to work well as an incentive to improve environmental outcomes it must be more cost effective to implement abatement measures than to just pay LBL fees.[24] The study found NO_x emissions had remained 'fairly stable' and concluded that 'the LBL scheme does not have a statistically significant effect on NO_x emissions' by licensees. This indicated that LBL fees during the period studied were not high enough to encourage abatement.[25] In comparison to other countries, such as Sweden where LBL worked effectively to reduce NO_x emissions, NSW LBL fee rates were much smaller: approximately 0.05 €/kg (NSW in 2008–09) versus 5 €/kg (Sweden).[26] Furthermore, it was much more expensive to abate emissions than pay the LBL fee, for example, by two to three times in some cases. Additionally, doubling fees once the threshold was reached was not enough to induce some licensees to implement abatement.[27] Where LBL fees are set too low, direct regulation, such as imposing PRPs on licences may produce greater environmental outcomes.[28] Ultimately, Ancev et al. suggested that LBL needed significant revision given that '[a]s it stands now, the LBL scheme seems more effective in raising revenue than in improving air quality'.[29]

In 2009 the Department of Environment and Climate Change (NSW) (which then incorporated the EPA) considered data covering a five-year period regarding the effectiveness of the threshold at which the fee rate doubles. The Department concluded that 'in about two-thirds of cases, [the threshold was] not providing any added incentive for LBL premises to improve their performance'. Essentially a number of the thresholds for different pollutants had been set well above the actual emissions being produced.[30] In response, multiple thresholds were reduced.[31]

Given the amount of time since these studies were conducted and the amendments were made, further information is required to determine whether the LBL scheme is now providing a sufficient economic incentive to force cleaner production. The current LBL review will hopefully provide greater clarity in this respect. The examples have, however, illustrated that LBL can be successful where pollutants can be diverted to another beneficial use rather than discharged.

13.2.2   Risk-based Licensing (RBL)

The EPA has recently adopted RBL. Higher levels of regulation are targeted towards licensees that pose the highest risk because of their compliance history and the potential environmental impact if an incident happens.[32] One component of RBL is that administrative licensing fees vary based on the licensee's environmental performance.[33] This aims to create an incentive to improve performance.[34] Licensees are placed into environmental management categories ('EMC') ranked A–E determined by a scoring system under which a licensee is allocated points for regulatory actions undertaken by the EPA, such as prosecutions, penalty notices and clean-up notices. Points are deducted (that is, the licensee receives credit) for environmental management systems and voluntary environmental improvement works and programmes undertaken at the premises. The higher a licensee's environmental management score the worse their EMC and the greater their administrative fees.[35] Licensees in the best EMC (category A) receive a 5 per cent discount. The worst performers (category E) will have their base fee, which ranges between AU$610 and AU$323 300, doubled.[36]

The RBL scheme has recently begun and applies to licensing fee payments from 1 July 2016.[37] Its effectiveness in practice as an economic tool to manage pollution is therefore unable to be assessed. However, serious design flaws exist that compromise its ability to operate fairly and effectively as an economic incentive. First, regulatory actions by the EPA may lead to fee increases that are (1) disproportionate to the particular incident and the need for an economic incentive to improve environmental performance, and (2) result in perverse fee increases for high-fee payers and nominal fee increases for low-fee payers. For example, under the scoring system a good category A performer may find themselves relegated to category D for a minor, unforeseeable incident if the EPA issues a penalty notice and clean-up notice. For the highest fee payers, fees would increase by nearly AU$194 000. For the lowest fee payers, fees would increase by AU$366.[38] The latter could be absorbed simply as a cost of doing business, providing little incentive to improve. In comparison, an issue arises regarding whether the high-fee payer needs such a large economic incentive to comply for a minor, unforeseeable incident. Notably, based on current sentencing trends in the Land and Environment Court of NSW ('LEC')[39] this amount would also grossly exceed any likely criminal penalty imposed by the Court had the breach been prosecuted.[40]

A second design flaw is with regard to credit given for environmental improvement works when calculating the EMC. A flat score reduction is applied to each environmental improvement work resulting in 'demonstrated environmental improvement' regardless of the level of enhancement.[41] One might raise concern that licensees may be tempted to carry out multiple small-scale projects of minimal environmental worth to achieve the greatest score reductions and lower licensing fees. The design flaws within RBL fees impact the scheme's ability to operate effectively as an economic incentive to improve environmental performance.

13.3   EMISSIONS TRADING SCHEMES (ETS)

The POEO Act gives the EPA power to implement an ETS as a 'means of achieving cost-effective environmental regulation or environment protection'.[42] The EPA has made little use of this tool – only two known ETS have been implemented, with both touted as successes. Both schemes were introduced before the POEO Act commenced but continue under that legislation. They are limited in geographical area and deal with only one pollutant 'type'.

The simple South Creek Bubble Licensing Scheme was established in 1996. It involves three Western Sydney sewage treatment systems licensed to Sydney Water Corporation that discharge pollutants into South Creek. It was introduced given concerns over high nutrient levels within the Hawkesbury-Nepean catchment, which can cause algal growth leading to other environmental impacts such as death of aquatic organisms.[43] The scheme was created through licence conditions establishing an annual nitrogen and phosphorus discharge limit as a total combined discharge limit for all three systems. Discharges can be adjusted between the three systems at the least cost as long as the overall pollutant cap is maintained.[44] The ultimate aim was to reduce phosphorus by 83 per cent and nitrogen by 50 per cent by 2004.[45] Phosphorus was successfully reduced by 88 per cent.[46] The figures for nitrogen are unknown by the author. The scheme was estimated to result in a AU$45 million reduction in necessary expenditure by Sydney Water to achieve the required pollutant reductions,[47] as opposed to the situation if uniform concentration limits had been specified for each individual plant.

The second ETS is the Hunter River Salinity Trading Scheme ('HRSTS'). This is discussed in more detail below before considering whether there is potential for greater use of ETS in NSW pollution law.

13.3.1   The Reasons for Introducing the HRSTS

The Hunter River can be naturally high in salinity because of underlying rock formations that derive from marine environments.[48] The catchment has a number of different commercial activities that use water within the Hunter River, including power stations, coal mines and agriculture.[49] Saltwater discharges from these businesses can significantly increase river salinity. This can, for example, decrease agricultural crop yields and impact aquatic ecosystems.[50] Concerns over salinity impacts on agriculture led to 'a serious conflict . . . between irrigators and mining companies',[51] compelling the EPA to implement different measures to reduce salinity. Previously, licensees had been allowed to release 'trickle discharges' (continuous small discharges of saline water) irrespective of current salinity or flow levels in the river.[52] The effects of this approach were that: (1) during low flow salinity levels would become 'excessive', and (2) licensees were unable to utilize the benefits of high flow where ambient salinity levels were lower due to increased water volume that would naturally dilute any saline discharges.[53] The EPA also prevented new developments from releasing saline water from 1992.[54] The costs of managing salt at new licensed premises became inhibitive, potentially stifling new development.[55] A number of different options were considered to manage salinity but, ultimately, an ETS was considered the most cost effective.[56] A pilot scheme began in 1995, which became formalized through regulations in 2002.[57]

13.3.2   The Way the HRSTS Operates

Licensees that wish to discharge saline water into the river must do so in accordance with the HRSTS and any licence limits.[58] During low-flow periods river salinity increases; during high flow the volume of water decreases salinity levels. The scheme's essential underpinning is its reliance on dilution based on natural river flows to ensure environmental impacts of saline discharges are minimized:[59]

- Low flow: no saline water discharges permitted.
- High flow: participants are allowed to discharge saline water. Each participant is permitted to discharge that part of the total allowable discharge amount ('TAD') that is calculated for the particular flow event, representing the proportion of credits the licensee holds. The TAD is determined so as to ensure river salinity will not exceed targets of 900EC (electrical conductivity) in the middle and lower sectors or 600EC in the upper sector of the river. Credits may be traded between participants either for a particular discharge event, specified periods or the credit lifespan.
- Flood flows: unlimited discharges can occur, provided river salinity levels are kept below 900EC. This is achieved by coordinated discharges between participants. If targets are exceeded, participants run the risk of the EPA imposing credit requirements on flood flows.[60]

The full costs of the scheme are recouped from the auction of credits, with any additional amount being recovered as contributions from scheme participants.[61] Costs cover matters such as managing and administering the scheme and monitoring systems.[62]

13.3.3   Has the Scheme Been Successful?

The HRSTS has received national and international recognition as a successful scheme.[63] It has achieved the set salinity targets with exceedances being attributed to either diffuse source pollution or natural causes.[64] However, an assessment of the HRSTS has found greater impacts on surface water quality in some sectors of the river than others. A lack of baseline data made it hard to assess the full effectiveness of the scheme in some sectors.[65] Nevertheless, the HRSTS has allowed the EPA to focus on cumulative impacts of licensed premises on environmental conditions within the catchment. This can be compared with its general approach of imposing discharge limits on individual premises without setting cumulative environmental targets.[66] This is important given that the EPA has been criticized for failure to properly consider cumulative impacts in licensing.[67] Indeed, individual licences are a process of negotiation between the EPA and the licence holder,[68] with the result that 'its terms may reflect a compromise between what is desirable and what is practicable'.[69] Graham and Wright (2012) argue that discharge limits seem to be based on achievability by the licensee, with cumulative impacts lacking any real consideration.[70]

The scheme has provided licensees with flexibility in managing salinity, namely by harnessing technology and/or by purchasing credits.[71] However, some factors are preventing participants from utilizing their full credit entitlements. Participants have only utilized an average of 25 per cent of the TAD, but this had risen to 43–47 per cent in 2010–12 due to a larger number of rainfall events.[72] Factors such as licence volume limits or insufficient time to prepare for a discharge within the permitted period have resulted in reduced opportunities to discharge.[73] Furthermore, salinity discharges by users in upstream tributaries that are not part of the HRSTS, particularly coal mines in the Goulburn River (which flows into the Hunter River), may impact on the discharge opportunities for scheme participants. This is because the upstream users are increasing salinity loads.[74] It was considered 'technically impractical' to include this area within the scheme because 'it is not possible to give these mines adequate advanced warning of discharge opportunities, as they are high up in the catchment'.[75] They are, however, subject to salt management plans under their licence arrangements.[76] Nevertheless, predicted expansions of coal mines that release saline water to the Goulburn River[77] have the potential to further compromise discharges by scheme participants. The inability to effectively utilize credits due to reduced discharge opportunities may impact on credit value and therefore effectiveness as a market mechanism. The EPA is considering options to manage these issues.[78]

Other factors within the scheme have the potential to affect the value placed on credits and therefore the price signal attached to saline discharges. Two examples readily illustrate this point. First, credits are not required in order to discharge during flood flows, meaning that participation in the scheme is possible without actually purchasing credits. The EPA concluded that '[t]his potentially undermines the value of credits'.[79] It therefore may impact upon the effectiveness of an ETS. However, it also indicates that the HRSTS may be encouraging participants to seek the most cost-effective solutions, namely releasing only during flood flows when credits are not required, while also achieving the desired environmental goals. Second, when it comes to trading credits between participants, it has been found that 'often a nil or token price is paid for credits – particularly where trades occur between mines which are part of a common corporate entity. This is an underestimation of the actual value of the credits traded.'[80] Again, undervaluing of credits has the potential to affect the effectiveness of an ETS. However, given that salinity targets are being met, the impact (if any) on environmental outcomes due to credit undervaluation is unclear. It is noted that the credit price at auction has varied, starting at an average price of AU$507 initially in 2004, steadily increasing to AU$1603 in 2010, rising markedly to AU$5737 in 2012[81] and then dropping significantly to AU$830 in 2014 (when the price paid for credits was determined based on the amount of the 'highest losing' bid, rather than the previous maximum bid price).[82] The impact of the changing credit price is hard to assess, particularly given that any shortfall in scheme costs is recouped from participants as contributions if credit auctions do not cover the full costs.

13.3.4   Is There Potential (and Willingness) for Greater Use of ETS?

While the HRSTS was designed specifically for the Hunter River catchment, the EPA has indicated that based on its success, it 'demonstrates the applicability of market-based instruments to achieving environmental goals and provides a sound precedent for the prospects of other similar reforms' in other geographic areas.[83] In a recent review of the scheme, the EPA again raised whether the scheme could be used as a model for other ETSs, either for salinity or other pollutants.[84] While the EPA has made such statements about the prospects of other ETSs, its willingness to actually introduce them or to extend the HRSTS to other pollutants is somewhat unclear. For example, stakeholders have suggested that the HRSTS should also address other pollutants of concern within saline discharges such as metals and pH.[85] In response, the EPA stressed the scheme had been introduced to address salinity issues and other tools, such as traditional licence discharge limits, could be used to control cumulative impacts.[86] The preference to limit the HRSTS to salinity may well be a sensible one given the success of the scheme lies in its simplicity of dealing with a single problematic pollutant that is easily measurable in 'real time'.[87] Yet the EPA's response ignores the fact that cumulative impacts have not been properly accounted for within the licensing process. Indeed, the HRSTS was adopted because traditional discharge limits were not effective in controlling cumulative impacts of licensed salinity discharges.

Graham and Wright (2012) give a number of examples of water catchments suffering from cumulative impacts of licensed discharges,[88] both from salinity and other pollutants. They argue that little has been done by the EPA to set 'acceptable maximum environmental concentrations' for pollutants, in order to address cumulative impacts within catchments or, in some cases, to set discharge limits at all.[89] They concluded that 'market-based approaches should be investigated to efficiently achieve catchment-wide targets for key pollutants and also to provide a real economic incentive to minimize pollution'.[90] Addressing cumulative impacts is therefore an issue that demands more attention from the EPA. Whether ETSs can effectively assist in reducing those impacts, either alone or in combination with other regulatory instruments, is a matter for serious consideration. For instance, given the lack of effectiveness of LBL in terms of NO_x emissions, Ancev et al. (2012) suggested consideration of an ETS as an alternative.[91] It is noted that an ETS for NO_x emissions was previously proposed[92] but never introduced, with emissions currently being controlled through licences, LBL and regulatory standards.[93]

It is not suggested that an ETS will be the most appropriate or cost-effective response for dealing with all pollutant issues. A number of schemes have failed. Yet even under the successful South Creek Bubble Licensing Scheme there was a point at which it became significantly more cost effective to offset nutrients off-site than carry out further reductions at any of the three plants.[94] Where other methods are ineffective, alternative legal instruments including an ETS should be considered. ETSs will be most relevant, and have been successfully employed, where multiple polluters (or premises) are causing cumulative impacts arising from discharge of the same pollutant or affecting the same physical parameter.[95] They will be especially applicable where the receiving environment can 'tolerate the introduction of pollutants on a cumulative basis'.[96] For example, in the HRSTS saline discharges are flushed through the system with high or flood flows. The particular environmental characteristics must be well understood. Data collection, modelling and trials occurred for the HRSTS over a number of years.[97] The targeted pollutants need to be easily measurable, allowing for 'real-time' modelling of pollutant levels[98] so that discharges and trading can occur quickly when monitoring indicates that current environmental conditions are optimal. It is also necessary to be able to set the goal sought to be achieved.[99] Where there are multiple stakeholders with conflicting interests, such as shared water users, effective negotiation of a goal acceptable amongst all users will be key to gaining support for the scheme.

13.4   MONETARY BENEFITS ORDERS (MBO)

When sentencing polluters, the LEC has the power to impose an additional penalty constituting the amount of any monetary benefit acquired by committing the offence.[100] This aims to prevent offenders from obtaining financial gain by committing crimes and achieving competitive advantages over lawfully obedient citizens.[101] Despite the clear merit behind MBOs, there is no known case of an MBO being sought by the EPA or other prosecutors. None has been made by the LEC. The EPA's 'Guidelines for seeking environmental court orders' state that MBOs 'will generally be sought whenever the EPA can quantify the benefit obtained and it is satisfied that the offender has sufficient funds to pay all or a significant proportion of the benefit obtained'.[102] The amount must be proven to the civil standard – that is, on the balance of probabilities.[103] In 2013 the POEO Act was amended to allow regulations to set out a protocol to calculate the amount of monetary benefit obtained.[104] No such protocol has been made. If the reason for not seeking MBOs is that it is problematic to calculate monetary benefits then a protocol must be swiftly developed.

In a number of cases, it has been argued that the offence was committed for financial gain, which is an aggravating factor in sentencing generally.[105] In some cases, that amount has been quantified but still no MBO has been sought. In *Environment Protection Authority* v. *BMG Environmental Group Pty Ltd*, evidence from forensic accountants led by the EPA showed that the defendant waste transportation company 'could have obtained a financial benefit of approximately AU$227000 by disposing of the waste [unlawfully at a property] instead of disposing of it lawfully'.[106] Justice Biscoe accepted that the company had 'obtained considerable financial gain' by unlawfully disposing of the waste, which put it at a competitive advantage compared to lawful operators. While his Honour also accepted the defendant mistakenly believed the circumstances fell within exemptions, Justice Biscoe held that the defendant was 'grossly negligent, bordering on reckless, in not checking whether this conduct was unlawful'.[107] No MBO was sought despite the EPA's evidence from forensic accountants and an absence of evidence establishing a lack of means to pay.[108] The company and its director were each fined AU$100000 (less than the company's estimated financial benefit) and made liable for the EPA's legal and investigation costs totalling approximately AU$175000.[109] The impact of this fine as an effective general deterrence mechanism in the absence of an MBO to recoup any financial gain is questionable.

In *Environment Protection Authority* v. *MA Roche Group Pty Ltd*[110] ('*Roche No. 2*') the defendant quarry operator had a history of exceeding the permissible tonnage limit set by its licence for a 12-month period.[111] It was prosecuted for breaching its licence conditions, being just over twice the permissible limit.[112] In an earlier prosecution for the preceding year the company had extracted nearly three times its limit (*'Roche No. 1'*).[113] In *Roche No. 2* the defendant estimated the net profit from the additional materials was approximately AU$50 000.[114] The exceedance was done knowingly or deliberately in both cases and was financially motivated, albeit that the purpose of surpassing the threshold was to offset the company's financial problems and keep the business afloat.[115] No MBO was sought in either case. It is noted this is consistent with the EPA's 'Guidelines for seeking environmental court orders', which state that the EPA will seek an MBO where satisfied the offender has sufficient means to pay. In both cases the Court could not determine the defendant's exact financial position on the evidence available, although it clearly took into account the financial problems in sentencing.[116]

The *Roche* cases demonstrate that the deterrent value of any court penalty may be significantly lowered where no MBO is sought. In both cases the Court emphasized the need for specific and general deterrence.[117] Indeed, in discussing general deterrence in *Roche No. 2*, Justice Craig stated that '[u]nless the penalty imposed rises above a level that is seen to be tokenistic, others will not be discouraged from complying fully with conditions of a licence'.[118] His Honour fined the defendant AU$52 000 and ordered the company to pay the EPA's legal costs of AU$9750.65. When the estimated financial benefit in committing the offence (AU$50 000) is offset against the fine, this leaves a net penalty of AU$2000. While no criticism is made of his Honour's judgement, particularly given that no MBO was sought and the defendant's financial problems were taken into account, the resultant penalty provides little incentive to those considering flouting the law for financial gain. In the absence of MBOs, the potential rewards may be seen to outweigh the 'tokenistic' risks involved. In particular, as companies in dire financial circumstances may find themselves tempted to flout the law for monetary gain so as 'to "trade out" of . . . financial difficulties',[119] the possible consequences should significantly outweigh the potential gain. The penalties imposed must be high enough to ensure appropriate processes for environmental assessment and approval are followed before production thresholds are increased. MBOs could therefore play an important deterrent role to encourage environmental protection.

13.5   CONCLUSION

Economic instruments under the POEO Act have been utilized to varying degrees and with differing outcomes. LBL has proved to be of mixed success, potentially more effective where pollutants can be diverted to another beneficial use than where clean technology needs to be implemented to abate pollution. Further studies are, however, required to determine its current effectiveness. RBL suffers from serious design flaws that may impact its ability to operate fairly and effectively as an economic incentive to improve environmental performance. There needs to be more thought into how RBL fees vary with environmental performance across the full scale of fees payable.

ETSs have been successful in achieving desired targets and addressing cumulative impacts. However, their use has been limited. The only two ETSs began before the POEO Act and are limited in geographical area and to single pollutant types. While successful, a number of factors within the HRSTS may be preventing participants from fully utilizing their credits or causing credits to be undervalued. This may impact the ability of the HRSTS to operate at its full potential as a market mechanism. However, there is clear value in considering making further use of ETSs, particularly in areas suffering from cumulative impacts arising from licensed premises emitting the same pollutant type.

While partial use has been made of some economic instruments, others such as MBOs appear to be all but forgotten. MBOs could play an important role in ensuring that offenders do not profit from crimes or receive 'tokenistic' penalties. They serve an important deterrent function. If they are not utilized because of problems with calculating monetary benefits then a calculation protocol should be introduced.

In short, economic instruments have proven to be capable of achieving beneficial environmental outcomes. Further reform is needed to make some existing instruments more effective, but consideration must be given to harnessing economic instruments to a greater extent in NSW pollution law.

NOTES

1. See Clean Waters Act 1970 (NSW).
2. EPA (2001), *Load-Based Licensing: A Fairer System that Rewards Cleaner Industry*, Sydney: EPA, p. 1.
3. See Murray, M. (2011), 'Pollution control and waste disposal', in D. Farrier and P. Stein (eds), *The Environmental Law Handbook: Planning and Land Use in NSW*, Sydney: Thomson Reuters, p. 341.
4. Protection of the Environment Operations Act 1997 (NSW) ('POEO Act'), ss. 6, 47–9; Murray, 'Pollution control and waste disposal', p. 346.
5. POEO Act, ss. 6, 43, 120, 122.
6. Ibid., s. 44.
7. Protection of the Environment Operations (General) Regulation 2009 (NSW) ('POEO (General) Reg.'), cls. 8–10.
8. Ibid., cls. 13–23.

9. Ibid., cl. 13(a).
10. Ibid., cl. 13.
11. EPA, *Load-Based Licensing*, p. 1.
12. POEO (General) Reg., cls. 14, 16, sch. 1.
13. EPA, *Load-Based Licensing*, p. 4.
14. Ibid., pp. 4–5.
15. Ancev, T., R. Betz and Z. Contreras (2012), 'The New South Wales load-based licensing scheme for NO$_x$: lessons learnt after a decade of operation', *Ecological Economics*, **80**, 71.
16. EPA, *Load-Based Licensing*, p. 5.
17. Murray, 'Pollution control and waste disposal', p. 377.
18. EPA, *Load-Based Licensing*, p. 9.
19. EDO NSW (2014), 'Submission to Legislative Council General Purpose Standing Committee No. 5, Parliament of NSW', *Inquiry into the Performance of the NSW Environment Protection Authority*, p. 11.
20. Graham, K. and I. Wright (2012), 'The potential and reality of the environment protection licensing system in New South Wales: the case of water pollution', *Environmental and Planning Law Journal*, **29**, 369.
21. Ancev, Betz and Contreras, 'The New South Wales load-based licensing scheme for NO$_x$', pp. 73–4.
22. Ibid., p. 74.
23. Ibid., pp. 70–71.
24. Ibid., p. 70.
25. Ibid., pp. 73, 75, 78.
26. Ibid., p. 75.
27. Ibid., p. 76.
28. Ibid., p. 77.
29. Ibid., p. 78.
30. Department of Environment and Climate Change (NSW) (2009), *Final Regulatory Impact Statement: Protection of the Environment Operations (General) Regulation 2009*, Sydney: Department of Environment and Climate Change (NSW), p. 44.
31. Ibid., pp. 44–7; POEO (General) Reg., sch. 1.
32. See EPA (2013), *Regulatory Impact Statement: Proposed Protection of the Environment Operations (General) Amendment (Licensing Fees) Regulation 2013*, Sydney: EPA ('*RBL RIS*').
33. POEO (General) Reg., cl. 10; EPA (March 2015), *Environmental Management Calculation Protocol*, Sydney: EPA ('*Environmental Management Calculation Protocol*').
34. EPA, *RBL RIS*, p. vi.
35. *Environmental Management Calculation Protocol*, pp. 3–12.
36. POEO (General) Reg., cl. 10.
37. Ibid., cl. 10(2).
38. See *Environmental Management Calculation Protocol*, pp. 4–12; POEO (General) Reg., cl. 10, sch. 1.
39. The LEC is a superior court of record that has equivalent status to the Supreme Court of NSW. It is a 'one stop shop' in relation to planning and environmental cases. It hears merit appeals, judicial reviews and civil enforcement matters, as well as criminal prosecutions: see Preston, B.J. (2008), 'Operating an environment court: the experience of the Land and Environment Court of New South Wales', *Environmental and Planning Law Journal*, **25**, 387.
40. See Baker and McKenzie (2014), 'Risk-based licensing for NSW environment protection licences', accessed 23 October 2014 at bakerxchange.com/rv/ff0018ad83656a1f4085f773d947b9ea307d7010.
41. *Environmental Management Calculation Protocol*, pp. 9–10.
42. POEO Act, s. 293.

43. Collins, D.J. and S.A.Y. Smith (1998), 'Economic instruments in environmental regulation experience by the NSW EPA', paper presented to First World Congress on Environmental and Resource Economics, Venice, 24–27 June, p. 11; Kraemer, R.A., E. Kampa and E. Interwies (undated), *The Role of Tradeable Permits in Water Pollution Control*, Berlin: Institute for International and European Environmental Policy, p. 19.
44. EPA (2013), 'South Creek Bubble Licensing Scheme', accessed 4 August 2015 at www.epa.nsw.gov.au/licensing/bubble.htm.
45. Ibid.
46. Mamouney, L., J. Stace and C. Heathcote (2009), 'Incentives for biodiversity conservation in NSW, Australia', *Stetson Law Review*, **38**, 368.
47. EPA, *Load-Based Licensing*, p. 11.
48. EPA (2013), 'Review of the Protection of the Environment Operations (Hunter River Salinity Trading Scheme) Regulation 2002: discussion paper', Sydney: EPA ('HRSTS discussion paper'), pp. 5, 23.
49. Ibid.
50. Ibid.
51. EPA (2001), *Regulatory Impact Statement: Proposed Protection of the Environment Operations (Hunter River Salinity Trading Scheme) Regulation 2001*, Sydney: EPA ('HRSTS RIS'), p. 7.
52. Ibid.
53. Ibid., citing Smith, S.A.Y. (1995), 'The Hunter River Salinity Trading Scheme: A harbinger of reform for Australian environmental regulation', BA (Honours) thesis, University of Newcastle, NSW, p. 51.
54. EPA, *HRSTS RIS*, p. 7.
55. Smith, S. (2004), 'What have we learnt from the Hunter River Salinity Trading Scheme?', in S. Whitten, M. Carter and G. Stoneham (eds), *Market-Based Tools for Environmental Management: Proceedings of the 6th Annual AARES National Symposium 2003*, Rural Industries Research and Development Corporation, p. 48.
56. EPA, *HRSTS RIS*, p. 8.
57. EPA, HRSTS discussion paper, pp. 24–5; Protection of the Environment Operations (Hunter River Salinity Trading Scheme) Regulation 2002 (NSW) ('HRSTS Reg.').
58. See HRSTS Reg., cl. 22(1)(b).
59. Department of Environment and Conservation NSW ('DEC') (2006), *Hunter River Salinity Trading Scheme: Working Together to Protect River Quality and Sustain Economic Development*, Sydney: Department of Environment and Conservation NSW, p. 4.
60. Ibid., pp. 4–5; HRSTS Reg., cl. 27. Credits have a ten-year lifespan, with 20 per cent of the credits expiring and being re-auctioned by the EPA every two years.
61. HRSTS Reg., pt. 7. Participants include individuals licensed to discharge saline water in accordance with the scheme and any other persons that hold credits: cls. 5–6; POEO Act, s. 295A.
62. See POEO Act, s. 295H(1); HRSTS Reg., cls. 78–81.
63. Smith, 'What have we learnt from the Hunter River Salinity Trading Scheme?', p. 47; EPA, HRSTS discussion paper, p. 20.
64. EPA, HRSTS discussion paper, p. 5.
65. Krogh, M. et al. (2013), *Hunter Catchment Salinity Assessment: Final Report*, Sydney: EPA, p. 45.
66. See DEC, *Hunter River Salinity Trading Scheme*, p. 7.
67. Graham and Wright, 'The potential and reality of the environment protection licensing system in New South Wales', p. 361.
68. Murray, 'Pollution control and waste disposal', p. 379.
69. *Macquarie Generation* v. *Hodgson* [2011] NSWCA 424, [55].
70. Graham and Wright, 'The potential and reality of the environment protection licensing system in New South Wales', p. 363.
71. DEC, *Hunter River Salinity Trading Scheme*, p. 7.

72. Krogh et al., *Hunter Catchment Salinity Assessment*, pp. 15–16.
73. EPA, HRSTS discussion paper, p. 8.
74. Krogh et al., *Hunter Catchment Salinity Assessment*, p. 47.
75. EPA, HRSTS discussion paper, p. 11.
76. EPA (2016), *Review of the Protection of the Environment Operations (Hunter River Salinity Trading Scheme) Regulation 2002: Report and Recommendations*, Sydney: EPA ('*HRSTS Report*'), p. 16.
77. Krogh et al., *Hunter Catchment Salinity Assessment*, summary.
78. EPA, *HRSTS Report*, pp. 14–16.
79. EPA, HRSTS discussion paper, p. 15.
80. Ibid., p. 17.
81. Ibid., p. 35.
82. See EPA (2014), *Hunter River Salinity Trading Scheme Credit Auction: 2014 Auction Report*, Sydney: EPA, p. 2.
83. EPA (2013), 'A basis for future market-based instruments', accessed 4 August 2015 at www.epa.nsw.gov.au/licensing/hrsts/precedence.htm.
84. EPA, HRSTS discussion paper, p. 20.
85. Ibid., p. 12.
86. Ibid.
87. EPA, *HRSTS Report*, p. 19.
88. Graham and Wright, 'The potential and reality of the environment protection licensing system in New South Wales'.
89. Ibid., p. 364.
90. Ibid., p. 369.
91. Ancev, Betz and Contreras, 'The New South Wales load-based licensing scheme for NO_x', p. 78.
92. EPA, *Load-Based Licensing*, p. 11.
93. See Protection of the Environment Operations (Clean Air) Regulation 2010 (NSW), pt. 5.
94. See Coggan, A., S.M. Whitten and F. Yunus (2006), *Conservation Incentive Design*, Canberra: Department of the Environment and Heritage (Cth), pp. 51–2.
95. See Kraemer, Kampa and Interwies, *The Role of Tradeable Permits in Water Pollution Control*, p. 25.
96. EDO NSW (2014), 'Submission to NSW Environment Protection Authority', *Review of the Protection of the Environment Operations (Hunter River Salinity Trading Scheme) Regulation 2002*, p. 5.
97. DEC, *Hunter River Salinity Trading Scheme*, p. 6.
98. See EPA, HRSTS discussion paper, p. 5.
99. Smith, 'What have we learnt from the Hunter River Salinity Trading Scheme?', p. 54.
100. POEO Act, s. 249.
101. NSW Government (1996), 'Protection of the Environment Operations Bill 1996: public discussion paper', Sydney: EPA, p. 28.
102. EPA (2013), 'Guidelines for seeking environmental court orders', accessed 9 March 2015 at www.epa.nsw.gov.au/legislation/environ_courtorders.htm.
103. POEO Act, s. 249(1).
104. Ibid., s. 249(2A) as inserted by the Protection of the Environment Operations Amendment (Illegal Waste Disposal) Act 2013 (NSW), sch. 1, item 8.
105. Crimes (Sentencing Procedure) Act 1999 (NSW), s. 21A(2)(o).
106. [2012] NSWLEC 69, [74].
107. Ibid., [107]–[110].
108. Ibid., [140].
109. Ibid., [144].
110. [2015] NSWLEC 29.
111. *Environment Protection Authority* v. *MA Roche Group Pty Ltd* [2014] NSWLEC 114, [4] ('*Roche No. 1*'); *Roche No. 2* [2015] NSWLEC 29, [25].

112.	*Roche No. 2* [2015] NSWLEC 29, [2].
113.	*Roche No. 1* [2014] NSWLEC 114, [2], [6].
114.	*Roche No. 2* [2015] NSWLEC 29, [42].
115.	Ibid., [32]–[33], [39]–[43]; *Roche No. 1* [2014] NSWLEC 114, [21]–[22].
116.	*Roche No. 2* [2015] NSWLEC 29, [43], [51]; *Roche No. 1* [2014] NSWLEC 114, [29].
117.	*Roche No. 2* [2015] NSWLEC 29, [54]–[55]; *Roche No. 1* [2014] NSWLEC 114, [30].
118.	*Roche No. 2* [2015] NSWLEC 29, [54].
119.	See *Roche No. 1* [2014] NSWLEC 114, [21].

Index